For Julius C. Berens
From A A B Ayres

COPYRIGHT, 1936
by L. L. B. ANGAS
Rights of Translation Reserved

Made, manufactured and printed in U. S. A. by
Mortimer and Walling
461 Eighth Avenue
New York

INVESTMENT
FOR
APPRECIATION

INVESTMENT FOR APPRECIATION

By

L. L. B. ANGAS

*Forecasting Movements in Security Prices
Technique of Trading in Shares for Profit*

SOMERSET PUBLISHING CO.
461 EIGHTH AVENUE
NEW YORK
1936

CONTENTS

CHAPTER		PAGE
I.	The Problem Outlined	1
II.	Investment Objectives	7
III.	Ethics of Speculation	11
IV.	The Semi-cyclical Switch from Bonds to Common Stocks	15
V.	Timing the Semi-cyclical Switch	27
VI.	Cyclical Policy for Bond Investors	30
VII.	Forecasting Interest Rates	35
VIII.	Cycles in Single Industries	44
IX.	Selecting Shares for Cyclical Profit	47
X.	Sectional Market Activity	62
XI.	How Prices Are Made	65
XII.	The Intermediate Movements (I. Their Causes)	69
XIII.	The Intermediate Movements (II. Their Exploitation)	81
XIV.	Short-run versus Long-run Speculation	90
XV.	Stakes and Stop-loss Orders	94
XVI.	Stop-loss Orders in England	100
XVII.	The Art of Using Charts	104
XVIII.	Fine Points in Chart Reading	118
XIX.	General Plan of Campaign	131
XX.	The Mind of the Broker	139
XXI.	Prosperous versus Unprosperous Industries	142
XXII.	The Case for Buying in Early Revival	145
XXIII.	Shares to Choose	149
XXIV.	The Timing of Buying	155
XXV.	Rules for Selling	158
XXVI.	Recapitulation	162
XXVII.	Occasions of Special Caution	163

CONTENTS

CHAPTER		PAGE
XXVIII.	Cyclical Stock Exchange Slumps	169
XXIX.	Panics	181
XXX.	Averaging	183
XXXI.	Pyramiding	189
XXXII.	Operating on Borrowed Money	195
XXXIII.	Living on Income or Capital	200
XXXIV.	The Human Factor	203
XXXV.	Qualities Required	212
XXXVI.	Bear Operations	214
XXXVII.	International Investment	218
XXXVIII.	Manipulation	221
XXXIX.	Sharp Practices	236
XL.	Treatment of Old Holdings Showing Losses	240
XLI.	Building Balanced Portfolios	256
XLII.	Don'ts	264
XLIII.	Survey of Rules for Investing in Ordinary Shares	270

APPENDICES

A.	Forecasting a Change of Trend in the Profits of a Single Industry	274
B.	Causes of the Business Cycle	290
C.	The Mechanics of Good and Bad Trade	310
D.	The Problem of Confidence	320
E.	How to Cure Unemployment	324
F.	The Influence of the Market on the National Economy	327
G.	A Method of Analyzing Securities	340
H.	Synopsis of Argument	345

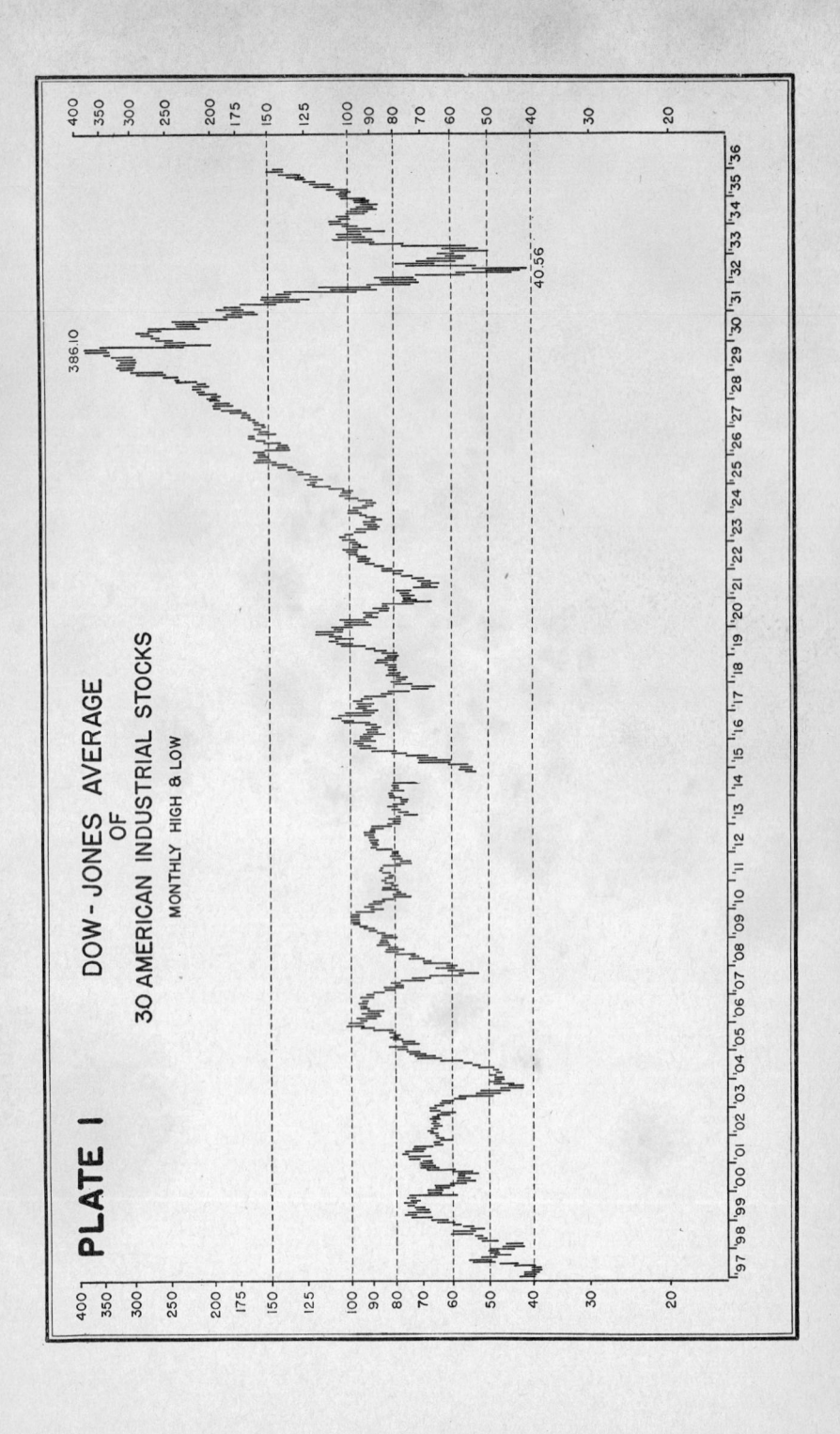

PLATE I DOW-JONES AVERAGE OF 30 AMERICAN INDUSTRIAL STOCKS
MONTHLY HIGH & LOW

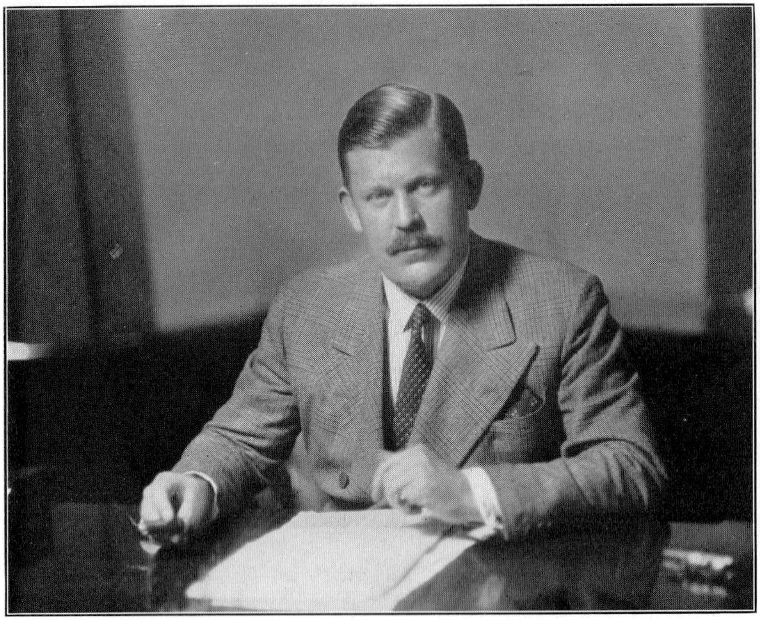

LAWRENCE LEE BAZLEY ANGAS was born of a British banking family on the 22nd of February, 1893. His great grandfather, George Fife Angas, founded the National Provincial Bank, the fifth largest bank in the British Empire.

The author was educated in England and France, and received the degree of M.A. at Magdalen College, Oxford. He entered the British Regular Army in 1914; served throughout the War in France and Italy; and received the Military Cross and the Croix de Guerre.

On peace being declared he resigned from the Army and was asked to stand for the House of Commons. He decided instead to specialize for some years in analyzing the causes of the business cycle, and the concomitant sharp fluctuations in profits and employment, his interest in Unemployment having been aroused by work carried on by his family in the slums of London.

In 1925, however, Major Angas came to the conclusion that in order to prove that his economic views were sound, it would be necessary to demonstrate publicly that his theories worked in practice. He therefore turned his attention to the public forecasting of Commodity and Stock Exchange movements. His success in this sphere with numerous published works has indicated that his theories are of a practical nature.

Recently he wrote a widely praised treatise on the *Problems of the Foreign Exchanges*. He also has in preparation two companion volumes: *The Problems of Money;* and *Methods of Preventing Unemployment.*

In addition to his literary work, Major Angas has been engaged in the banking and stock-broking business in London. Recently he retired, and his possession of a British quota permit has enabled him to settle in America, where he now concentrates on the management of individual portfolios.

INTRODUCTION

To be successful an investor requires a clear picture (i) of the various short- and long-run factors which influence security prices and thereby create either profits or losses. He also requires (ii) a knowledge of what pitfalls particularly to avoid; and, in addition, (iii) a series of clear-cut rules which it will *normally* pay him to follow.

There is, further, (iv) a definite technique of trading in shares to be learnt, for the investor should know how best to treat his losses and profits, and how to protect himself against unforeseen contingencies.

The forecasting of security prices is not an exact science, but apart from the gains occasionally to be made owing to luck, flair or inside information, consistent profits can only result from scientific methods of analysis and dealing.

The quality of "flair" deserves special mention: it is fully realized that some of the most successful men in the Market are those who doubt the practical utility of rules, statistics, charts and theories; they prefer to rely on their own instinctive gifts and on the methods which they have subconsciously learnt in the course of a life-time's experience. Experience in the realm of finance, however, is apt to prove expensive; while if a close study is made of the behavior of men who possess "flair," an acute observer is able to tabulate certain "attitudes towards market movements" and certain "conditions preferred for buying and selling," which of themselves constitute a series of useful Investment Principles.

This book does not undervalue the quality of "flair," but suitable emphasis must also be given to the complementary subjects of long-run forecasting and market technique.

INTRODUCTION

In the following pages an endeavor is made to explain the chief aspects of investment and speculation in their proper perspective, and thereby to provide the reader with the economic knowledge and mental outlook necessary for success.

The general procedure adopted is as follows:

1. To analyze the causes of the General Business Cycle.
2. To show how to forecast a change of trend in the profits of Single Industries.
3. To explain the causes of the short-run fluctuations which occur in the Stock Market as a whole; and
4. To provide the investor with a Scientific Method of exploiting these short-run and long-run fluctuations.
5. To furnish a definite Set of Rules (based on economic probability) for the Timing of both buying and selling.

The book is intended not only for private investors but also for those engaged professionally in finance.

L. L. B. ANGAS

55 Onslow Gardens   *and*   The Waldorf-Astoria
London, England   Park Avenue, New York

February, 1936.

PLATE II. London and Cambridge Index of 20 English Industrial Ordinary Shares

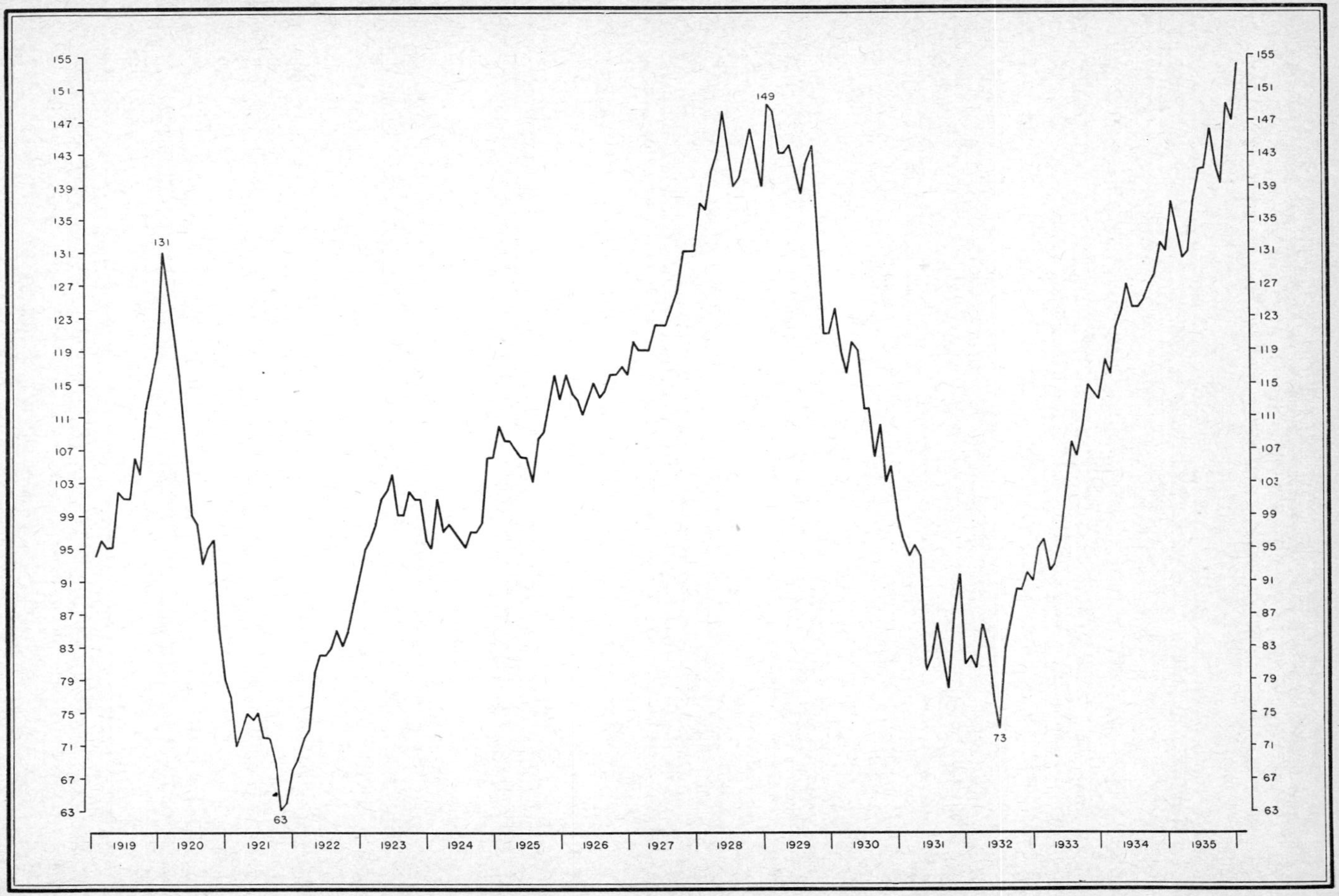

CHAPTER I

OUTLINE OF OUR SUBJECT

Exploiting laws of probability.

Stock market forecasting is a branch of economics; but economics is not an exact science; it consists merely of Laws of Probability. The most prudent investor, therefore, is one who pursues only a general course of action which is "normally" right and who avoids acts and policies which are "normally" wrong.

Market movements.

The movements in the common-stock market, taken as a whole, and decade by decade, are of three different kinds, and they occur simultaneously:

1. Major or cyclical—usually lasting two or more years.
2. Intermediate—usually lasting two or more months.
3. Minor—usually two or more weeks, but frequently shorter.

Day-to-day and hour-to-hour movements are also always in progress, but are of interest only in so far as they are components of the minor trend. There may also be a secular trend spread over several cycles.

The normal business cycle.

General business, stock and bond prices swing in cycles. These cycles of prosperity, strain, collapse and depression are analyzable and largely predictable.

Extraneous forces (political and otherwise) can admittedly intervene to disturb the "normal" sequence of change. For instance, in an era of managed money, the policy of the Managers may require exceptional attention.

In the absence, however, of special factors, there will occur the "normal" cycle of: prosperity; boom; strained credit; collapse; depression; revival; prosperity; and repeat.

Long-run strategy.

During revival and prosperity, common stocks rise with increasing profits.

Prosperity, however, tends to increase the demand for loan money and to raise interest rates. Bonds therefore tend, with a lag, to decline.

Intense prosperity, in its turn, especially if coupled with rising prices and speculation, tends to strain the banks. This strained credit position usually leads to collapse.

During the credit crisis which ensues, both bonds and stocks for a while fall simultaneously.

Industrial collapse, however, gradually reduces the demand for loan money, and interest rates fall. Bonds, therefore, begin to rise (usually well in advance of common stocks).

When bonds have advanced, common stocks tend to rise in their wake, and to gain cumulative upward momentum as business revives.

Cyclically speaking, therefore, the correct investment policy is to hold high-grade bonds in the falling half of the cycle, and common stocks in the rising half.

Short-run tactics.

The stock market, however, does not move exactly simultaneously or parallel with industry as a whole, for it is subjected to alternating waves of mass optimism and pessimism, and to "technical conditions" relating to the amount of savings available for new investment. The general market thus swings violently astride its cyclical mean.

These "intermediate" swings are due to share prices being affected not only by "internal" factors, i.e., matters relating to the industry and company, but also by "external" factors, e.g., stock market conditions such as psychology or temporary variations in the amount of money either available for the market, or wanted out of the market.

These intermediate swings, which usually last several months and give scope for large profits, are subject to definite study and there is a science of forecasting their probable movements. See Chapter XII.

* * *

Single industries also have definite business cycles of their own, and there is a science of determining their turning points. See Chapter VIII and Appendix A.

Individual stocks also follow a fluctuating course astride their mean angle of cyclical ascent or descent.

to sell on "Intermediate" boomlets in any given market, or in the market as a whole,—for even good stocks can become temporarily too dear.

Attempts to anticipate the intermediate or "secondary" fluctuations are, however, only an incidental feature of our recommended general policy.

Little or no attempt should be made to exploit the "minor" and day-to-day movements.

* * *

Summarized, the general policy which we advise is:
 (i) To take advantage of the cyclical swings in given industries and given groups of securities.
 (ii) To switch from shares which have risen unduly (even though their industrial trend may still be favorable), into others with equally favorable industrial trends, which nevertheless appear to be "cheaper" on actualities or prospects.
 (iii) Only to sell out of cyclically promising industries and companies when either
   (a) Prices seem too high either absolutely, or in relation to other securities; or
   (b) The technical position seems definitely dangerous.

There is, of course, no infallibility in this system. Its economic and market philosophy, however, is sound. Excellent results should therefore mature to Investors who steadfastly follow its principles.

CHAPTER II

INVESTMENT OBJECTIVES

Types of investors.

Broadly speaking there are three different types of investors:

1. Those concerned mainly with the preservation of capital.

2. Those concerned mainly with obtaining as high an income as is possible from a limited amount of capital.

3. Investors who aim, in the main, at capital appreciation.

1. *Investors concerned mainly with the preservation of capital.*

The attainment of this goal requires recognition that industry and interest rates move in cycles.

Many investors believe that safety can be obtained only by choosing those bonds or common stocks whose recent record in the market has proved continuously good over the last four or five years. Since, however, both interest rates and industry move in a cycle, this policy of buying only those bonds, or common stocks, whose *recent* record has been exceptionally good, although intended to be ultra-conservative, as a general rule means buying near the top. The quest of safety thus often leads to a heart-breaking series of losses.

Sometimes short-term bonds, sometimes long-term bonds, are a safety-first medium, but in view of the fact that prosperity in any group of securities, whether bonds or common stocks, tends, in the modern competitive world, to set in motion forces which eventually breed its termination, the safest way of preserving capital intact is, at most stages of the cycle, to buy only securities which still possess economic chances of further appreciation; and in the case of every purchase the chances of a rise should be greater than the chances of a fall; and this involves buying common stocks at certain stages of the business cycle.

2. *The second type is the Investor concerned with obtaining as high an income as possible from limited capital.*

Sometimes both bonds and common stocks can be bought to give a high income, but in many cases high income is obtainable only as a result of subjecting one's capital to great risks; *i.e.,* the buying of stocks in companies whose management is known to be unenterprising, or in industries with an unpromising trend. This, however, is not always the case.

Since general industry moves in a cycle, it is often possible, even though interest rates are low, to obtain comparatively high yields from the shares in certain industries; not because they are in a dangerous position, but solely because they do not possess so much scope for a cyclical increase in profits as have certain other industries.

Investors, however, must realize that, as a general rule, they cannot obtain the dual amenity of high income and large scope for appreciation.

3. *The third type of Investor is the one who aims, in the main, at capital appreciation.*

This need not necessarily be at the sacrifice of safety, although normally the quest of capital gain involves accepting a lower current, as distinct from future, yield than that obtainable on shares whose "comeback" possibilities are smaller.

During the early stages of revival, the three most promising groups for capital appreciation and eventual higher income, are usually:

    (i) The industries whose profits fluctuate considerably throughout the course of the business cycle; *e.g.,* the raw material, constructional and luxury industries.

    (ii) The industries for whose products a huge deferred replacement demand has piled up during the course of depression.

(iii) The industries with an especially promising future in the present decade, such as aircraft, Diesel engines, air-conditioning.

If sound companies in these industries can be found possessing high leverage in their capital structures, the prospect of profit is further enhanced.

Long- and short-run traders.

As regards investors seeking capital profit, these again divide themselves into four classes:

(i) Day-to-day traders.
(ii) Intermediate-trend traders.
(iii) Long-term cyclical investors.
(iv) Permanent investors.

Any individual may, of course, purchase certain of his holdings as a temporary speculation, and others as a long-term investment. He should, however, be certain in his mind why, and for how long, he has bought each security. Nothing is more dangerous than confusing one's Time-factor, for certain shares may be promising gambles though dangerous lock-ups, and others promising lock-ups though unpromising for the short run.

A knowledge of what securities are suitable for various purposes is important.

Incidentally, the right policy to pursue may vary from investor to investor. Influencing factors are: Temperament, knowledge, time available for study, age, health, amount of insurance held, current earning power, prospects, nature of dependents (children, etc.), standard of living, probable future annual savings, how much able and willing to lose, future liabilities, inheritances, etc.

Methods to pursue.

Broadly speaking, successful investment requires five separate studies:

I. Analysis of the fundamental economic and monetary forces which cause the business cycle in *industry as a whole.*

II. Analysis of the factors which cause the cyclical transition from boom to depression, and vice versa, in *single* industries.

III. Analysis of the factors, both monetary and psychological, which cause the "intermediate" swings in the stock market *as a whole.*

IV. Analysis of single companies in promising industries so as to determine those which are the most soundly situated.

V. Analysis of the technical condition of individual stocks and bonds, so that purchases and sales may be made in periods of temporary under or over valuation, resulting from technical market conditions.

* * *

The foregoing is a general outline of our problem—and its solution. Let us now proceed to a more detailed study of the subject.

CHAPTER III

THE ETHICS OF SPECULATION

The social need for a stock market.

That a Stock Exchange is necessary in a capitalistic society is obvious. Industry requires capital. There are not sufficient rich men to provide single-handed all the finance required by each industry. Some form of co-operative investment, such as the Joint Stock Company, is essential.

Small men, however, will not invest their savings in a company unless they are more or less sure that they can get them out quickly, and at a fair price. Such savings might be suddenly required for illness, old age, house purchase and so on.

The merit of the Joint Stock form of capitalism, which has led to such rapid advances in industry, is that, with the aid of a Stock Market, people can be fairly sure of getting their monetary savings to all intents and purposes "out of" industry at a fair price, although the "real" capital has been irrevocably sunk.

This, of course, requires a Stock Market, with a continuous supply of buyers.

The social need for speculation.

Markets, however, must be reasonably free. If a market were not free, and an investor in a company required to raise money, he might not be able to find a buyer except at a great sacrifice in price. Such conditions would check the continuous investment of savings in industry.

It is therefore theoretically desirable that there should exist a large, and preferably rich and intelligent, body of professional investors and operators who when they see a share falling in value on the market to below what they think is its intrinsic worth, should step in and buy. Conversely, this group of men, when they see a market rising too high on account of a wave of over optimism or over saving on the part of the public, should step in and sell either their own holdings or sell short.

If such a body of men exists the tendency will be for the market to fluctuate comparatively little and for such fluctuations to occur astride a level which indicates the probable intrinsic merits of the company.

Socially, in fact, in a capitalistic community, it is highly desirable that there should exist a large body of *well*-instructed speculators. Ill instructed speculators add to the swings in the market instead of levelling them out. Intelligent speculation, however, does just the reverse. And if speculation is to exist at all—as is socially, as distinct perhaps from ethically, desirable—the sooner it becomes intelligent the better—which I hope is a partial justification of this book.

Personal ethics.

But although it may be socially desirable for intelligent speculation to exist; and although speculators may reap large rewards for the risks they run in the market for the services they indirectly render to industry, it does not say that any individual participating in a prolonged series of speculative operations can justify his existence ethically, except on the above rather indirect grounds.

Living by one's wits is always somewhat contemptible. Savings, however, have to be invested; and certainly an investor, in justification to his family, is unjustified in losing his savings. He should, therefore, try to invest wisely. Moreover, if general intelligence is shown, little new money will be put into any industry unless it deserves it. Intelligent speculation will therefore check the influx of new money into an industry at the wrong time, and save the nation wasting its capital.

On self-deception.

But the speculator should not bluff himself. He, for the first part, will continuously be trying to pass on shares which he personally distrusts to the less well-instructed in the hope of their unwisely, though voluntarily, holding his own discarded securities. The individual, therefore, must fight this problem of ethics out within himself. Perhaps he will be able to ease his own conscience (a) on the ground that he may personally be wrong; and (b) on the ground that what he discards is not necessarily bad, but that he happens to think that *he* can find something *even better*.

Dow-Jones Index for 30 Representative Industrial Common Stocks (U. S. A.)

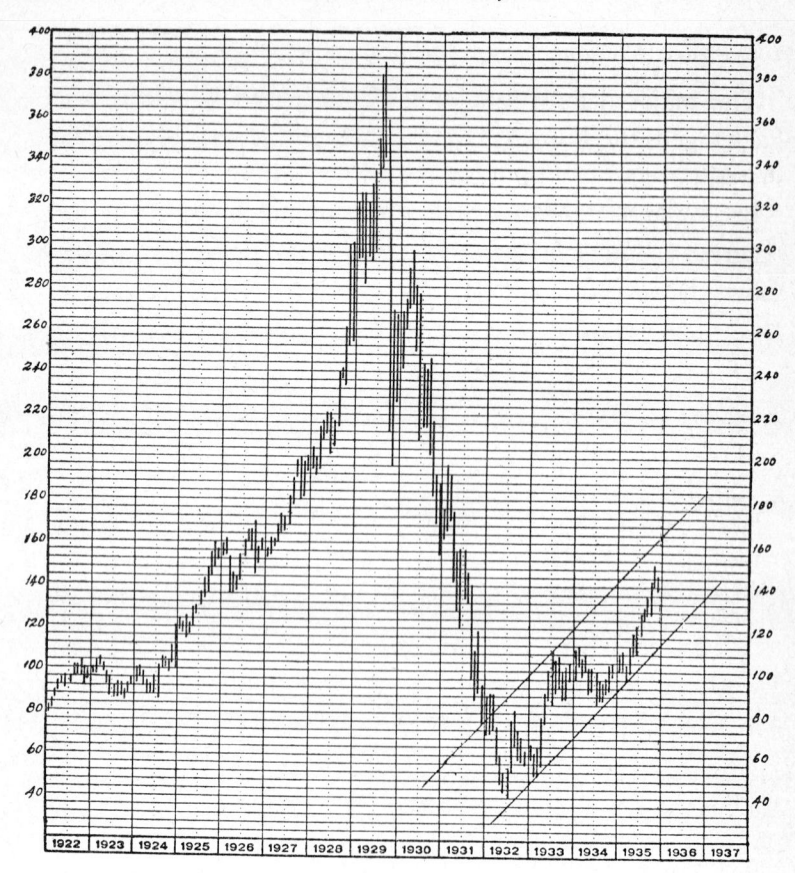

CHAPTER IV

THE SEMI-CYCLICAL SWITCH FROM BONDS TO COMMON STOCKS

The trade cycle and its influence on all securities.

The major determinant of price movements on the Stock Exchange is the Business Cycle, which affects not only ordinary shares, but also fixed interest bearing securities.

In England, industrial booms and slumps have, in the past, occurred at intervals of five to eleven years; the following table shows the years of boom:—

Boom years	Interval
1928	8 years
1920	7 "
1913	6 "
1907	7 "
1900	10 "
1890	8 "
1882	9 "
1873	7 "
1866	9 "
1857	10 "
1847	11 "
1836	11 "
1825	7 "
1818	8 "
1810	9 "
1801	5 "
1796	

Average period, 8 years.

In America, hitherto, the cycles have been shorter for reasons —agricultural and financial—which are now (I think) disappearing.

In all these cycles, the majority of industries have moved in the same direction more or less simultaneously; this is partly because high earnings in one industry augment, directly or indirectly, the demand for the products of others; and partly because the changes in currency and banking conditions, which largely govern the trade cycle, affect all industries simultaneously.

Monetary and banking factors, however, although the chief, are not the only causes of cyclical fluctuations in general industry. Others are harvests, invention, speculation, over-saving, bad income-distribution, and so on.

The five normal stages of the business cycle are:—
Revival.
Prosperity.
Boom and credit crisis.
Collapse.
Depression.
And repeat.

The reason for this sequence of events is to be found in the reaction of any given set of circumstances upon business men, consumers, investors and bankers. Each of these groups fears loss and seeks profits; each, therefore, rationally adopts at each stage of the cycle a course of action which seems to him logical, and which therefore tends to produce the next stated stage. Thus the cumulative change goes on until a complete cycle of slump and boom is engendered; then history begins to repeat itself with only minor variations, because like conditions usually produce like results.

The normal course of the business cycle.
The typical movements of each cycle are:—
Healthy conditions breed good confidence.

SEMI-CYCLICAL SWITCH FROM BONDS TO COMMON STOCKS

Good confidence encourages borrowing from the banks, and expansion.

This leads to increased production and to an expansion in industrial incomes which are largely paid out *before* any new production is *completed*.

This results in increased consumption and a lowering of dealers' stocks. Additional orders are therefore given to makers.

Conditions of prosperity are gradually created.

* * *

Prosperity, however, breeds credit expansion and elation; and elation normally breeds either over-speculation in commodities and a rise in their prices, or, alternatively, such an expansion in productive plant that the extra output can no longer be sold at the old level of prices, or be managed by the quantity of currency and bank credit available.

The banking position thus becomes strained, partly because of increased demands for credits and partly because there are usually large withdrawals of legal tender from the banks for additional wage-paying, pocket-money, and till-money purposes.

Credit then becomes dear and possibly is contracted.

Middlemen try to let stocks run off.

Few new orders are given to manufacturers.

Manufacturers therefore pay out less.

Consumer-income declines. Buying from the shops simultaneously decreases.

Trade then gradually gets worse.

Confidence disappears.

* * *

[The foregoing is the normal course of events during most trade cycles; there may, however, be slight variations in the way in which consumer-demand eventually fails to absorb all factory output. But these factors are too complex for the contents of this chapter. (See Appendix B.)]

Eventually, however, revival develops in the following manner:—

Bad trade and general depression lead to the cutting of retail prices and wages.

Less legal tender is taken out of the banks. The banking position is gradually strengthened.

Depression simultaneously breeds efficiency among workmen and producers.

Manufacturing costs are reduced.

Prices in consequence gradually decline, and meanwhile consumers' goods wear out.

Eventually a position is reached where continued consumption, facilitated by gradual re-expansions of bank credit, eats into stocks of commodities faster than they are reproduced.

Middlemen then give more orders to producers. Producers pay out additional incomes.

Consumption tends to increase proportionally.

Confidence is gradually restored.

Revival is thus set in motion.

Healthy conditions have again matured.

The cycle then repeats.

* * *

Throughout the cycle, ordinary shares tend to rise and fall with the earnings of their companies; and since most industries move together, ordinary shares taken as a whole move up and down with general business—though perhaps a few months in advance.*

* This "lead" in share movements is due mainly to insiders learning of earnings before the public, and buying or selling shares prior to annual reports being published.

SEMI-CYCLICAL SWITCH FROM BONDS TO COMMON STOCKS

The influence of long-term interest rates on securities.

Fixed interest bearing securities* are influenced by other considerations. They tend to rise and fall inversely with the long-term rate of interest.

If the long-term rate rises from, say, 5% to 7%, bonds paying only 5% will fall below par. On the other hand, if the market rate falls from 5% to 3%, financiers will borrow at the lower rate to buy the 5% bonds, and this will force their prices up. Hence the prices of fixed interest securities vary inversely with the long-term market rate of interest.

The same set of influences works to some extent in the case of ordinary shares: falling interest rates tend, other things being equal (i.e. unless industrial earnings are falling even faster), to force ordinary shares up; while rising long-term interest rates tend to force ordinaries down. The influence of long-term rates on ordinary shares is, however, often swamped by the earnings factor; the result is that ordinary shares do not invariably fall with every rise in the market rate of interest, and vice versa. As a generalization, however, it is always true that, *other things being equal,* a rise in the *long*-term rate of interest affects *all* securities simultaneously.†

This matter of interest rates is so important as to deserve some slight enlargement.

How industry governs interest rates.

The long-term market rate of interest (i.e., the price that borrowers will pay would-be lenders for money) is governed

*Which for brevity we call "bonds" throughout this book.

†Beware of confusing long-term, and short-term "call," rates of interest. Rises in the short-term "call" rate for Stock Exchange loans often occur *without* affecting security prices adversely. This may happen if people confidently foresee an early rise in shares which they think justifies them in temporarily paying high rates.

mainly by the profits which people expect to be able to make in industry,* and this rate varies with the general industrial outlook.

The trend of industry, therefore, by affecting interest rates, governs not only the prices of ordinary shares, but also, indirectly, the prices of fixed interest securities as well. Fixed interest securities fall with a lag when industry booms, and rise with a lag when industry slumps.

These several matters may be graphically represented as follows:—

PLATE IV

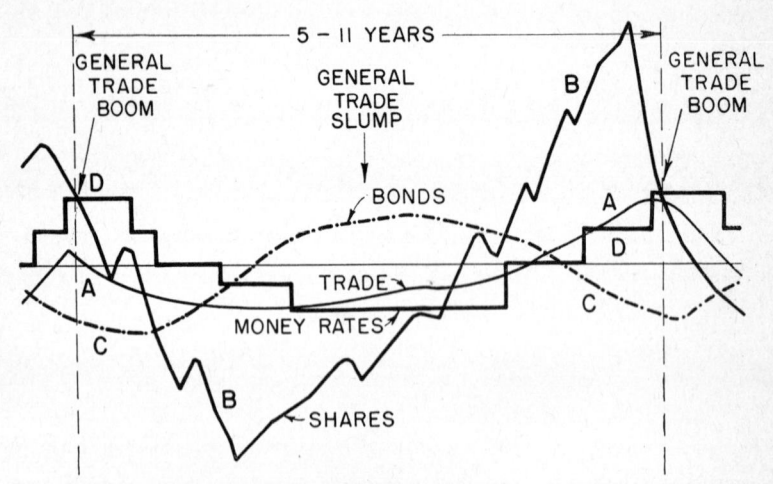

[Figure: Plate IV — shows curves over 5–11 YEARS, with GENERAL TRADE BOOM at left and right, GENERAL TRADE SLUMP in middle; curves labelled BONDS, TRADE, MONEY RATES, SHARES, and A, B, C, D.]

Curve A. The declared profits of industry.
Curve B. Industrial share index.
Curve C. Bond index.
Curve D. Long-term money rates.

*Government borrowing is *as a rule* only a minor influence, though sometimes it becomes of dominant importance. If the borrowing is done by the government from the public it tends to raise interest rates: if from the Central Bank to lower them (under most banking systems). See Chapter VII.

SEMI-CYCLICAL SWITCH FROM BONDS TO COMMON STOCKS

Comments on the above chart.

During the major part (roughly two-thirds) of each business cycle, bonds and ordinary shares normally move in opposite directions. At the crisis stage, however, both bonds and ordinary shares slump together usually for about nine months; conversely, in the early stages of revival they simultaneously rise (usually for at least a year and a half). The bond movements are far less violent than those of ordinary shares and normally precede them by about fifteen months.

Bonds in each cycle usually fluctuate only about 10% astride their cyclical mean; speculative ordinary shares about 50%; thus giving normal increments from bottom of about 20% and 200% respectively.

National production throughout the cycle usually varies only about 15% as between slump and boom. Industrial profits usually vary some seven times as much, or, say, 100% from bottom (speaking nationally).

Share prices fluctuate even more than trading profits, but normally reach their peaks and bottoms several months in advance of published trading profits.

* * *

Incidentally we would add that during the rising half of each trade cycle ordinary share prices tend to run ahead of earnings on prospects, so that yields gradually fall (throughout the rise) until they reach, perhaps, a 3% or 4% basis. On the other hand, during the falling half of the cycle, shares usually fall even faster than earnings, in the expectation that profits next year will be lower than last. Hence shares swing gradually on to a high-yield basis.

The following chart represents these movements in the yield basis.

PLATE V

CHART REPRESENTING THE CYCLICAL SWING IN ORDINARY SHARES

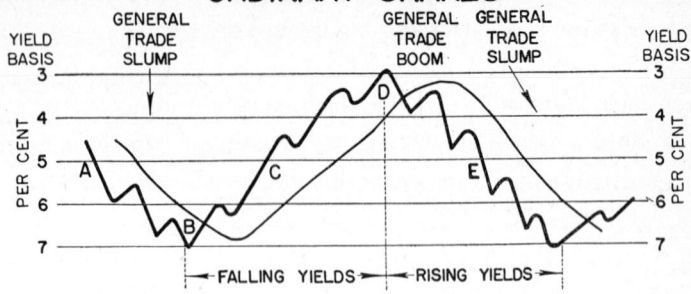

———=Index of ordinary-share prices.
A B C=A period of high yields, bad trade, low earnings.
C D E=Low yields, good trade, big earnings.
  B D=Improving trade prospects, and falling yields.
  D F=Declining trade prospects, and rising yields.
———=The course of industry.
N.B. The bond yield fluctuates mildly astride a central mean.
Beware when the phase C D is reached.

Investment policy should alter semi-cyclically.

The conclusions to be drawn from the foregoing remarks on the trade cycle and on interest rates are that the long-run investor who aims mainly at capital appreciation should change from ordinary shares to bonds when general trade starts slumping; and from bonds to ordinaries when it starts to revive.

This semi-cyclical switch is usually necessary every four or five years.

Most trade booms, however, end with a credit crisis lasting about nine months, and during this period almost all securities, both bonds and ordinary shares, fall simultaneously. Thus, at the peak of each cycle, it is usually advisable, after selling one's ordinary shares, not to re-invest in bonds at once. The money should be left on deposit until the fall in bonds appears to be over, and until the bond index has itself started turning upwards a point or two, i.e. until about the time when the bank rate is first lowered after the boom and crisis.

Then one should invest in long-term bonds (preferably ones which have a low nominal rate of interest and which stand well below their redemption levels; see Chapter VI): these bonds will gradually appreciate as the interest rate goes on falling.

The six successive stages of the cycle.

Broadly speaking, the common stock movements throughout the cycle divide themselves into six successive stages:

(1) *Recovery from fear* and forced selling, after a period when the market has been driven to unreasonably low levels by banking conditions, when equities are offered for whatever they will bring, and are thus depressed to levels not logically justified even by the depression. This stage represents a re-bound, usually quite swift, though not yet based on true fundamental recovery, but simply on return to rational thought as distinct from unreasoning panic.

(2) The second stage which follows is a period during which security prices *respond to actual improvement* in business. This advance is usually slower and less general than the first stage.

(3) The third stage is a phase of *over-enthusiasm;* when security prices go higher than they should, on hopes of continued future improvement.

(4) The fourth stage is the simple *reaction from over-enthusiasm* and a return of prices to a level more nearly justified by current conditions.

(5) The fifth stage is the *response of securities prices to declining business* and reduced profits.

(6) The sixth stage is a period when fear again replaces reason, and when forced selling drives prices down once more to levels below those justified even by current low business activity.

Scope for profits.

As regards the cyclical scope for profits in the common stock market: No exact figures can be suggested, as variations occur from cycle to cycle.

Certain mathematical factors should, however, be considered as per the following graph, where we have drawn an imaginary curve for the common stock market over a period of eight years, wherein the rise from the bottom of the slump at the end of the third year, to the top of the boom at the end of the eighth year, is from an index level of 50 to an index level of 250, i.e. 400%.

The graph is drawn on an arithmetical and not on a geometric scale.

If an investor buys at the bottom of the slump, with the index at 50, and sells at the top of the boom, he makes 400%.

If he buys at the 100 level, he makes only 150%.

If he buys half way up the boom at the 150 level, he makes only 66%.

Whereas, if he buys at the 200 level he makes only 25%.

In this last case it is to be noted that although a rise from 200 to 250 is the same, in terms of "points," as a rise from 50 to 100, in the former case an investor makes only 25% whereas in the latter he makes 100%. The earlier, therefore, one can buy in the course of the cyclical upswing, the greater one's chances of mathematical gain.

But since hitting cyclical nadirs is exceptionally difficult, early

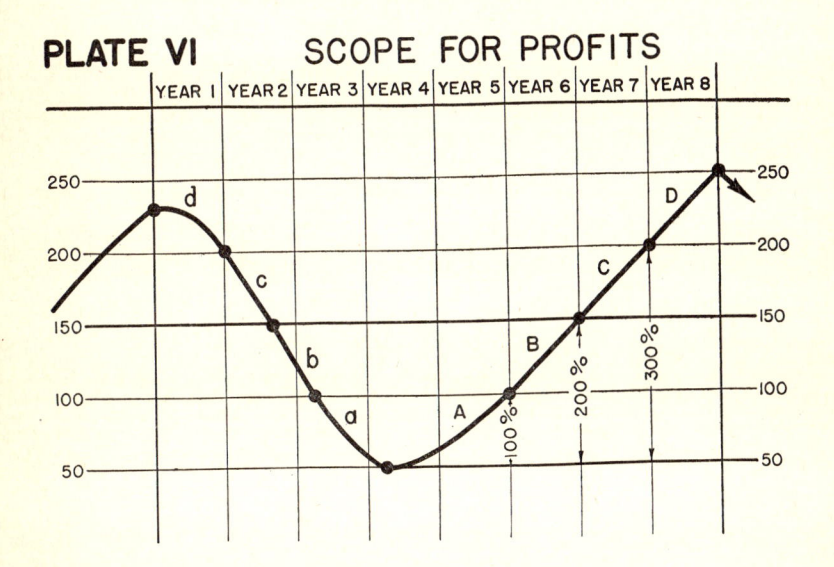

SEMI-CYCLICAL SWITCH FROM BONDS TO COMMON STOCKS

PLATE VI — SCOPE FOR PROFITS

SEMI-CYCLICAL SWITCH FROM BONDS TO COMMON STOCKS

in the second year of revival, as shown by a share index graph, is probably the safest time to buy.

* * *

On the bear tack, a fall of 50 points from 200 to 150 gives only a 25% profit.* A fall of another 50 points from 150 to 100 gives a 33% profit; and a fall from 100 to 50 gives a 50% profit.

There is perhaps, therefore, not so great a need to be early in commencing one's bear operations during depression, as to commence one's bull operations during revival, and since bear squeezes are particularly likely during the boom period of the cycle, it is probably more dangerous to try to hit a cyclical top for bear operations than a cyclical bottom for bull operations. Indeed, buying too soon (before a slump has ended), say in Section b in the downswing (see Plate VI), is probably safer than going bear in Section C of the upswing.

Incidentally, it should be added that a man who buys too soon in Section b makes more cyclical profit, if he holds his position to the top of the next boom, than if he buys in Section C of the upswing. The latter investor makes slightly over 25%; the former slightly over 66%—although of course he will suffer several years of financial worry before he sees his profits.

Margin traders should, of course, avoid buying too soon in the cycle (say in Section b) lest they be squeezed out before they see a net appreciation in their holdings in Section C of the upswing.

* Strictly speaking, this profit cannot be measured in terms of percentage of money put up (although it is convenient to talk in these terms), because one may not put up any money at all. The profit is really one measurable in terms of the percentage depreciation on the shares one has sold short.

CHAPTER V

TIMING THE SEMI-CYCLICAL SWITCH

Broad general rules.

Although it is easy in a book to prescribe that a switch should be made from bonds to common stocks, and vice versa, at the bottom and top of each cycle; it is, of course, in actual practice far from easy to decide when a top or bottom is being reached.

The forces which bring about a change of direction in general trade are certainly subject to economic analysis; and in Appendix B an outline is given of these economic forces. But the actual moment at which the stock market itself begins to change direction is a matter of mass psychology; and no satisfactory rules can, I think, ever be laid down, to time the movement exactly. Indeed the bottom never occurs except at a time when it is not yet expected.

Broadly speaking, however, there are several rough and ready rules which will provide the investor with an indication of when the general economic tide is likely to turn.

There are, for instance, five rough signals for which an investor should probably wait before buying common stocks in a period of depression, viz.:

1. Three years of slump.
2. A fall in the bank rate to 3%.
3. A fall in the index for industrial ordinary shares to somewhere near the low level of the previous trade cycle.
4. A rise in the average yield on common stocks until it exceeds the yield on high-grade bonds.
5. Incipient revival in one or two industries, although trade as a whole has not yet revived.

Conversely, the following are the normal indications of a probable cyclical downswing in general industry and shares:

1. A rise in the common stock index until the yield on common stocks is below the yield on bonds.

2. A rise in the bank rate until it becomes higher than the yield on either common stocks or bonds.

3. A flattening out of the curve (if available) of the profits of general industry.

* * *

Numerous other indications also exist, but a separate book would be required to discuss them in any convincing detail. Appendix B and Chapter XVII, however, are devoted to analyses which may throw some further light on the subject.

A policy of "graduality."

Since, however, even the most perfect economic study will never provide the investor with a guaranteed method of hitting the peaks and nadirs, a policy of half measures and "graduality" is probably advisable.

It is exciting to attempt to hit off the bottoms of depressions, but more money is probably lost in trying to do so, particularly with the aid of borrowed funds, than at any other stage of the business cycle.

The following procedure of "graduality," therefore, is recommended in preference to the more full-blooded method of a 100% simultaneous switch from bonds to equities:

1. To switch, say, 25% of one's bonds into common stocks (preferably during a temporary collapse in the market), at a time *before* one thinks that the actual cyclical change in trade has come. (This will give one a sporting chance of buying perhaps at the absolute bottom, during a period of market panic.)

2. Then later, when one sees an occasional industry showing

signs of revival after its own cyclical slump, to switch another 25% into common stocks—preferably during another intermediate relapse in the common stock market as a whole.

3. Then later, when one is more or less convinced that the general cyclical upturn has come, to switch another 25% into common stocks.

4. Finally—switch the remaining 25% when you think there is a chance of the bank rate shortly being raised, and of the cyclical collapse in long-term bonds commencing.

* * *

The same procedure of gradually switching out of common stocks into bonds might also be adopted during the boom and prosperity phases of the cycle.

* * *

The foregoing procedure of graduality certainly precludes one from effecting a spectacular, and 100% right, switch at the tops and bottoms of cycles, but it secures the investor more peace of mind; and few are those who, in a 100% simultaneous switch, ever hit the tops or bottoms precisely.

CHAPTER VI

POLICY TO BE FOLLOWED BY TRUSTEES AND OTHER SAFETY-FIRST INVESTORS

Introductory.

Although, theoretically, the best form of long-run investment is to switch from ordinary shares to bonds, and back, semi-cyclically, most trustees are required by deed to keep all their funds in bonds throughout the cycle. Many insurance and trust companies, too, find it necessary to keep a large portion of their funds always in loan issues. Numerous investors also favor this compromise; consequently it is desirable to set down a series of rules as to how best to manage these funds even though industry as a whole may be improving and interest rates may be rapidly rising.

Bond prices and the date of redemption.

The first fact which must be recognized is that individual bond-prices, though they may fluctuate over a substantial range, are to a great extent regulated by the date of redemption. A bond issue is, in essence, a loan; the original offer specifies not only the rate of interest, but also the date and price at which the loan is to be repaid. It is usual for loans to be repaid at par, even when they are issued at a discount; occasionally the redemption price is fixed at a slight premium.

The influence of redemption arrangements, in determining the price of bonds, is often a question of actuarial probabilities. Some bonds are redeemable by drawings spread over a period of years (the final date being fixed), while in other cases the repayment must be effected at a specified date. The nearer this date approaches, or the greater the probability of repayment within a short time, the more reluctant will the market be to vary the quotation from the repayment price.

Thus if a bond is paying 4½% (nominal), when the current interest-rate is 6%, the natural price of the issue (apart from redemption) would be 75. But if the loan is to be repaid at par within the next three years, financiers could advantageously buy at that price, in order to receive a repayment amounting to a bonus. For this reason, prices will be marked up until the quotation discounts the probability of imminent repayment.

Thus when interest-rates are rising and bond-prices are therefore declining, there will be a relative stability among issues with a nearby date of redemption. When the trend of industry and of interest-rates turns downwards, the longer-dated securities will tend to improve; but the short-date bonds will be less inclined to move.

The semi-cyclical switch from short- to long-date bonds.

In this way investors who are restricted to Government bonds can enjoy some of the benefits to be derived from cyclical trade fluctuations. The course indicated is to sell long-date bonds and re-invest in short-term issues, as soon as rising interest-rates are in prospect. Then later, while interest-rates are still high, but as soon as the first credit-crisis is over, the investor should switch again into long-term Government bonds; in this way he will benefit from the capital appreciation which occurs when both trade and interest rates begin to fall.

These long-term Government bonds should be of a low nominal rate of interest (3% or 4%) rather than of a high rate (6% or 7%); for, assuming redeemability in both cases to be somewhere near par, a 3% long-term bond standing at 50 and yielding 6% (and redeemable at 100) will, if the long-term market rate of interest falls from, say, 6% to 4%, rise much faster than a 6% bond standing at 100 and also yielding 6% (if it too is redeemable at 100 at the same date). The 6% bond may rise only a few points. The 3% bond may rise to 75, i.e. 50%.

Types of long-term bonds to buy during the rising half of the cycle.

During the period when trade has revived and when interest rates have begun to rise, we have so far assumed only *short-term* bonds should be held.

This is certainly true as regards high-class *Government* securities, but there is considerable scope for making capital profits by operating in and out of certain *industrial* bonds.

Although it is a fact that bonds as a whole decline as industry and interest rates rise, it often so happens that depressed bonds in certain industries go on rising even despite the rising long-term trend of interest rates. This frequently occurs in those industries which are recovering after a depression.

For instance, when industrial revival begins and certain industries begin to improve, the bonds of these depressed though reviving industries usually rise much faster (in their early stages of revival) than do first-class Government stocks—which will probably have risen considerably already.

Similarly, later on in the cycle when general trade is at last definitely prospering, by switching out of bonds in industries that have already revived into bonds of industries that have been recently depressed but are now also showing signs of revival, considerable profits can be made.

Convertible debentures are also good purchases in industries that are improving.

Suggested behavior throughout the cycle.

Looking at the trade cycle as a whole the following behavior seems correct for bond investment.

Stage	Probable Duration	Signs of the Times	Type of Bond Investment
I. Credit crisis and general Stock Exchange slump.	6 to 9 months.	Very high bank rates. All securities slumping.	Money on deposit in the banks or in short maturities. (Or possibly abroad if foreign trade cycles are not simultaneous.)
II. Industrial collapse—most trades slumping.	1 to 2½ years.	Sharply falling bank rates. Bonds rising; ordinary shares falling.	Long-term Government bonds with a low nominal rate of interest.
III. Industrial stagnation—most trades depressed; some slightly improving.	1 to 4 years.	Low bank rates. Sharply rising bonds. Rising ordinary shares.	Long-term bonds of an industrial as well as of a governmental character. Convertible debentures.
IV. General revival—most trades improving although a few still slumping and others becoming over-invested in.	1 to 4 years.	Slowly rising bank rates and long-term rates. Bonds fairly steady. Ordinary shares rising fast.	Convertible debentures in prosperous industries. Long-term bonds in reviving though recently depressed industries. (These latter usually rise with their trades despite the rise in interest rates.) Short-term securities of high character.
V. Boom.	½ to 2 years.	Sharply rising long-term rates and bank rates. Bonds slumping. Ordinary shares still rising.	Short-term bonds. Convertible debentures. Or money on deposit or abroad.

The assessment of relative safety.

In assessing the relative safety of bonds and preference shares in different companies, do not think that because the prior charges of one company are covered by earnings, say, ten times, and those of another only three times, that the former are *ipso facto* the safer. An exaggerated illustration from a company whose earnings are say £1,000,000 will demonstrate this danger.

POLICY FOLLOWED BY SAFETY-FIRST INVESTORS

Capital of Company	Dividend Requires	Earnings Available	Times Covered	Percentage of current earnings required
£	£	£		
5,000,000 in 4% 1st Mort. Debs.	200,000	1,000,000	5	0-20%
4,000,000 in 5% 2nd Mort. Debs.	200,000	800,000	4	20-40%
1,000,000 in 6% 1st Pref. Stock	60,000	600,000	10	40-46%
100,000 in 6% Pref. Ord. Stock	6,000	540,000	90	46-46.6%
10,000,000 in Ordinary Shares		534,000		

This table shows that the 4% debenture dividend is five times covered, whereas the 6% Preferred Ordinary Stock can be met ninety times: but it is obvious that the 4% debenture is safer than the 6% Preferred Stock. The 4% debenture holders would receive their dividend so long as earnings were 20% of their present amount; 46½% of current earnings would, however, be necessary to meet the claims of the Preferred Ordinary Stock-holders. These facts are shown in the right-hand column. This "percentage" method is the only safe method of assessing relative security. "Times covered by current earnings" is totally unreliable.

CHAPTER VII

THE RATE OF INTEREST*

Why important.

The long term rate of interest is, as already stated, a vitally important factor in investment, because it is an "external" factor which influences the general level of *all* securities.

A 3%, as distinct from a 6% long term rate, tends to double the price of all securities, other things being equal.

The quoted rate is a loan rate for "Money."

The first thing to note about the rate of interest is that it represents a hire price of Money and not of goods (as so many economists have suggested), even though goods can, of course, be bought with the borrowed money. The interest rate is, in fact, the loan price of borrowed Monetary purchasing power.

The pure rate and the additional risk rate.

Any given *market* rate of interest contains two elements:
1. The pure rate of interest.
2. An additional Risk-rate in accordance with the credit of the borrower in the eyes of the lender.

This risk element partially determines the *market* rate at which a capitalist will, in practice, lend to a borrower.

The rate of interest is, however, determined by the forces of demand and supply; and it is necessary to split these two sets of factors into their separate component ingredient parts.

* NOTE.—This (rather difficult) chapter is inserted here, because the Rate of Interest is one of the dominant factors in investment theory. The reader, however, might skip this chapter for the moment, and read it prior to reading Appendix A.

The demand for loan-money.

Broadly speaking, there are three separate types of demand for loan-money:

(i) Demand by profit-seekers, e.g., business men.
(ii) Demand by non-profit seekers, e.g., governments and municipalities—for public works, unemployment relief, war, etc.
(iii) The Distress Demand such as matures during a financial crisis.

As regards the profit-demand: as business improves and the prospects of profit grow, the demand for capital to exploit these prospects naturally grows with it. The prospective profit rate is, in fact, the "normal" major determinant of the current long term market rate of interest.

Governments and municipalities can, however, twist the current market rate away from the anticipated profit rate on account of their demands for capital for non-profit making processes, e.g., wars, public works, and so on.

Thirdly, at the crisis stage of the business cycle when nerves become shaken (so that few people are willing to lend), and when the velocity of money stagnates so that businesses do not receive income as punctually as was originally anticipated, a Distress Demand for loan-money, so as to meet current obligations, matures. The result is that although the profit rate of industry is falling, the demand for loan-money, and the price of it, may temporarily rise.

Foreign demands.

Although the domestic demand is, in most countries, the dominant factor, foreign influences may be considerable, either for profit making or non-profit making purposes.

For instance, if the rate of interest in England is much higher than the rate of interest in America, there will be a tendency for English financiers to borrow in the American market so as to re-lend in England, with the result that American interest rates may be forced up by this foreign demand—and English rates lowered.

Foreign influences are particularly likely to influence the domestic loan rate, if the foreign exchanges are rigidly fixed, as under the old gold standard.

The short rate and the long rate.

The demand for loan-money may be either short term or long term; so also may the supply.

In the depression stages of the business cycle the short rate is usually below the long rate:—

(a) Because bank reserve ratios will probably be unstrained;

(b) Because the commercial and speculative demand for loan-money will be small owing to the reduced scale of commercial transactions, the low level of commodity prices, and to the general absence of speculation.

On the other hand, in the prosperity stages of the business cycle the short rate normally exceeds the long rate for opposite reasons.

* * *

The short rate and the long rate are essentially distinct and different; although, of course, they, to some extent, influence each other because of the Law of Substitution; for if the short rate is much higher than the long rate people will prefer to borrow long rather than short; and vice versa if the long rate is much higher than the short rate.

* * *

But the Demand for loan-money is not the only factor which influences its market price. Supply also must be considered.

The supply of loan-money.

The supply of money comes from three separate sources:—

(i) Bona fide savings on the part of the public.

(ii) Loans by the banks.

(iii) The foreign supply.

It is, however, important to note that the supply of loan-money is of two separate sorts:—

(a) Bona fide savings by the public out of income.

(b) Artificially created loan-money, created artificially by the banks.

Some economists and bankers deny the ability of banks to create deposit-currency. But in this they are wrong.

Modern money is 80% bank money, namely the typewritten or hand-written entry in a customer's passbook and in the bank's ledger. This is what circulates among the public as money, transferable, of course, by cheque.

The modern bank can create this money. The modern bank has, in fact, usurped what is called in England one of the prerogatives of the Crown, namely the minting or creation of the money in practical use.

Some people, disputing this theory, say, firstly, that the public would never be so silly as to use for money something created at the whim of a mere banker. Secondly, they say that a bank never lends what it has not got. Therefore, it never creates money.

But when a bank lends to one client the deposit which is still spendable by another, two spendable deposits come into existence and the bank has created money, even though he, the banker, did not actually lend what did not already exist. That is the trick of banking.

Banks can, in fact, by lending money to the public, or by buying investments from the public, create bank-credit-currency which possesses purchasing power, and which circulates as money.

The extent to which the banks are able to lend or invest in this way, depends, however, on their cash reserve ratios. If they have excess reserves their tendency is to compete to lend and to invest, with the result that the thus artificially created supplies of loan-money tend to force the market rate of interest down to below what it otherwise would have been (if the only form of loan-money had been the bona fide savings of the public made out of income).

Governmental influences.

A particularly curious feature of the modern monetary system is that if a Government borrows from the Central Bank and pays the proceeds to contractors and others who bank with member banks, the so-called reserves of these member banks with the central bank are increased, so that they in turn can pyramid additional loans upon these so-called reserves.

In fact, a Government by borrowing from the reserve bank, as distinct from the public, can actually set in motion monetary forces which tend to lower the market rate of interest (because the potentially creatable supply of bank money is augmented by the foregoing reserve-inflation process), even though the Governmental demand for loans has increased.

Governmental demand from the Reserve bank, as distinct from the public (or the *member* banks), thus tends to lower, rather than to raise, the market rate of interest. A curious anomaly in the modern monetary system!

The effect of banking behavior upon the actual market rate.

The net result of the ability of the banking system to create loanable money out of nothing, is that, on certain occasions although the profit rate may be rising in industry, with a tendency for the demand for loan money to exceed the bona fide savings of the public, the fact that the banks may be glutted with cash reserves, may keep the market rate of interest (both short and long) abnormally low, even though the profit rate in industry is rising.

Conversely, it is possible, particularly in the crisis phase of the business cycle, when bank loans are being contracted owing to cash reserve ratios having become strained, for the calling in of short term loans by the banks, and the selling of long term investment (which constitute a market demand for the long term bona fide savings of the public), to cause the market rate of interest to rapidly rise, even though the profit rate in industry is not rising, but falling.

Thus we see that fluctuations in the artificial bank-made supply of loans (due to fluctuations in the cash reserve ratios of the banks), may tilt the market rate of interest considerably away from what it would otherwise be if there were no alternate expansion and contraction of what we have called the "artificially" creatable (and extinguishable) supply of bank-made money.

Cyclical movements.

Having discussed the influence of the artificial supply of loan-money on the actual market rate of interest, let us now consider seriatim the normal influence of trade itself upon the long term rate, throughout the course of the business cycle.

In the early stages of cyclical revival, i.e., before most factories have become fully employed, the demand for long-term loan-money for expansion purposes remains small, and tends to grow less rapidly than bona fide savings, which will be increasing *pari passu* with general incomes.

When, however, trade revival has progressed sufficiently far to make most factories fairly fully employed, a demand for long term money will spring up for factory enlargement.

This additional long term demand will tend, more or less suddenly, to raise the long term rate; particularly if at the same time the short term rate is itself increasing owing to commodity prices rising, more trade being done, and more speculation breaking out, and thus straining the credit resources and reserve ratios, of the banks.

It is, in fact, when the capital goods industries begin to revive, for expansion purposes, somewhat late on in the rising half of the trade cycle, that the long term rate of interest normally begins to rise most.

This high rate tends to continue not only during the boom period, but also slightly afterwards; for, even when the subsequent slump has begun, the rate tends to stay high for perhaps nine months owing to the outbreak of Distress demands; and owing to a large additional risk element over and above "pure" interest, entering into the market rate.

Eventually, however, as trade goes on declining, and as the desire to erect new plant subsides, the long term demand itself tends to diminish; and the short term demand also diminishes because speculation dies as commodity prices fall and the volume of commerce diminishes.

Thus, with a lag, both the short and long term demands decline; and this influences both short and long rates even though the available supply of long term money is *also* probably diminishing (though not at so rapid a rate as the demand).

Furthermore, as the slump progresses and retail prices and wages fall, less and less legal tender is required in public circulation for wage paying, pocket money, and till money purposes. More and more of it returns to the banks, and cash reserve ratios are thereby augmented.

The banks, therefore, being profit seeking institutions, and since they are unable to find any large *commercial* outlet for their resources, tend to invest their surplus resources in well secured Government bonds, and to force up their prices, thereby forcing down the long term rate of interest.

There will, it is true, be some risk-element over and above pure interest in the price of government bonds during depressions (owing to tax receipts having probably fallen with the declension in general trade), but even so, since safe industrial investments, without a falling profit trend, will be hard to find, high class government bonds will be particularly sought after even despite their risks.

Indeed, unless there is a crisis in the credit of the Government, the rise in Government bonds will continue until at last trade revival, and the consequent demand for industrial capital, has once more led to a rise in the long term rate of interest.

I should add, however, that when recovery begins, and as the Government budget becomes better and better balanced, actual recovery in Government bonds will continue for a while (owing to the risk factor in governments diminishing), even though the profit trend in industry is simultaneously rising—a factor which, other things equal, would have caused interest rates, and Government bonds, to fall, if there had *not* previously existed a risk-factor.

Interest rates during inflation.

As already said, the market rate of interest represents a hire-price for money itself.

If, however, a rapid price inflation is occurring money itself will be depreciating in real value owing to its purchasing power over goods falling. Lenders will, therefore, if they are wise, demand an extra high price for their monetary loans to offset the "real" depreciation which is likely to occur in the purchasing power of money itself during the currency of the loan. Lenders will, in fact, if they are wise, tend to hold off the loan-money market proper, and to invest their available resources in equities, commodities, or foreign exchange, which will *appreciate* in terms of money as the inflation progresses.

The supply of loan-money in the long market proper is, therefore, likely to decline.

Meanwhile, the demand for loan money will rapidly increase; for, during a period of rapid price inflation, it is highly profitable, in terms of money, to be a debtor and to speculate with one's borrowings in equities, commodities and exchange.

During price inflations, therefore, interest rates tend to rise particularly high. Indeed in Germany in 1923, the short term rate rose for a while to 108%.

Conversely, during a price deflation opposite forces operate, and interest rates tend to become abnormally low—at all events until the deflation itself has led to a crisis in the banks or in Government finances; when market rates of interest usually soar, for Distress reasons, reflecting abnormal risk.

Avoid bonds during inflation. Borrow rather than lend.

Normal effect of a change in the bank rate.

A change in the bank rate, *if widely anticipated,* may have little effect on either common stocks or bonds. A sudden *unexpected* change, however (say, upwards), always sends both bonds and common stock down for a while. But if such a rise occurs in the rising half of the cycle, common stocks usually recover afterwards, although bonds may continue to remain depressed on the lower level, owing to general interest rates having risen.

Theoretically, a change in the money rates tends to affect all securities simultaneously in an equal degree; but other factors of a different nature may subsequently cause common stocks to swing on upwards (or downwards), whereas no such factors may operate to cause a similar movement in bonds.

CHAPTER VIII

CYCLES IN SINGLE INDUSTRIES

Industries have their own private cycles.

Although most industries prosper and slump together as a result of the major trade cycle, and although much profit can be made by effecting a complete semi-cyclical switch from ordinary shares into bonds, and vice versa, at the transition stages of each cycle, additional gain is to be made by studying single industries separately.

History shows that in most trade cycles there is rarely a single year during which the profits of some industry are not at their maximum, while the profits of some other are at their minimum. For instance, in 1922 in England, when most industries were slumping, artificial silk enjoyed considerable prosperity.

In a few instances single industries have undergone the abnormal experience of two or more independent cycles within the compass of the major trade cycle.

In view of these facts single industries should be studied separately on their merits, even though a study of the trade cycle as a whole throws much light on the prospects of individual industries.

Why certain industries fail to move with the majority.

The reasons why single industries do not all prosper and slump simultaneously with the general trade cycle are either:—

(*a*) Because of government demands; because of changes in fashions; because demand becomes saturated; or because of the successful competition of some rival new industry.

Or more probably—

CYCLES IN SINGLE INDUSTRIES

(*b*) Because supply fluctuates peculiarly on account of variations in plant and resultant output.

In single industries, particularly during periods of prosperity, the supply factor is often more changeable than the demand factor: to watch it is therefore particularly important.

The normal cyclical course of a single industry.

The usual sequence of events in any single industry is:—

1. Prosperity and high profits.
2. Big influx of new capital.
3. Increased supply as soon as the gestation period of the new plant is over.
4. Competition and cutting of prices; and simultaneously—
5. A gradual saturation of demand.
6. Resultant over-production and competitive marking down of prices to prime costs.
7. Several years of stagnation; during which there is—
8. A gradual reduction of costs, coupled with closing down of the weaker companies.
9. Gradual wearing out of the products already in private use; leading to—
10. A revival in demand.
11. Renewed prosperity.

In this way eras of good profits eventually lead to eras of bad profits;* augmentation of supply is usually the major cause of the change.

Since, however, this happens in different industries to different extents and at different times, their prosperity is not always

* Early slump after boom is much more certain than early revival after slump—a point in favor of the long-run bear tack during the fever-periods of boomlets.

simultaneous; shares consequently pursue different courses. The investor, therefore, must watch each industry separately; and if any one bids fair to slump while another bids fair to revive, he should switch his funds from the one to the other. It is not, as a rule, advisable to hold the same ordinary shares throughout the whole of the rising half of each cycle.

Appendix A describes how to forecast the profits of single industries. The matter is not treated here, since it would break the flow of our argument.

CHAPTER IX

SELECTING SHARES FOR CYCLICAL PROFIT

Factors to consider.

Assuming the rising half of the cycle to have been reached, it is desirable to categorize the industries and companies which will probably show the greatest profit in the market during the rising half of the business cycle.

In the rising half of the trade cycle when commodity prices normally rise, various influences are at work which affect different industries in different degrees. It is, therefore, well to sift these influences, to ascertain how the profits of different industries are likely to respond.

The factors to be considered divide themselves broadly into four main groups:

(i) Factors likely to influence demand.

(ii) Factors likely to influence supply costs.

(iii) Factors relating to the company itself.

(iv) Political influences.

Although a given company may be subjected to influences belonging to any or all of the above four groups, it is desirable for us to isolate the phenomena, so as to emphasize the importance of each factor separately.

Sequence of revival.

First of all, not all industries begin their cyclical revival simultaneously. The capital goods industries, and the super-luxuries frequently tend to lag behind.

The consumer goods industries, on the other hand, particularly those for which a large deferred replacement demand has grown up, tend to rise first.

Shares, however, do not always move exactly simultaneously with industrial profits; although there is certainly a tendency for the shares in industries whose profits recover first, also to rise first;—unless perchance the shares in the industries which revive late happen to have been marked down abnormally in depression, in which case they also may recover early.

Narrow range cyclical fluctuators.

Some industries have a bigger range of swing in the course of the business cycle than others.

Those which normally fluctuate least throughout the cycle are the necessities and semi-necessities, like foodstuffs and passenger travel; and perhaps certain semi-necessities like tobacco and motion pictures.

Representative industries.

Medium range fluctuators are what might be called the Representative Industries, namely, industries whose sales fluctuate more or less proportionately to general business, e.g., jute (the world's wrapper), the paper trade, chemicals, the cable and telegraph companies, railways, shipping and the newspaper trade (which depends upon advertisement revenue).

Since, however, the profits of such companies fluctuate roughly parallel with the general volume of business, a distinction must be drawn between them and the industries of a more stable nature, such as foodstuffs, and public utilities.

These latter improve slightly, it is true, when general trade revives, but their shares have little in the nature of a "comeback" like the truly Representative Industries.

The three violently fluctuating groups.

The industries which fluctuate most throughout the cycle and in which most cyclical profit is therefore to be made by the investor, are in three main groups:

(i) The raw material industries,

(ii) The constructional industries, including machinery, and

(iii) The luxury industries.

Raw material industries.

The raw material industries have certain interesting features. Sometimes what they produce rises in price very early in the cycle, even though the demand for the raw material for true "consumptive" purposes has not yet greatly increased. That is rather interesting. They rise rapidly in price *without* an increase in true consumption.

The reasons for this are usually threefold. Firstly, just when a cyclical slump is nearing its end and most raw material industries have got into trouble, the people in an industry usually get together and institute a scheme for restricting supply.

Secondly, the anticipation of the restriction of supply, and the anticipation of a resultant rise in price lead to a speculative demand for the raw material, and this often sends prices up sharply for a second reason.

While thirdly, if, owing to better confidence, retailers begin to stock up their inventories again, more orders will be given to producers, and there will thus mature a big, quick "shiftback" or disappearance of raw material stocks from the published statistics.

The "apparent" statistical position of raw materials is thus improved; although real, true, final consumption has hardly moved at all.

That is what happens in almost all trade cycles.

The net result of these three influences is that raw materials tend to rise to above costs so that a small profit is made.

Thereafter, however, there is usually a long pause until the continued upward swing of the general cycle has so increased demand that the restriction schemes are gradually abandoned. Then when true scarcity subsequently matures, owing to expanding demand, a further sharp upward movement in prices occurs.

Of course, all the different commodities do not enjoy these jumps in prices simultaneously. Consequently, an index number of raw commodities tends on the whole to make only a steady and gradual rise.

Single groups, however, get concentrated "runs"—lasting perhaps 18 months; and then later usually lie dormant for perhaps a full year.

To catch these intermittent industrial movements as they begin is part of the art of scientific investment.

The constructional industries.

Next let us consider the constructional industries. When existing factories are under-employed there is little demand for new plant for expansion. The replacement demand for machinery is also usually postponed until finances are stronger and the prices of machinery have been lowered.

For example, if the normal replacement demand for machinery is 10% of all standing plant, this demand is likely to be postponed during trade depression, so that actual output may fall to one-fifth of normal in periods of prolonged depression.

During trade revival, however, when expansion is occurring, not only does postponed replacement demand come into action, but there is likely to be added to these delayed replacement demands an additional demand (perhaps also of 10%) for expansion purposes. The result is a doubling of normal demand in booms, as opposed to a subnormal demand (of say only one-fifth of normal) in slumps.

The difference may be some 1000%. This is the reason for the excessive fluctuations in the constructional industries as between general prosperity and depression.

The housing industries.

There is, however, another sort of capital goods industry, besides the plant industry; namely, the housing group.

For the housing group to prosper, the public must have enough money to pay the rents required by speculative builders who finance their operations with borrowed money. The effective market rent rate must, in fact, be above the long-term market rate of interest. There may, for example, be a "social" shortage of houses, but the public may not have enough money to pay the rents required on new buildings, and to make their social demand an "effective" demand on an extensive scale.

Three factors can, therefore, cure this state of affairs by providing builders with a profit, and thus stimulating the housing industry:—

1. A fall in building costs.
2. A fall in the rate of interest.
3. A gradual enrichment of the general population, as a result of further revival in other industries.

To consider these factors separately:

1. Building costs rarely fall appreciably in the rising half of the cycle.
2. Interest rates usually remain low for the first few years of revival, but "nominally" cheap money is not always made "actually" cheap to builders in practice. Very often it is necessary for governments to guarantee housing loans in order to make nominally cheap money really "effective."

If there is no government intervention more often than not it will only be when the consumer goods industries have revived so extensively, that the constructional industries also begin to revive, that general incomes will prove adequate to cover, on a very wide scale, the rents which speculative builders require, even despite the low market rate of interest.

Housing shares, however, should of course rise in anticipation of coming prosperity.

The luxury industries.

As regards the luxury industries: here a distinction should be made between the luxuries supplied to classes with virtually fixed money incomes and those supplied to the classes mainly dependent on profits for their incomes. For instance, cheap beer, tobacco and cinemas may prosper during general trade slumps owing to most of their clientele having (in England rather than in America) fairly fixed money incomes and becoming "really richer" as retail prices fall.

Luxuries sold to the relatively richer classes are in a different category. Their sales depend chiefly on the surplus spending power of the profit-earning classes. In depressions it is to be expected that this type of company will suffer a heavy decline in receipts. In booms they should prosper abnormally.

* * *

If then the bottom of a trade cycle has at any time been reached, there is a prima facie case for purchasing shares in raw material, constructional and luxury enterprises. Such purchases must be founded, it is true, on economic theory and faith. But since no depression has ever yet been permanent, eventual revival will doubtless occur—although no one can predict with complete accuracy the date of revival in each industry.

Deferred replacement demand industries.

Besides these three big swingers, namely raw materials, constructionals and luxuries, there exists a second big group of "big swingers" in which huge profits can usually be made in the early stages of revival; and that is the deferred replacement demand industries.

Whereas, after a slump, there is no deferred replacement demand for railway traffic, telephones, oil, beer, etc.; there is definitely a deferred replacement demand for motors, railway equipment, paint, apparel.

Take for instance paint. If consumption went down to 30% of normal during the slump, it may, as prosperity returns, rise not only to normal, but to double of normal, owing to deferred replacement demand. Thus the index of paint consumption may quite easily rise from 30 to 200, or more than 500%.

The ultra promising infant industries.

Another group of industries well worthy of study are the highly promising infant industries, which seem to possess the characteristic of super-charged economic pressure behind them.

In the 1920-29 trade cycle, the industries which went ahead faster than most others were: radio, rayon, cigarettes (because of ladies' new habits), motors, office equipment, sound pictures, cement and electrical supply.

Industries which suggest themselves as having these "geometric" qualities in the present 1929-19... trade cycle, as well as perhaps in the last, are: air-conditioning, the Diesel engine, rayon, aircraft, beer cans, bus companies, television, financing of installment buying, the pre-fabricated house, industrial alcohol, certain metal alloys, the mechanical refrigerator, and so on.

If one can cleverly pick the best companies in these industries, one obtains the chance of exceptional gain.

Rapidly growing ancillary industries.

A peculiarly promising type of investment is the growing ancillary of a growing industry; e.g., unbreakable glass for motors, in the last trade cycle. But the question must be asked: Can rival factories be quickly set up; and, Do patents fail to prevent the development of competition and encroachment?

Shares with high leverage.

The capital structure of companies should also be studied. Presuming an Investor is right in his choice of industries, he should try to find shares which possess a highly geared equity in their capital structure; that is to say, companies which have very few ordinary shares and a large amount of fixed prior charges, so that a small percentage increase in net profits means a highly geared increase in the percentage available for the ordinary shareholders.

Such common stocks suffer particularly in slumps but benefit particularly in booms.

For instance, if at present only one-tenth of total profits is available for the ordinary shares, a ten per cent rise in net profit would mean a 100% increase in the amount available for the common stock.

Industries with a heavy proportion of fixed overhead charges.

Certain industries, even if they do not have any leverage in the capital structure of their companies, nevertheless have an element of leverage, which will help their common stocks, owing to technical conditions within the industry itself. I refer to industries whose costs do not rise, even though they sell more, so that all extra business is equity profit.

Falling under this heading, in either greater or lesser degree, are: newspapers, with their advertisement revenue; such utilities as draw their power from water; hotels, as regards their bedroom as distinct from their restaurant business, and so on.

Indeed, industries with a high percentage of capital costs, and with relatively low raw material or wage costs, tend to benefit particularly from industrial expansion. This condition applies particularly where such industries are able to raise their prices.

The telegraph and motion picture companies fall into this class. Unlike, say the automobile industry, practically all increased revenue becomes net profit.

Inflation stocks.

If it is believed that general prices will rise, it is important to analyze how the inflation will affect companies:

> a. On the demand side.
> b. On the supply side.

Industries selling at a stereotyped price, like the five and ten cent stores; or industries catering mostly to the fixed income classes; or industries whose prices are regulated by law; or industries (like mail-order concerns) who have to produce a catalogue some six months or more ahead; run the risk of being squeezed either by rising costs or diminished demand.

Other industries, however, tend to benefit from inflation, particularly if they cater for the relatively rich; if they hold large inventories which can be marked-up in price; or if their overhead, even though relatively heavy, is somewhat rigidly fixed.

Personally, I do not greatly favor real estate as an inflation investment, unless it is heavily mortgaged or in a residential area popular among those who will benefit particularly from so-called profiteering.

Heavily mortgaged property, however, might be a promising equity purchase in inflation.

Vertical combines.

Another type of company particularly worthy of support, either during inflation or at the bottom of depressions, is the so-called Vertical Combine, that is to say, a corporation which produces not only a finished product but also its own raw materials.

During depression when the prices of most materials fall to below average costs of production, vertical combines, unless they are abnormally cheap producers, fail to enjoy the benefit which rival firms enjoy by buying their raw materials at prices below costs. Not only are their losses on their inventories great, but the raw material portion of their enterprise becomes a loss-making asset. On the other hand when trade revives and prices rise, vertical combines make abnormal gains; they enjoy appreciation in their inventories, and their costs of raw materials do not rise with market prices.

Lateral combines on the other hand, consisting, for instance, of chains of retail shops or combines of manufacturers not possessing their own raw materials, do not benefit so greatly in booms unless they are virtual monopolists and can charge what price they like.

In slumps, however, such companies, if they are monopolistic and are not purveyors of super luxuries, suffer, as I have said, very little.

Avoid industries which have recently boomed.

A particular type of industry which the Investor should avoid is one that has recently enjoyed an especial boom.

Any industry which has recently enjoyed an abnormal boom tends to attract an excessive influx of new capital which, on coming to fruition, tends to flood the world with too many goods. Competition to sell and keep factories employed becomes fierce; and the industry, having outgrown its sister-industries, normally suffers for a lengthy period a decline in the exchange ratio of its products with other products, via and in terms of money; and experiences a long period of difficulty until other industries themselves have had time to grow up and expand to an equivalent extent, or marginal producers have been eliminated.

Depression in such cases tends to become exaggerated (i) if the product takes a long time to wear out; and if replacement demand is consequently small, e.g., as in phonographs as opposed to silk stockings; or (ii) if the finances of *all* the rival companies are strong, so that it is a long while before any one company is eliminated. (Compare the influence of the financial strength of the tin and rubber companies after their 1926 booms.)

Usually industries which boom wildly in one trade cycle do not boom much in the next. They have usually to wait for another trade cycle, i.e., until other industries have had time to catch up with and at last outstrip them.

(N.B.—Steel boomed in England in 1920, but it hardly boomed at all in 1928. I expect it to prosper violently again in the mid-nineteen thirties.)

Degressive industries.

Another type of industry particularly to avoid is one which is suffering from displacement on the part of a rival "artificial" industry (like the horse plow); or one which is dying out due to a change in fashion (such as hair pins);—although, of course, it must be realized that fashions may change, and a recently degressive industry may once more become a progressive industry.

Indeed, fashion industries may be highly promising, although the greatest care must be exercised not only in their selection, but also in timing the right moment to sell in order not to be caught when the public taste changes.

Politically dangerous industries.

Another type of industry to be avoided is that likely to be singled out for political attack either because its function is considered deleterious to the health or morality of the nation, or because political capital is to be made by attacking it with a view to getting lower prices for the consumer, particularly the housewife.

And one should also be cautious about such industries as armaments which might be affected by a Peace Conference; and upon industries likely to be hurt as a result of tariffs, foreign quotas, and so on.

Incidentally, it is to be noted that if a country insists upon imposing numerous import tariffs, the automatic equation of the foreign exchanges, particularly under a paper standard, is likely to cause the exchange rates of the country in question to swing in a so-called "favorable" direction, thereby causing, in time, a check to the majority of export industries which sell in competitive markets abroad.

Violent changes can come about in an industry because of exchange and tariff factors.

* * *

An eye should also be kept on the possibility of new subsidies being given to an industry, or of existing subsidies being removed.

Prefer industries depressed due to under-consumption.

The Investor, having selected the chief groups in which it is theoretically advisable to place his funds during slumps, must examine the recent history and present position of each industry individually with a view to selecting only those industries whose existing depression is due more to general under-consumption than to positive over-enlargement of plant.

Industries which have recently over-expanded in relation to other industries should studiously be avoided—unless their shares stand sufficiently low in the market to make them on that account attractive.

The best industries to choose at the bottom of the Trade Cycle are those in which depression is due to normal cyclical decline in demand, i.e., to temporary under-consumption, like in chemicals, rather than to saturation of demand or to over-enlargement of plant during a previous boom (e.g., wheat, and as was well illustrated after the World War: copper).

The oft-advocated policy of boldly choosing the financially strongest companies in the most depressed industries can only be recommended if careful attention is paid by the Investor to the above factors.

Prefer under-employed companies with scope for profits come-back.

If a manufacturing company is only partially employed and yet is still showing a reasonable earnings yield on market price, profits can be enormously increased when trade revives without the aid of additional capital, especially as overhead costs will fall as output increases. Such companies near the bottom of slumps are frequently desirable.

The equity shares of holding companies.

Another promising type of investment is the highly geared equity shares of holding companies whose holdings are themselves chiefly highly geared equities. If the management of such companies is good, and if, at the same time, the industry is suitable, they are obviously to be considered promising purchases, in the rising half of the business cycle.

Choose high-cost producers with a low profit-margin.

It is interesting to add that if any Investor is tempted boldly to invest in a depressed raw material or manufacturing industry (like automobiles), in the expectation of an ultimate revival in the commodity price, he should theoretically, for cyclical capital appreciation, choose low profit-margin companies and the higher-cost producers rather than the high-profit margin companies and low-cost producers. For instance, if current prices are 100 and A's profit margin is 50, while B's is 10; a 10 per cent rise in the current commodity price will raise the profits of B by 100 per cent, although only raising those of A by 20 per cent. (Of course, however, if prognostications prove wrong, B shares will particularly suffer.)

Consider prices.

Although there have been enumerated different categories of shares and industries either to be preferred or to be avoided, it must be clearly realized that the selections made are purely in terms of prospective profit movements. The vital question of market price in relation to profit-prospects has been entirely omitted.

The point to be made is that although certain industries may be highly promising on account of their prospective economic and profit trends, the prices of their shares may already stand in the market so high as to make a purchase undesirable.

Conversely, although an industrial profit trend may not be highly promising, the price of a share may stand so low as to make a purchase desirable. Relative cheapness, in fact, must be considered just as carefully as prospective movements in profits. Only buy if the price, as well as the profit-prospects, justifies a purchase.

The ideal selection.

It would be interesting to find a company in an ultra promising and fairly young industry, for which there is a deferred replacement demand; which is at present working on a small profit margin; whose factories are at present under-employed; whose recent slump was due to under-consumption, rather than over-production; which purveys a semi-luxury for a class which benefits particularly in good times; where the capital structure is highly geared; which is not greatly subjected to foreign competition; which stands at a price in the market which shows a reasonable current earnings yield, despite low profits; which has a high ratio of capital costs to labor and raw material costs; or which alternately is a vertical combine, and the price of whose products can be raised during scarcity.

Such would be an ideal company at the revival stage of the general business cycle.

CHAPTER X

SECTIONAL MARKET ACTIVITY

Since single industries have their own private cycles which vary in length, range and time-incidence, the investor should attempt to switch from one industry to another as occasion seems to demand.

The shares of companies do not, however, always move in strict conformity with their actual profit curves.

Fashion influences the Stock Exchange as much as any other sphere of life. Different shares or groups of shares are wont to come into public favor at different times, and then later to be forgotten. But behind the fashions of the Stock Market there is normally some basic improvement in the economic outlook of the company or group; it is this, or the expectation of it, which sets the process in motion.

The usual sequence of events is:

(a) For a share or group of shares to be fairly valued.

(b) For economic improvement to take place and for the group automatically to become undervalued.

(c) For the under-valuation to lead to buying by those with inside knowledge.

(d) For the Press to comment on the buying and for the public then to buy too.

(e) For the rise to be carried too far, through excess of zeal on the part of small investors.

(f) For a minor relapse to follow.

(g) For stagnation then to occur—with fluctuations in a narrow range, buyers roughly equalling sellers and the public thinking the price about right.

SECTIONAL MARKET ACTIVITY

(h) After an interval of perhaps a year, the same cycle may once more be repeated.

In the case of some shares there are several upward sweeps of the foregoing nature in each complete cyclical upswing in the industry. Occasionally there is only one major movement.

As a general rule the appearance of movements of the above sort when plotted on a share chart is somewhat as follows:

First a rise from one zone to another; then a minor reaction of about a third of the rise; then a fairly flat period, followed by another rise into a new zone, and so on—the shares fluctuating in a grand manner astride their cyclical long-run mean, thus:

PLATE VII

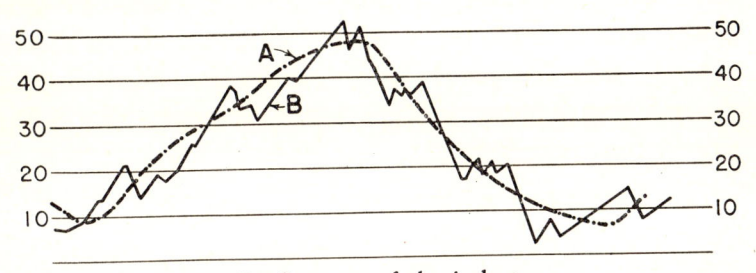

A = Profit curve of the industry.
B = Share index curve.

Sometimes these spasmodic sectional movements last only a few months; more usually they last well over a year. Investors should try to exploit these large scale swings in groups of shares, and try to stand clear when the swings are apparently over.

We would add that public fashion for particular groups of shares becomes especially pronounced in the revival stages of the cycle, when industry after industry begins to show signs of improvement. The "fashion" factor gradually loses in importance as prosperity becomes more widespread.

In the early stages of revival investors should concentrate on deducing which few industries appear the most attractive for early improvement, and should place their funds for the most part in these particular groups, in the expectation that their various merits will shortly bring them into public favor.

CHAPTER XI

HOW PRICES ARE MADE

The forces governing prices.

Investors often ask how precisely share prices are made and what is it that exactly governs them. Is it the actions of the jobber in England, or of the specialist in America; the actions of insiders; or the actions of the investing public? Is it market sentiment; demand and supply; or earnings, assets or prospects? Or is it something to do with technical market conditions, e.g., the volume of savings; the supply of credit; the amount of stock that jobbers hold on their books; the dearness of money; and so on?

The inter-action of these various forces may be described as follows:

Demand and supply within the market.

On various parts of the floor of the London Stock Exchange there stand various groups of jobbers. (A jobber is a middleman who deals, not with the outside public—this is done only by brokers—but with brokers direct). Jobbers quote a price at which they will buy and another at which they will sell. This "turn" represents their normal profit, which is sometimes increased, sometimes diminished, by a rise or fall in the shares which they are holding.

Each jobber specializes in certain types of securities. In all the chief markets like Oils, Rubbers, and so on, there are various competing jobbers. Some or all of them probably hold on their books a supply of the shares in which they deal. If their holdings are already rather big in view of their private finances and their view of the outlook, they will be unwilling to take more stock on their books except at lower prices. If, therefore, a broker goes up to a jobber, and after being made a buying-and-selling quotation, succeeds in selling the unfortunate jobber 1,000 shares that he did not really want, the next broker who comes up is almost sure to be quoted a lower price. Thus, the price will gradually or rapidly fall on account of supply exceeding demand, at the old price, in the actual market.

On the other hand, if demand exceeds supply and if brokers with buying orders exceed those with selling orders, jobbers' stocks will be reduced, and prices will be marked up.

The supply of shares coming on to the market may result either from investors becoming nervous, from bankers calling in loans, from pessimism as regards the industrial outlook, from deceased estates, from switches into what appear more attractive securities, from "bear" sales by the public, from sales because of adverse rumors or adverse news, such as reduced dividends, reduced profits, hostile tariffs, political trouble and so on.

The same set of factors, with signs reversed, can cause an increase in market demand.

Average opinion governs prices, through so-called demand and supply.

The *fundamental* factor governing price, however, is the "average" opinion of the general public. Any price current in the market will at the time be thought too high by some people, too low by others, and just about right by a certain number.

Those who think that the market price is too high will sell, *at the market price,* via brokers and jobbers, to those who think it is too low. If, however, the public's average opinion changes adversely, so that, on an average, they think a share over-valued at the price, more sellers will come in than buyers, with the result that jobbers' stocks will increase and prices will be marked down.

If, on the other hand, the price falls so low that "average" opinion thinks it too low, or if average opinion about prospects changes and the belief gains ground that the share is undervalued, more buyers will come in than sellers, jobbers' stocks will be affected, and the market price will rise, until it once more reflects the "average" opinion of the public.

This opinion, as was said earlier, is affected by rumors, news, prospective earnings and the apparent relative cheapness or dearness of other alternative securities.

The "relativity" factor in relation to ready money.

Looking at the price problem as a whole, however, prices are essentially "relative" expressions. Two opinions about value are always at issue (i) concerning the shares themselves, and (ii) concerning money or rather monetary savings. Indeed, matters relating to ready money, and the value temporarily put on liquid resources by the public, may be just as important an influence on security prices as are prospective movements in industrial earnings.

It can thus occur that a temporary scarcity of *bona fide* savings due to an all round reduction in industrial dividends, or to a glut of new issues such as absorbs *bona fide* savings, or a temporary calling in of loans by banks, or a desire on the part of investors to get in cash reserves because of lack of confidence about the future, a need to pay taxes or holiday expenses, or for the purpose of transferring money abroad into foreign securities, may cause a sudden rush to realize securities and thus lead to a violent collapse in share prices even if industrial earnings, actual and prospective, are unchanged.

Short run rises and falls on the Stock Exchange can well be caused *solely* by matters relating to Money and Sentiment. Hence the whole theory of Conjunctures. (See next Chapter.)

External, i.e., market and monetary conditions may thus, in the short run, affect "average opinion" and security prices just as much as internal, i.e., industrial factors.

CHAPTER XII

THE INTERMEDIATE MOVEMENTS. (I. Their Causes)

The short-run swings.

As already stated, each upward and downward swing of the business cycle is interrupted by sizable Intermediate movements against the general cyclical trend.

These movements are due either to fluctuations in the amount of money available for new investment, fluctuations in the amount of money wanted out of old investments, or to fluctuations in market sentiment.

During each of these intermediate movements there is a powerful tendency for all types of shares to move roughly together. This point is clearly indicated by any graph of any representative index of ordinary shares.

This being so, the object of the short run, as distinct from the long-run investor, should be to sell in the intermediate boomlets—when he and the public are probably full of confidence; and to buy in the succeeding reactions when the public's, and probably his own, nerves have probably been severely shaken.

Indeed to do what "feels" to be eccentric at the time is usually right in investment.

Above all let the short-run investor realize that the only way to make profits is to buy shares when they are cheap and to sell them when they are dear. Shares, however, are rarely cheap except during fits of market weakness. Successful investment therefore largely depends on buying when the public, and probably oneself also, feels hesitant to buy and somewhat nervous.

With the further implication that in order to be able to buy in the short-run slumps, one must habitually sell in the short-run boomlets, so as to accumulate liquid resources for use in the next intermediate slump. This involves selling when the public, and probably oneself also, is eager to buy and full of confidence. It also implies that half the art of investment is to keep one's funds idle for perhaps two or three months on end out of every six.

Usually, when shares are cheap, nobody has any money—they have spent it all in a preceding boomlet. Wherefore get in cash in the boomlets. Try not to be like the general public.

Factors governing share prices—(a) Internal, (b) External.

Short-run general movements are so important as to require extra special attention. As already said:

Share prices can move for two sets of reasons, "internal" and "external." The *internal* influences are those connected with the fortunes of the industry or the company; the *external* are those resulting from technical Stock Exchange conditions and sentiment. It is quite possible, without any change in internal conditions, for market prices to fluctuate 20% to 50% within a few months; this may happen solely for *short-run external* reasons.

The conjuncture.

Normally there are always some forces operating to push the market as a whole down, while others are simultaneously operating to push it up. The net effect of this "conjuncture of forces" determines the current general trend.

The intermediate swings, which are the subject of this chapter, have, like the cyclical swings, definite economic causes; and the "conjuncture of forces" which brings them about can be split up into its various separate psychological and mathematical elements, both of demand and supply. Indeed to make rational forecasts as to the "intermediate" swings, it is necessary to adopt this "splitting" form of analysis.

The three groups of influences.

There are three separate causes of the Intermediate Swings:

I. Purely *Emotional* factors, i.e., fortuitous waves of mass fear and confidence.

II. Variations in mass *Opinion as to Value,* i.e., as to whether the market is too high or low on prospects. This, although psychological, is something more rational than pure emotion. It implies a varying long-distance economic view of the future; and suggests alternate public waves of over-optimism or pessimism.

III. Purely *Quantitative* factors relating to savings, speculative bank loans, the open bear position, etc., which have nothing to do with either fear or opinions as to the underlying economics of given companies or industries. These quantitative factors are essentially mathematical, and determine the "technical," as distinct from psychological, condition of the market. They comprise the amount of money *statistically* available for share purchases as compared with the funds which investors wish to withdraw from the market.

Market action is, of course, decided upon by the brain, but decisions are influenced by the statistical as well as by the two psychological factors. Let us analyze these three vital factors: *(I) Sentiment, (II) Valuation* and *(III) the Quantitative factors.*

Fortuitous waves of fear (or enthusiasm).

No matter how favorable the technical (non-psychological) condition of the market; nor how favorable the long run outlook for industry, it is *always* possible, at every stage of the cycle, for an unexpected wave of fear, actuated either by political or economic factors, domestic or foreign, to cause buyers suddenly to hold off the market, and to stimulate a wave of sales. The demand-supply ratio in the market may thus become upset, and the index of shares may collapse.

No man, unfortunately, can scientifically forecast these for-

THE INTERMEDIATE MOVEMENTS

tuitous waves of mass fear. All he can do is to keep well informed, and be particularly careful when conditions are developing which look politically or economically threatening, and which *might* create a sudden wave of mass pessimism.

Alternate errors of optimism and pessimism.

It is, however, a characteristic of almost all markets, whether rising or falling, to swing astride their cyclical mean angle of ascent or descent. Indeed, the "typical" shape of the graph of any market is as per chart IX on page 108.

The arrows represent the apparent (guessed) cyclical trend. Point (A) on Figure 1 represents an error of pessimism. This error, when discovered, usually gives rise to an error of optimism (B); which, when discovered, usually gives rise to another error of pessimism (C).

PLATE VIII
REPRESENTATIVE INTERMEDIATE FLUCTUATIONS

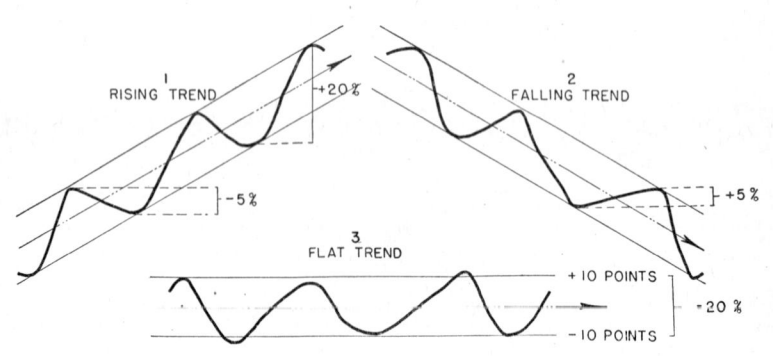

1 RISING TREND +20% −5%
2 FALLING TREND +5% −20%
3 FLAT TREND +10 POINTS / −10 POINTS

Danger and safety zones.

It is the economic or trade situation (or the general rate of interest) which causes the upswing in the "mean" line; it is alternations of optimism and pessimism, coupled also with certain non-psychological factors (discussed later) which engender these normal swings astride the cyclical mean.

When shares are above the apparent (guessed) mean angle of cyclical ascent, they are "probably" getting into a dangerous position from a short run point of view; whereas if they are below the mean, they are "probably" safe. This, of course, is not an infallible rule; but if an arrow line is drawn through the middle of the "apparent" mean trend or track of a market; and if thin lines are drawn more or less parallel to it joining the sequence of tops, and the sequence of bottoms; one gets what might be called the upper and lower parallels; and it is amazing how often, when shares reach their upper apparent (cyclical, intermediate, or minor) parallels, they relapse; and how often, when they reach the neighborhood of their lower parallels, they recover. (Compare the 1929-32 slump in U. S. A., page 14.)

Of course when a market which is fluctuating sideways, as in Figure 3, starts changing its general direction, either downwards or upwards, this rule of safety at the lower parallels (and danger at the upper) breaks down; for a change of direction, say upwards, implies that the graph *must* break through its normally dangerous upper parallel. But most of the time, the rough rule is most valuable, both for rising, falling and horizontal parallels.

The supply of funds in relation to demand. (Statistical Factors.)

In addition, however, to casual variations in Sentiment, and to alternate errors in Valuation, certain purely *mathematical* factors must be considered by forecasters of the intermediate or "conjunctural" short-run swings in the market.

These mathematical factors are:

A. *Funds available for investment; and*

B. *Funds required by investors, to be withdrawn from the market, i.e., Disinvestment.*

A. Funds available for investment.

As regards "A": The various funds with which securities can be bought may be classified as follows:

1. *Unexpended bona fide savings (either new; or old, i.e., hoarded).*
2. *Money borrowed from the banks.*
3. *Funds flowing in from abroad.*

If all these funds are being reduced simultaneously, or if the net effect of their variations is a reduction, stock exchange prices can suffer, even though trade may be improving. Conversely, if the net effect is an expansion, stock prices tend to benefit, even though trade may not be improving. Perfect statistical measurement is impossible, but reasonable calculations can be made.

The investor, therefore, should carefully study these three funds and try to forecast their short-run movements.

1. *Bona fide savings.*

It is estimated that, of America's bona fide savings, there often accumulate and become available for purchase of new or old securities about $2\frac{1}{2}$ billion dollars a year, or say, 200 million dollars a month; and the only way these funds can permanently disappear is in:

(a) Commissions and expenses.
(b) Withdrawals for private spending, or for transference abroad.
(c) Repayments to the banks.
(d) Subscriptions to new issues.

Except in the case of bank credit contraction, subscriptions to new issues are *usually* by far the most important of these various savings-absorbing factors. If new issues fall much below the accumulating savings of about 200 million dollars a month, savings gradually pile up and eventually get spent on *old* securities. This forces up their prices and tends to cause a conjunctural boomlet (*unless* the banks are simultaneously squeezing speculators, or unless foreign selling absorbs the money). Thus a paucity of new issues is good for old stock exchange securities.

Conversely if new issues (requiring *new* money) are occurring at a rate *faster* than new savings are accumulating, it is *probable* that indigestion will occur and that there will be a short-run slump—unless, as occasionally happens, the deficit is made up by foreign or banking funds. (A vivid illustration of such an exception was offered by the boom which took place in the United States in 1929.)

Pessimistic sentiment, it is true, may retard the spending of such savings as have become available, but if people do not permanently hoard their bona fide savings (and if these savings are not entirely absorbed by new issues, and if the banks are not calling in loans), common stock prices tend to rise as savings accumulate, even though the general industrial situation may *not* be improving. Indeed prices may rise for some months on end even though trade is mildly declining. (Compare March to June in America, 1935.)

It is essential, therefore, that speculators and investors should study the new issues position continuously. Throughout large parts of the normal business cycle, the volume of new issues being offered is a governing factor in the intermediate conjunctural movements.

2. *Banking funds.*

In considering Banking Funds, the first thing to look at is the reserve positions of the banks, i.e., (i) the gold flowing into and out of the country, (ii) the notes flowing from the banks into internal public circulation.

When, in either case, there is a definite (and non-seasonal) flow outwards from the banks, the investor should beware; for if the flow persists unduly the central or reserve bank will probably raise its rates, and bankers will call in loans from speculators; sellers will, in consequence, outnumber buyers, and prices of stocks will accordingly begin to fall.

A continuously strained banking reserve position always causes calling in of stock exchange loans and a collapse in security prices (unless the paper or gold currency is being inflated at the time).

It should, however, be added that the banks *might* on occasions call in loans from the speculators even though their reserve ratios were *not* strained. This might be a deliberate policy of the banks, possibly instigated by the Government. This factor of deliberate government interference so as to check unhealthy and wild speculation will have to be carefully watched for in the future.

3. *International funds.*

International movements of funds are difficult to measure statistically. They are, however, governed by the relative attractions for speculation or investment of the different international centers. Newspapers usually report with accuracy which way the tide is currently flowing, if at all.

B. Disinvestment.

As regards "B": So far we have considered only the supply of money available for purchases of old Stock Exchange securities. There exists, however, the converse case of Withdrawals, i.e., attempts by shareholders to get money "out of" shares, for one or more of the following reasons:

1. The need for cash for holiday, Christmas or tax-paying purposes. These demands are largely seasonal.
2. Withdrawals for private spending, or for transference abroad.
3. Sales made in order to subscribe to new issues of securities.
4. Sales made because shares are thought too high, and because idle money is regarded as a better investment, at current share prices.
5. Sales to pay off loans called by banks, or to meet extra margins if required by brokers.
6. Sales made because of general fear and a desire to get liquid.

But note this: Although a single individual can get money "out of" the Stock Exchange; if he does so, someone else must simultaneously put it in. The public *as a whole* can never get money out of, or put money into, old securities or the Stock Exchange—for the seller receives what the buyer invests; and neither the national supply of shares nor the national supply of monetary savings is affected.

Attempts, however, to get money out of the Stock Exchange at a rate *faster* than buyers are willing to put it in, lead to the demand for money (i.e., cash savings) exceeding the supply, and the supply of shares exceeding the demand. Prices therefore must decline for these mathematical demand-and-supply reasons, until buyers and sellers once more equate, the former being eventually attracted, the latter repelled, by cheapness.

The following point, however, concerning temporary market momentum, and the Law of Supply and Demand, should be noted: Lower prices *eventually* attract demand, but prospective falls in prices temporarily check it.

Intermediate momentum.

When, after a period of extensive speculation, a market begins to look too high on prospects, the more cautious element in the investing community begins to take profits and sell. This tends to cause reactions in shares, and general nervousness; and speculative buying begins eventually to dry up.

Bears then begin to comb the market for weak spots and their selling tends to give downward momentum to the fall. Stop-loss orders then begin to be caught, and one seller thus breeds many others. As prices fall, margins are called; and further forced sales eventuate. Nervousness spreads, and buying dries up further, and the movement thus tends to gain cumulative momentum.

Normally the swing goes on until most weak positions have been cleaned up; meanwhile shares usually move to below their imagined real value on prospects, i.e., to below their apparent mean angle of cyclical ascent, and into the region of their lower graphic parallels.

Then, since they look cheap, and since the market looks firmer and well sold out, new buying on the part of those who sold at higher prices begins, usually of the leaders; and when a rise in the leaders has occurred, less important shares begin to rise in their wake and the whole process, with signs reversed, continues in an upward direction until an unhealthy condition has once more matured and a new conjunctural top eventuates.

An interesting feature of these intermediate market swings is that the percentage of trading swings towards "blue-chip" stocks near each conjunctural bottom, or towards "speculative" issues near each conjunctural top. This change in the character of activity usually happens about half way between the two parallels; and itself often provides a warning.

THE INTERMEDIATE MOVEMENTS

Conclusion.

Quite apart from changes in the general state of political and economic Sentiment, and quite apart from "internal factors," i.e., changes in the prospective earnings of a company or industry, shares can decline (or rise) for technical market reasons of a purely mathematical nature, such as fluctuations in bank loans, new issues of securities, and foreign operations.

Normally, intermediate reactions occur in a market every few months. If, however, the underlying technical conditions remain sound; and if sentiment is not shattered; and if trade is rising so that no overvaluation is maturing, the general market *can* rise for six or twelve months on end, without there being any normal intermediate reaction at all. Though general reactions every few months are admittedly "normal," they are not to be regarded as "inevitable."

* * *

Certain points, however, briefly touched upon above, deserve some further elucidation.

New issue indigestion.

New Issues are usually paid for by instalments, i.e., with payments spread over several months. It is therefore possible for a wave of New Issues to occur and to be all applied for and over-subscribed, despite the total value having already exceeded all likely or possible savings within the period. The first few instalments may be paid with great ease, but when the final instalments, which are usually the largest, fall due, it may be found that their total exceeds the concurrent accumulation of savings.

The actual subscribers may possibly have funds enough to pay all the Calls as they fall due, but in all probability this involves a diversion from old securities of funds that might normally have been used to meet the continuous trickle of sales which is always occurring for purposes of private expenditure, winding up of estates so as to purchase Trustee investments, death duties, taxes, and so on.

Thus the supply of "old" shares on offer may exceed the demand maturing (a) from concurrent bona fide savings, and (b) from such funds as speculators may see fit to borrow from the banks.

The net result is a general decline in the market due to previous over-inflation of new issues, and to market indigestion. It is really a question of over-supply of securities in general, within a period, in relation to market demand.

No general market recovery is usually possible until the extra securities have been digested by the gradual accumulation of additional bona fide savings; or until the fall in prices has been so great as to induce speculators to step in with borrowed bank money.

Good securities in the meantime will fall along with the bad; and it will not be merely the prices of the new issues alone that will suffer. All groups in fact will probably suffer simultaneously.

It should incidentally be added that for new securities to "go" at all, they must be offered at prices which are competitive with existing securities, and that the gradual offering of better and better terms often causes investors to sell old securities in order to subscribe to the new issues which look cheaper. Thus the market as a whole may steadily fall, even though there may not have occurred, as yet, any real statistical Indigestion.*

---

* A knowledge of conjunctural theory is of obvious value to new issue houses and "stags."

CHAPTER XIII

THE INTERMEDIATE MOVEMENTS

(II. Their exploitation)

Survey of the short-run external factors which constitute so-called Market Conditions.

Looking back at the combined influence of the various "conjunctural" factors described in the last chapter, what we find is that although the general long- or medium-run trend of any given share or industry may be upwards, downwards, or flat, short-run zigzag movements occur astride this mean to the extent of anything from plus and minus 5% to plus and minus 30% or more; the biggest movements, of course, take place in the more speculative counters. Skilled timing, therefore, may enable a buyer to buy 20% lower and sell 20% higher than he might otherwise do. Indeed, a study of the "external" factors which constitute the Timing problem is just as important to short-run operators as is the forecasting of long-run industrial trends. The subject is also of interest to long-run investors if they are to time their buying and selling to the best advantage.

Long-run investors would do well to follow a simple policy of buying mainly in conjunctural slumps, i.e. when the conjunctural share index curve has been depressed for about ten weeks, and again starts turning upwards.

Short-run speculators would also be well advised to buy in the main in the conjunctural slumps—with a view to selling the major part of their holdings, though not necessarily all, in the next conjunctural boomlet.

THE INTERMEDIATE MOVEMENTS

Conjuncture charts.

In order to get a bird's-eye view of the factors which, in conjunction, cause general Intermediate movements, it is advisable for the investor to keep weekly graphs (preferably on millimetre squared paper) of the following statistics:

1. Such foreign exchange rates as (under a gold system) are likely to govern an influx or efflux of gold which, in its turn, will influence bank reserve ratios, and possibly bring about expansion or contraction of bank credit.

2. A graph of the actual national gold holdings (assuming the country to be on the gold standard). Rises and falls in the total stock will tend to indicate forthcoming credit policy.

3. A graph of the bank rate itself, with the 3 months bill rate alongside. A rise in the bill rate towards the bank rate, or a fall away from it, will tend to indicate not only prospective changes in the bank rate, but also the prospective credit policy of the banks.

4. If the country is one where Open Market Operations are resorted to by the Central Bank, keep a graph of its total Loans and Investments; changes in these figures may indicate changes in its open market policy.

5. Keep a monthly graph of such new issues as absorb *new* money, so that changes in totals may be clearly indicated. When this curve is above the average mean beware. Where it is well below, begin to regain confidence.*

6. Since, however, new issues are normally paid for by instalments, it is also desirable to keep say a ten weeks' moving

---

* In England weekly figures for New Money Absorbed are published by *The Economist* newspaper.

average which will give a somewhat better picture of new calls, plus maturing old calls, together.*

Excursus.

It is difficult to determine the magnitude of the surplus or deficit of money required to cause a conjunctural boomlet or a conjunctural slump on the London Stock Exchange; it has been estimated, however, that even so small an unabsorbed surplus as two million pounds is capable of eating quite a large hole in jobbers' stocks and of causing a rise within a few weeks of 5% to 10% in the majority of speculative ordinary shares, even though the sum of two million pounds itself represents only about 1% of total annual national savings. (See Appendix F for a full enlargement of this important subject.)

In other words, the spending of only a few million pounds can cause capital appreciation on paper of several hundred millions.

Conversely, public competition to encash paper profits and to extract from the Stock Exchange even so small a sum as two million pounds—when no new savings or bank funds are available—can, if jobbers are nervous about taking extra stock, cause a capital depreciation of several hundred millions.

---

* Statistical allowance should, of course, be made for new issues which only very temporarily absorb the public's savings, e.g., issues for the redemption of debentures; issues by investment trust companies; new issues containing much water, i.e., representing large reinvestable profits on new flotations of old companies), and so on.

N.B.—New issues for paying back debts to banks permanently, absorb new savings permanently, and incidentally constitute deflation of bank credit currency, unless the banks re-lend the money at once, or spend it on buying Stock Exchange securities, buildings, etc.

Conjuncture charts (continued).

7. Keep also a curve of the index for industrial securities; it indicates general Market Sentiment and shows whether the public have recently been predominantly bullish or bearish. A continued rise over several months (particularly if approaching the higher parallel) suggests the building up on borrowed money of a dangerous bull position, which assuming bad political or industrial news may suddenly burst.

8. A graph of brokers' loans, and of banking loans against securities, is also desirable if statistics are available.

9. A curve for volume of deals might also well be kept. Huge volume usually means the building up of weak speculative positions.

10. It is also desirable to draw some sort of picture of the quality of the new buying and selling. The tail end of an Intermediate upward movement in the market is usually characterized by an increase in volume of dealing in low grade securities, and a relative decline in high grade securities; just as the early part of a rise is usually characterized by high grade buying with only a small percentage of so-called cats and dogs.*

I personally ascribe particular importance to this gradual change in the "character" of buying and of activity which normally is visible at the two ends of a "normal" Intermediate movement.

11. It is also desirable to keep a curve of the share index of important foreign curves (e.g. New York for Londoners and London for Americans) since foreign booms and foreign collapses may have international repercussions, and the two Stock Exchanges, at times, may be mutually competitive for world

---

* At the time of writing (1936) excellent graphs portraying "character of activity in America" are published by Investographs, Inc., 31 Gibbs Street, Rochester, N. Y.

savings. For instance, if New York slumps, international shares may be dumped on London. English funds will probably flow abroad to pay for them; and English savings will be absorbed just as much as if there had been a sudden wave of English new issues.

Similarly (curiously enough) if New York booms, funds may also flow abroad to exploit the rising market, and the English market may suffer!

12. Important Foreign bank rates might also be kept, since their movements may, with a lag, influence the domestic bank rate, and may also lead to change in the flow of short-run international funds to or away from the domestic market.

13. Also plot weekly or monthly curves for statistics concerning general trade and production. Changes in the course of these curves may also cause changes in the course of shares, although shares *usually* begin to move in advance of changes in production and profits.

* * *

The information provided by charts of the foregoing figures will not, as a rule, be non-contradictory. Various factors will point to a rise; others will point to a fall. And above all there will always exist the unchartable factor of ever varying Political sentiment. The investor, however, with the limited evidence available, must make his short run guesses as best he may.

He will, however, obtain considerable extra assistance from the empyrical method of chart reading (itself a branch of the economic Laws of Probability) to be described in Chapter XVII.

General rules.

In making practical use of the Conjuncture Chart, investors should hesitate to buy anything while the weekly share index curve is falling, since it is an indication that sellers as a whole for the moment still outnumber buyers. Investors should wait until this adverse general condition has apparently ended and there is a flattening out of the index curve or a minor upturn.

It is also usually dangerous to buy:

(a) While gold is flowing outwards.

(b) While the three months' bill rate is rising and approaching the level of the existing bank rate. (This latter condition indicates a growing tightness of bank money and a possible rise in the bank rate.)

(c) While new issues for the last three months are high above the average of the last calendar year.

Investors should also be careful of buying if the weekly share index curve has been rising for ten weeks or more, and now looks high in relation to its apparent recent mean slope. (See Chapter XVII.) Such continuous rises usually lead not only to over-speculation among the public, and to the creation of a weak technical position on the Stock Exchange, but also to a glut of new issues on the part of company promoters, which, later on, when calls fall due, will cause indigestion and a scarcity of funds and bring about a market reaction—especially in those groups of shares which are speculatively over-valued.

Policy advised.

The rule, therefore, is first to analyze the four main conjunctural factors (i.e. sentiment, the banking position, foreign funds, and the new issue position) and then to decide whether the net position appears absolutely favorable or unfavorable. Then having come to a private conclusion, decide not to act until the share index curve itself (which indicates how the public, as distinct from you yourself, are reacting to the underlying conditions) starts to change direction upwards. Rarely act contrary to the current trend of this curve, which represents General Market Sentiment. Let its up-turns be your major guide. Never, on principle, run against the current trend of the general market.

Further hints on using this curve are given in our chapter on Graph Reading (Chapter XVIII).

What to sell in unfavorable conjunctures.

Of course, whether or not one sells when conjunctures look unfavorable, depends on whether one is a long-run or short-run investor. But, assuming one's mind is somewhat divided, the following principles may prove of assistance.

When a conjuncture becomes unfavorable, it is not usually necessary to sell everything. Certain types of shares, however, stand out as the most suitable for sale, as follows:

1. *Prospect shares,* i.e., those which have been marked up say to some 30 or more times current earnings, without much prospect of them reaching a 5% earnings yield basis within the next year.

2. *The wide movers,* i.e., those which habitually swing far up and far down in each intermediate swing. If they have risen much faster than the average, and if they possess this characteristic habitually, it is usually wise to sell them when the conjunctural situation has come to look dangerous.

3. *Narrow market shares* which have risen sharply. When a reaction begins, shares with narrow markets are difficult to sell, and a little selling causes sharp declines. It is, therefore, usually advisable to consider selling them while the market is still strong, and before it appears to have entered a technically weak and dangerous position.

4. *Shares bought as a short-run, intermediate speculation.* If shares were bought for the short-run rise, the investor should keep to his plan and intentions, and sell them when that rise has occurred and when the market condition appears to be becoming dangerous.

5. *Shares bought on borrowed money.* It is dangerous to hold shares on borrowed money at what looks like the top of a conjunctural rise.

6. *Shares which have behaved badly.* It is also sometimes wise to sell shares which have behaved badly in the last upward swing. Such behavior often indicates a sharp drop in the forthcoming period of weakness.

What not to sell.

On the other hand, the following shares might normally be kept, unless held on borrowed money:

1. Shares bought for the long-run cycle, unless they have moved very rapidly ahead and have been subjected to wild speculation.

2. Cheap and promising shares with a high earnings yield.

3. Small swingers, i.e., those which do not normally fluctuate much in each conjuncture.

4. Forgotten shares in which there is no bull position but whose industrial outlook is still considered promising.

5. Shares concerning which good (*unexpected*) news is expected shortly by your well-informed self, though not apparently by the public. (Publicly expected good news is normally well discounted in advance.)

6. Shares with a sharply rising profit curve, and which still show a reasonable earnings yield. These shares rarely relapse appreciably during conjunctural reactions.

7. Shares which look safe on the graph. But if they too are grossly overvalued, it is usually wise to sell them also even though their graph looks good and their long-run prospects seem favorable.

8. It is normally not unwise to be half in cash at the peak of any conjuncture which looks dangerous if shares as a whole are overvalued.

When to act.

The actual timing of one's sales is a difficult problem. Usually, however, it is worth considering selling:

(a) When almost all groups have had a rise. (But as a general rule one should expect several groups to escape popular attention.)

(b) When stock market activity is attracting wide attention in the popular Press and articles are appearing on the front page. Usually when this has occurred for several days running, it is a sign of gross overspeculation and technical danger. (Too much company.)

Since, however, bull markets are capable of going to extremes, and since it is wise to have a personal predilection for (cutting losses and) letting profits run, it is, as a general rule advisable to defer action until the market has given its own signal. That is to say, until the rising graph quits its recent upward zigzag track and begins to curve over on the downside. This subject is too lengthy to discuss here, although I propose to deal with it in Chapter XVII on Chart Reading.

CHAPTER XIV

SHORT-RUN VERSUS LONG-RUN SPECULATION

Introductory.

Having considered the way in which shares are affected
(a) By the general trade cycle, and long-term interest rates,
(b) By actual industrial earnings,
(c) By confidence and popularity,*
(d) By conjunctural factors,

let us now examine how best to make money out of these different movements.

Is long-run or short-run speculation the best?

The first question to arise is, whether one should be a long-run (say, three or more years) investor or a short-run (say, three months) speculator.

A study of share prices during past trade cycles shows that the rises from bottoms to tops in most industries are usually well over 300%. Hence if these rises take place within about six years the investor will reap roughly 25% per annum cumulatively on his capital.†

If, however, a glance is made at the curve of any single share throughout the course of its upward cyclical swing, it will be obvious that the sum of the minor rises vastly exceeds the aggregate total of the rise. At first sight, therefore, it might be thought that more profit could be made by in-and-out opera-

---

* Manipulation is dealt with in Chapter XXXVIII.

† 100 units at 25% cumulatively becomes 305 units at end of 5 years, and 381 at end of 6 years.

tions than by a policy of long-run lock-ups. In actual practice, however, this is not necessarily so.

Dual accuracy required both for selling and re-buying.

First, few short-run fluctuations exceed 20%, and if one misses the actual bottoms and tops by, say, 5% each, and adds in jobbers turns and expenses, which may (in England) amount to about 6%, only 4% is left as net gain.

Thus it can be seen that to succeed in short-run speculation is, in practice, not nearly so simple as it at first sight appears. Unless one is exceptionally skilful or lucky the long-run system is undoubtedly safer and usually much more profitable. And yet if investors are to get the best results from their capital, and if they have time to study short-run influences, they should certainly try to profit *to some extent* from the conjunctural and other short-run fluctuations in shares which occur for external reasons. This constitutes somewhat of a dilemma.

Admittedly a system of in-and-out short-run speculation, pursued as regards *the whole* of one's holdings, conjuncture by conjuncture, would almost certainly fail, for the simple reason that if one looks at past index curves for English, as distinct from American, ordinary shares in general, one rarely finds that any conjunctural movement greatly exceeds 7%. And since in-and-out expenses absorb perhaps 6% there is very little profit to be gained.

The following points, however, should be noted. A 7% rise in the general index may be due to half the shares, for example, standing still and the other half rising 14%; or to one-half falling 7% and the other half rising 21%; or to one-third falling 7%, one-third standing still, and the other third rising 28%. If, therefore, one could pick out the widest movers in each conjuncture, reasonable profits might be made.

Allowing for errors.

Looking at the matter without optimism, however, no short-run system of speculation seems worth while unless one has a chance of making at least 10% net on one's capital (i.e. 100 units on a capital of 1,000).

No short-run speculator, however, can reasonably hope to be 100% right; indeed throughout the course of this book we shall regard 70% as a reasonable optimum.

If, then, out of any ten selections, three are almost certain to go wrong, say to the tune of 15%, this will give a gross loss of 45 units. In-and-out expenses (including jobbers' turns) on all the ten shares will in addition come to (at least) 3% on each, which equals 30 units.

Total losses and expenses will thus be 75 units.

But since 100 *net* units of profit are required to give 10% on the 1,000 units capital, 175 units *gross* will have to be made on the remaining 7 successful shares, i.e. 25% on each. Few short-run speculators can reasonably hope to get seven 25% rises out of every ten selections in say three or four months; the short-run system, therefore, does not appear mathematically very promising.

On the other hand, to hold shares doggedly for four or five years on end regardless of whether they sometimes become grossly over-valued as a result of intermediate boomlets is to forfeit the chance of gain that a more active policy might provide.

Probably the ideal programme, therefore, is to adopt a *compromise* between the two above policies and to follow a system involving a lock-up, *if necessary,* of something longer than the normal conjunctural period and yet definitely shorter than the completed cycle of industry as a whole.

SHORT-RUN VS. LONG-RUN SPECULATION

Policy suggested.

The system we suggest is to buy only in conjunctural slumps and to envisage lock-ups of eighteen months or more *if necessary*—so as to give shares a reasonable opportunity eventually to enjoy an appreciable enhancement in price (and so as to get the benefit of probably three successive conjunctural rises) —with, however, the preconceived intention of taking good profits if in the meantime public fashion, or conjunctural factors, or manipulation, should luckily cause the shares to rise until they look over-valued.

This we believe to be the most speedy method of augmenting one's capital (i.e. to be prepared to wait for say two years, *if necessary*). People in a greater hurry rarely make profits so quickly.*

* * *

We would here add that whenever one sells shares after a conjunctural rise, one must normally expect to wait for several months before re-investing. Ability to wait with funds idle until revival begins after the *next* conjunctural slump is one of the highest tests of self-control and character in investment.

To re-invest immediately after selling is rarely right in short-run speculation. Selling times and buying times are not normally identical.

---

* See later, Chapter XX on the high-pressure broker.

CHAPTER XV

STAKES AND STOP-LOSS ORDERS

Have a mathematical system.

Another factor of importance in all types of investment is the simple mathematics of trading in shares—quite regardless of the special art of forecasting. To be a good forecaster does *not* automatically insure success; the mathematics of one's trades must also be scientific.

It has already been suggested that no investor can reasonably hope to be right in his selections much more often than seven times out of ten, for even the best laid plans will go wrong; and unfortunately no one can recognize in advance on which three occasions out of each ten he will be unsuccessful.

The first thing, therefore, for every investor to do is to adopt a system which, provided he is right in the *majority* of his selections, will insure him a net profit. Such a profit, we would emphasize, does *not* automatically mature just from being right more often than wrong. Two factors may combine to cause a net loss even though one is right on an average, namely:

(a) Not having a loss-taking system which is compatible with one's profit-taking system.

(b) Not balancing one's stakes properly.

(N.B. Although we use the convenient word "stakes," we do not wish to convey any idea of blind gambling.)

Loss-taking and profit-taking systems must be mutually compatible.

As regards profit and loss-taking systems: the majority of investors (under the influence of their brokers) snatch readily at their profits but allow their losses to run on. Most investors have in consequence a sheaf of securities in their banks which were once worth hundreds of pounds and are now worth only a few shillings. These losses are always the result of well-laid plans going unexpectedly wrong. In many cases the losses on single holdings exceed the gains on numerous other sales.

The preventive is to decide in advance, however strongly one may believe in any share which one buys, that one will not lose, under any circumstances whatever, more than a fixed amount of money in it. One should further aim at preventing losses on any one holding ever exceeding probable gains on any other. The wise investor, accordingly, gives his broker the order to stop his losses, i.e. to sell, as soon as the share falls to a certain level.

What, however, often happens to the average man buying ten different shares is as follows:

Seven shares rise, say, 15% and give a profit of 105 units.

Three shares, however, fall 40% and give a loss of 120 units.

Final result: a loss, *despite* being right seven times out of ten.

The point is that, mathematically speaking, if small profits are taken, it is essential to take equally small losses. It is ruinous to snatch small profits and let losses run on. One must have loss-taking and profit-taking systems which are mutually compatible.

Long-run investors expecting long-run profits of 50% or more might possibly give large stop-loss orders of 30% or more.

A rigid system of loss-taking is essential.

Short-run operators, however, expecting only 20% profits *must* give relatively small stop-loss orders. The shorter the run you intend to allow for each share, the smaller should be your stop-loss order.

Of course, to take a fixed and rigid percentage loss on any *one* single share regardless of prospects is just as irrational as it is to take a rigid percentage profit regardless of prospects; but if one is investing in a series of shares—after deliberately spreading risks over several securities, instead of in only one security—one must have a scientific system as regards the whole that will prevent any loss on any one holding wiping out the likely gains on perhaps four or five others. Indeed, the correct treatment of losses on a single share in a joint list may differ from that appropriate to the same share if it is a solitary holding. Our contention is that if risks are deliberately spread over, say, ten shares (so that even a total loss on one holding can never wipe out more than one-tenth of one's total capital), one should also follow it up with a rigid loss-taking system which will prevent a few unlucky selections wiping out the whole of the profits on a large number of the others.

Of course, it is psychologically difficult to sell on a fall, just when one invariably feels that a recovery is most likely; but in the long run, if one is going to invest scientifically, a rigid loss-taking system is essential.

Any share, no matter how good it appears to you (who lack complete information concerning the company itself, and the conjunctural factors), can fall 50%, either fast or imperceptibly, even if the directors appear both efficient and honorable, and even though everything appears promising and serene on the surface. The first duty of every investor, therefore, is to prevent such a disaster *ever* happening to himself.

If investors snatch their losses early, profits will normally look after themselves. It is easy, moreover, to make back small losses; big losses are hard to regain.

Amount to put in each share.

The next matter to consider in the problem of investment is Stakes. In securities where risks are approximately equal stakes should be approximately equal as well.

What, however, most people quite rationally, though to some extent wrongly, do, is to try to assess risks in advance and then vary their stakes accordingly. The result is that after careful thought a man may put £2,000 into an ordinary share about which he is confident and only £200 into another about which he is rather nervous. The unexpected, however, is always happening, and quite often those shares about which one is most nervous rise fastest and soonest, while those about which one is most confident fall rapidly and soon. Thus, although seven out of ten selections may be right, the three that fall may unluckily be those in which one has the largest commitment.

The result may be:
Seven gains of, say, 50% on £200 = £700.
Three losses of 15% on £2,000 = £900.
Net result = A loss of £200, although one's selections were brilliant in practice.

Of course, it is quite right to vary stakes in, say, War Loan on the one hand and mining gambles on the other, but taking high-class ordinary shares as a whole stakes should be fairly equal.

A useful rule concerning stakes in *doubtful* cases is to decide that you will never on any occasion lose more than some fixed proportion of your capital (say 2%, or £100 if your capital is £5,000) in any one share, or homogeneous group of shares like tins, and then to balance your stakes *and* stop-loss orders accordingly. If you think that stakes can be safely raised, then lower your stop-loss orders so as to limit your loss to the fixed sum of, say, £100. On the other hand, if you think that you ought to give bigger stops, lower your stakes proportionately. Stops, however, should rarely be more than 20% (nor less than three jobbers' turns in England).

STAKES AND STOP-LOSS ORDERS

The following table may be useful in guiding investors as regards their stakes and their stop-loss orders:

Grade of share (as defined in next column)	Imagined maximum feasible depreciation within 6 months	Stake £	Maximum loss £
A	10%	1,000	100
B	20%	500	100
C	33⅓%	300	100
D	50%	200	100

Give stop-loss orders which will be caught when your loss approximates to £100.

Preferably distribute your funds over ten or more securities.

N.B.—If you adopt several buying schemes whose principles are different, allot a fixed proportion of your capital to each Scheme and apply an appropriate system of staking and of loss- and profit-taking to each.

Recapitulation.

To summarize: To be right in one's selections more often than wrong, although difficult, is by no means enough. One must also have a methodical system of staking and of stop-loss order giving, which will almost guarantee a net profit provided one's selections are right on the whole.

Above all do not try to introduce economic "judgment" into a mathematical system when once adopted—for the simple reason that the whole object of rigid mathematical rules (as regards losses, for instance) is to make you a winner *despite* occasional errors in "economic" judgment. Do not, therefore, try to flavor your entirely reliable mathematics with extra doses of unreliable judgment. The temptation to do so, of course, is strong; but always carefully avoid it. Have the strength of mind to abandon Hope and to sell shares that fall even though they may *still* attract you mentally. This is a mathematical rule which *must* be applied by economic forecasters in *scientific* investment.

Any share can suddenly halve in value. Never dare to forget it.

CHAPTER XVI

STOP-LOSS ORDERS IN ENGLAND

Although stop-loss orders are theoretically sound (who does not regret not having used them in 1929?), in actual practice the majority of brokers do not always find stop-loss order systems satisfactory; the technical difficulties of watching and executing them are great, and the prices obtained for shares may cause friction with clients unless the latter are fully conversant with the actual Stock Exchange detail.

In America stop-loss orders are usually executed at a price extremely close to the figure given, particularly in the case of the market leaders; but in England numerous difficulties arise, and the purpose of this chapter is to outline them briefly.

A stop-loss order cannot be caught except in a falling market, and a falling market is itself a sign that jobbers (similar in character to a specialist in America) already hold more shares than they want. Brokers, therefore, will always find difficulty in making the jobbers buy more.

It is generally imagined that two separate prices are always quoted by jobbers in the market, a buying price and a selling price, for instance 20s.—21s.

At no given moment, however, will jobbers themselves both be bidding for shares and offering them. Strictly speaking, there is no such thing among the jobbers in any given market, say oils, as a fixed and definite buying and selling price. And since these two figures are not fixed there is no precise middle price either.

A client, of course, who wishes to limit his losses to 20% on shares bought at 20s. would like to be able to rely on getting exactly 16s. for them; but it is impossible in a falling market for a broker to know when the shares are precisely 16s. bid. In such a market, jobbers will be calling out their selling prices only, and if the jobber is calling out that he will sell at 16s. 6d., it will be purely guesswork if the broker assumes that his buying price is 16s. The actual buying price may be 16s. 1½d.; and under these conditions no broker would be justified in slaughtering the shares for only 16s. (when he might have got 16s. 1½d.). And yet, if he does not make a guess of this nature, the next price called out by jobbers may be 16s. 4½d. sellers, and the best bid obtainable by the broker may be only, say, 15s. 9d. He will, in fact, as a result of not having taken 16s. 1½d. for the shares, have landed his client with an extra loss of 4½d.

And yet if he had sold them at 16s. 1½d., and the shares instead of falling further had risen immediately, the client would (perhaps) have complained that the shares were wantonly sold (for the sake of the commission) before the stop-loss figure was actually reached.

For this reason no broker will guarantee any given price being secured; nor will most brokers take stop-loss orders based on the market's buying price.

Further, most brokers will not, so far as I know, accept stop-loss orders based on middle prices. The middle price is merely a guess; and if the broker's guess seems to the client wrong, as it may do if the shares start suddenly rising, the client may demand an explanation—which, in the nature of things, will prove unsatisfactory, and leave the client with a feeling of resentment; and the broker with, perhaps, a "legal" liability for having acted too soon.

Most brokers, therefore, will only accept jobbers' selling prices as a basis for cutting limits. They require that the order shall be given in the form "sell when the market are so many shillings sellers."

Even then, however, a client giving an order of this character must understand the nature of the business. If the market are sellers at 16s. they will clearly not buy except at a lower figure, i.e., under 16s. A client giving a stop-loss order therefore worded "when the market is so much sellers" must, if he wants to get 16s., allow for the normal jobbers' turn in the share (plus a little bit extra because of the fact that when a market is falling the difference between the buying and selling prices of jobbers normally tends to widen). Thus, if he wants to get about 16s. for his shares, he must give his order at say "16s. 9d. sellers."

Even then, however, his broker may not get as much as 16s. for the shares. For example, if the share in question is in, say, a mining company, and a local earthquake is reported overnight, the shares which closed near 16s. 9d. sellers on the first day may open at 14s. sellers on the next; and the best bid obtainable in the market may be only 10s. or 12s. Thus, a client who wished his loss limited to 20% on shares bought at 20s. may, if sudden bad news is published, make a loss of nearly 50% if his broker sells "at best," according to instructions as soon as the shares have fallen in the market to "16s. 9d. sellers."

In view of this danger, and in view of the fact that the implication behind a stop-loss order is that the broker should sell "at best" as soon as the market is selling at or below a given price, it is advisable for the client to give low limits, below which the broker is not to sell (after the market has touched 16s. 9d. sellers) without further reference to the client.

For instance, the stop-loss order might well be worded thus, "Sell my XYZ shares, bought at 20s., when they fall to 16s. 9d. sellers; but do *not* sell if the best bid obtainable is 13s. 9d. or below."

I personally advise this kind of order; it seems to me the

wisest. A client thus avoids an unexpected 40% loss being taken when he wishes to take about 20% only.

* * *

Now, although all brokers will do their best to see that stop-loss orders are carried out efficiently, no broking firm is big enough to detail separate dealers to stand at each and every point in the Stock Exchange listening to the ever-varying prices of the 5,000 odd securities that are quoted. It is true a broking house can inform the various jobbers that it is probably a dealer (whether buyer or seller would not be stated) at somewhere about a certain specified price; and in such a case the jobber will (probably) telephone the broker when the market quotation has fallen to the region of the specified figure. No broker, however, can guarantee that this will be done, and no broker can afford to have men detailed continuously to watch all the shares in the market.

Prudent brokers therefore merely say that "they will do their best," and as a rule will take no responsibility either for getting a specified figure or even for carrying out orders given. Dealers, of course, do their best; but clients must clearly understand that such orders are accepted only on the basis of "when the market are sellers at a certain figure," and "without any legal or moral responsibility."

Indeed many brokers in England, in view of the difficulties, refuse to take stop-loss orders altogether; although they are usually ready (without responsibility) to inform their clients when certain lower prices are approached.

CHAPTER XVII

THE ART OF USING CHARTS

Although in the foregoing chapters we have frequently referred to buying during the short-run slumps and selling during the short-run boomlets, nothing conclusive has yet been said as to how to time such actions to the best advantage.

Actually there does not exist any totally reliable set of rules; but the following notes on graph reading will prove of much practical use not only for the intermediate, but also for the major, swings in the market.

Merits and limitations of charts.

More nonsense, however, is talked about chart reading, both by its protagonists and antagonists, than about any other subject in the sphere of investment.

Some graph readers, it is true, are fanatics. The sane graph reader, however, rarely uses charts to determine what to buy, i.e., for Selection. Economics tell him this. He merely uses his graphs to suggest to him what might be bought, and to tell him when (and when not) to buy securities which, on economic grounds, attract him. Graphs tell you *when* to operate, but not *why* to operate; and since Timing is often as important as Selection, charts can prove extremely useful.

One writer, misunderstanding the whole subject, asserts that graphs are entirely useless since the future cannot be foretold from the past. Another writer, however, in a book now out of print, puts the matter very neatly (somewhat) as follows:

Graphs are *not* a method by which chartists try to foretell the future from the past; nor does the modern graph-reader postulate that a given set of conditions in the past provides a good and sufficient reason for expecting a recurrence of such conditions in the future. There may be a few chartists who think in this way, but the sensible graph-reader never expects history to repeat itself without variations.

Charts, however, are a tool which, when used *in conjunction* with other recognized means of forecasting, improve the trader's chances of accurately determining the trend of the market.

* * *

A chart is a pictorial record of the market's action in the past. It is in no sense a guarantee that the same action will again prevail.

Over many years, however, it has been found that individual stocks and the market as a whole, as represented by well-known averages, often move in such a way as to produce certain easily recognizable patterns and formations.

As Mr. Roland says: Some of these patterns have definite significance. If a chartist's examination of past records shows him that in eight out of ten times, whenever formation "X" has appeared, the market has subsequently declined, he has a reasonable expectation—an empirical Law of Probability—that a decline will again take place when he sees this formation developing on his charts.

These "Graphic Laws of Probability" are well worth studying, even though they are never 100% right.

They *should* be used to "influence" one's judgment, even though the investor should never allow his charts to do his thinking for him.

Charts are, however, of considerable value in reaching a decision when other (economic and psychological) factors are in doubt.

Incidentally, apart from the portrayal of suggestive formations, charts perform another valuable function. Memories are notoriously short; and we are all prone, when concentrating on the developments of the day, to lose sight of what has come before, and consequently at times have a distorted impression of the market and its position a few weeks or months previously. A chart, practically at a glance, corrects this human tendency.

A chart, moreover, portrays the recent trend of market demand in relation to market supply, and since price movements in any direction, either sideways, upwards or downwards, tend to influence the minds of watchful investors, and tend to make them behave in a certain way—which will produce yet *other* shapes and formations—certain shapes and formations are highly suggestive.

These "laws" of probable future mass behavior, following upon previous mass behavior (as shown by a chart), are only probabilities, not certainties, but they should be learned by heart, and borne continuously in mind.

Due allowance, however, must, of course, be made for earnings at current price, industrial prospects, the general Technical Position, and other factors not susceptible to simple graphical treatment.

* * *

The great value of a chart for a single share, especially when studied alongside curves representing

    (a) The conjuncture,

    (b) other companies in the same industry, e.g. the industry index, and

    (c) industry in general,

is that it shows how the company and its shares have been faring compared with other companies and shares. It gives a picture of comparative movements, and suggests underlying *relative* trends.

Share charts, however, have other uses.

Different shares have characteristics and "followings" of their own. Some shares fluctuate widely each conjuncture, or each month and year; in others the movement is narrower. Some shares fluctuate seasonally; others tend to become active only near the ends of their financial years, when insiders become acquainted with results *before* the general public. Charts reflect these characteristics. They may in fact indicate the character of directors.

If annual profits and dividends are plotted on each share chart,* and marks made to show when the financial year ends and when the subsequent report is usually published, inside selling or buying is often reflected on the share chart as soon as insiders have learned what annual profits have been. Such apparently well-informed selling or buying, if it occurs *before* the report or dividend is published, is often worth following.

Share charts may also throw light on the market policy of powerful interests. For instance, if no upward movement takes place on the publication of *un-*expected good news (when the shares are in a high zone, especially if the conjuncture is favorable), it often indicates unloading by big holders or pools.

If the investor will consider charts as a supplement to, rather than a substitute for, market judgment, he is bound to derive a considerable amount of benefit from their use.

The three chief graphic rules.

Broadly speaking, there are three major rules in chart reading. (Various refinements will be described in the following chapter.)

---

*Excellent charts of this nature are published in America by "Investographs, Inc.," who have supplied me with loose copies of their advertisement brochure so as to illustrate my point.

RULE I. THE THEORY OF THE PARALLELS

As was said in Chapter I, the upward *cyclical* track of the common stock index tends to fluctuate astride a more or less *straight* line (although frequent exceptions occur to this rough rule).

The actual graph, however, follows a zig-zag movement astride the (more or less straight) upward cyclical mean. The result, of course, is a rising path or track.

By running a straight line roughly through the successive rising Intermediate tops, and another more or less parallel straight line through the successive rising Intermediate bottoms, one obtains what might be called the upper and lower parallels (on either side of the rising cyclical mean). See Plate IX.

The cyclical tendency is, in fact, for the market graph to fluctuate conjuncturally, between the so-called upper and lower parallels.

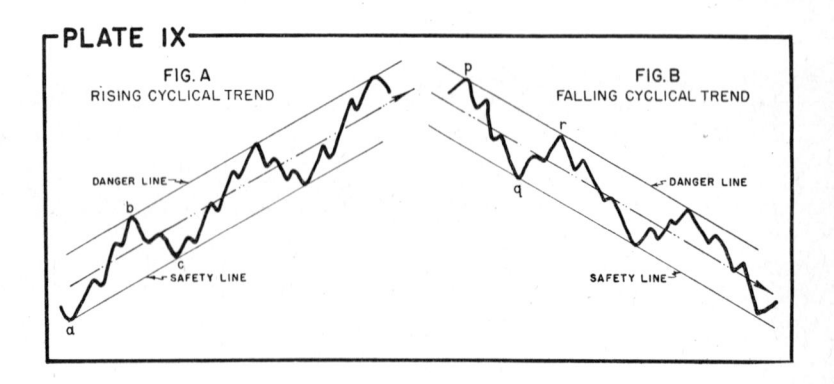

PLATE IX

FIG. A
RISING CYCLICAL TREND

DANGER LINE
SAFETY LINE

FIG. B
FALLING CYCLICAL TREND

DANGER LINE
SAFETY LINE

As regards constructing the parallels: If two bottoms (a and c) have formed, the second higher than the first, in an apparent new upswing, without *two* tops having yet formed, draw the lower parallel first (through a and c); and then draw the upper parallel, parallel to it, through the single top (b).

Conversely, in a fall: if p, q and r have formed, join p and r, and then draw the lower parallel (through q) parallel to it.

The upper parallel suggests when market is in temporary danger.

As regards reading such a graph:

When the market figure (portraying the index for industrials) rises and approaches the higher parallel (i.e., the upper edge of the apparent mean track of the rising zig-zag), the investor ought to be careful, and consider taking profits. The higher parallel area is a normal short-run danger zone.

On the other hand, when a fall lasting some months has occurred and the graph has fallen below what appears to be the mean line of ascent, the investor should, as soon as it is near the apparent lower parallel, become more confident and consider buying back the shares which he sold some months earlier, or others which may appear more suitable.

The lower parallel is a "normal" short-run safety zone.

Mental doubt must usually accompany all wise market actions.

It is to be noted, however, that the very essence of this system is to sell when the market as a whole has been good; and to buy when the market as a whole has for some months been suffering from a bad fit of nerves, i.e. in the so-called semi-panics.

Everyone agrees, in the abstract, that such action alone is sound. Experience shows, however, that most investors, while paying full lip service to this policy, are constitutionally incapable of following it in practice. Such bold action, however, is normally wise for the following reasons:

Always get in cash in the boomlets.

Even if the shares which he sells near the higher index parallel do not relapse, others which are equally attractive will probably relapse instead of them; and there is little except an unscientific sentimentality for wanting to hold continuously onto some single specified share throughout the whole course of its business cycle, for it will *undoubtedly* pursue a violent zig-zag course.

Moreover, even if one's original favorites do not relapse appreciably, the upward swing of trade in general, and of single trades in particular, will bring into the limelight certain other companies and industries whose shares are undervalued in view of recent amelioration of their industrial position.

Never be afraid, therefore, to get in cash in the conjunctural boomlets; indeed, the art of investment is to get in cash and remain "uninvested" for, perhaps, two months out of every six—waiting for the development of a market fit of nerves and the gradual maturity of an ideal investment opportunity, i.e., so-called panic conditions.

Have, therefore, during each boomlet, when the graph is in a dangerous position, the mental imagination to envisage an unforeseen series of adverse market factors which will probably soon cause shares to relapse—away from their upper parallels —even though the market as a whole is at present still optimistic, and no one else, at the time, pessimistically foresees a reaction. Such reactions, however, almost *always* occur; so have the gumption to know it, and act accordingly "on sound chance," as soon as the right indications are given (see Chapter XVIII).

Resolve, in fact, to buy only in the short-run panics and to sell in the short-run boomlets. Act, in fact, in the manner to which you pay lip service, but the wisdom of which you will invariably doubt *at the actual time.*

Let the market give its own signal.

Intermediate movements, however, astride the cyclical mean, are largely psychological, and are, therefore, capable of going to extremes, i.e. beyond the two parallels. It is consequently desirable to find some method of deciding when an Intermediate upswing or downswing is *probably* terminating and changing direction, e.g., by letting the market give its own signal, either by rolling over after a rise, or saucering out after a fall.

Here again graphs are capable of being most useful (as will be shown in the next chapter).

Graphs are useful in telling one "When" it is probably right to take a course of action which one has already decided is probably right.

Graphs indicate, in fact, what the Public, including insiders, (as distinct from oneself) is beginning to think and to do in the market—and it is after all the Public and the insiders whose actions make the market for oneself. It is, therefore, dangerous —since markets often go to extremes—ever to buy or sell until the public majority also seem to be *beginning* to act in the way one has thought for some time they ought to. This brings us on to Rule II.

RULE II. BREAKING BELOW RISING BOTTOMS (AND ABOVE FALLING TOPS)

Examination of a large number of graphs, during past swings in previous trade cycles, shows not only that intermediate oscillations occur for the most part astride a more or less "straight" mean line of ascent, but also that, in most cases, the successive conjunctural summits, and successive conjunctural nadirs, occur on higher and higher planes in a rising market (and lower and lower planes in a falling market).

The normal track in a rising market.

The economic explanation of this important phenomenon (see Plate IX) is as follows:

If at some given moment a share, or a group of shares as represented by an index, is fairly valued on the Stock Exchange, any amelioration in the fundamental economic position of the company or industry will automatically justify a rise.

Usually such a rise, when it has once begun, acquires cumulative momentum and becomes exaggerated, on account of the advertisement that a share gets if it once starts rising.

At last, however, market critics become convinced that the rise has gone, for the moment, too far; selling occurs, and a reaction is produced, usually equaling about one-third of the recent appreciation; the graph itself moving from the upper parallel to the region of the lower parallel.

In the course of time, however, further cyclical amelioration in the economic position of the company or industry will make the shares, which have reacted, once again look cheap; and a further upward movement becomes justified.

Shares thus rise in zig-zag fashion, each successive conjunctural top and nadir *normally* being higher than the previous top and nadir. (See Fig. A on Plate IX.)

Conversely, during each cyclical downswing, gradual deterioration in the economic position of a company or industry causes zig-zag downward movements in the graph of the shares —the successive bottoms and successive tops being normally successively lower. (See Fig. B.)

Assessing a cyclical change of direction.

From what has been said, it follows that if a cyclical change of direction occurs, say downwards after a major upward swing, the graph will, shortly after the change has begun, fall below

THE ART OF USING CHARTS

the last of the recent rising series of conjunctural bottoms. This will show that the market has *probably* lost its previous upward cyclical momentum and is not unlikely to change direction downwards.

It is, moreover, *impossible* for any cyclical change of direction to occur *without* this graphic phenomenon being produced. A good rule, therefore, is, after a period during which the curve has been zig-zagging, say, upwards, for several years, and making successively higher Intermediate tops, and bottoms, to sell as soon as the graph falls below the last of these recent rising *bottoms*. (See Figures A and B, Plate X; and also Plates XIII and XIV.)

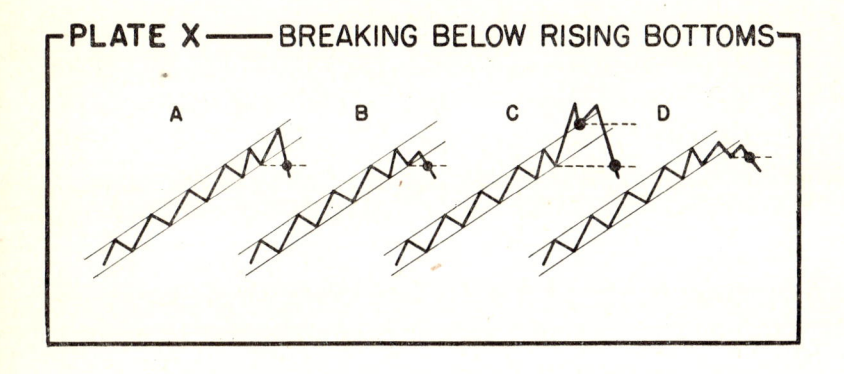

PLATE X —— BREAKING BELOW RISING BOTTOMS

As we shall shortly show (in our remarks about Track-breaking), breaking below a bottom which lies near the *upper* parallel (Fig. C) does not signify much until the fall has gone on to a point *outside* the *lower* parallel.

THE ART OF USING CHARTS

Conversely, when a graph has been zig-zagging downwards during a cyclical slump, buy when the line at last rises above the last of the falling conjunctural *tops*. (See Figures A and B on Chart O.)

Temporary (as distinct from permanent) exceptions, of course, can occur to this empirical cyclical rule, but the rareness even of the temporary exceptions confirm its *general* utility and soundness.

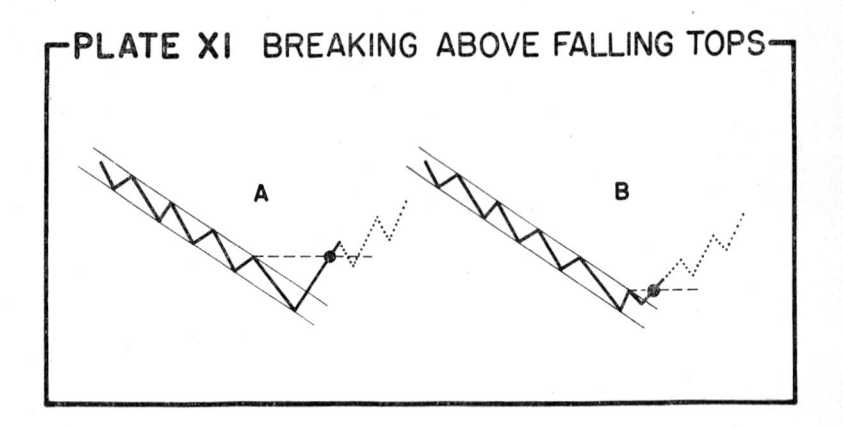

PLATE XI   BREAKING ABOVE FALLING TOPS

RULE III. TRACK BREAKING

A third invaluable graphic rule, useful for assessing a cyclical (or for that matter, Intermediate) change of direction (as distinct from a *temporary* danger point), is what might be called Track-breaking, or the Crossing of Trend-lines.

As we have already explained, shares usually pursue a zig-zag track astride a more or less straight mean.

PLATE XII QUITTING THE TRACK

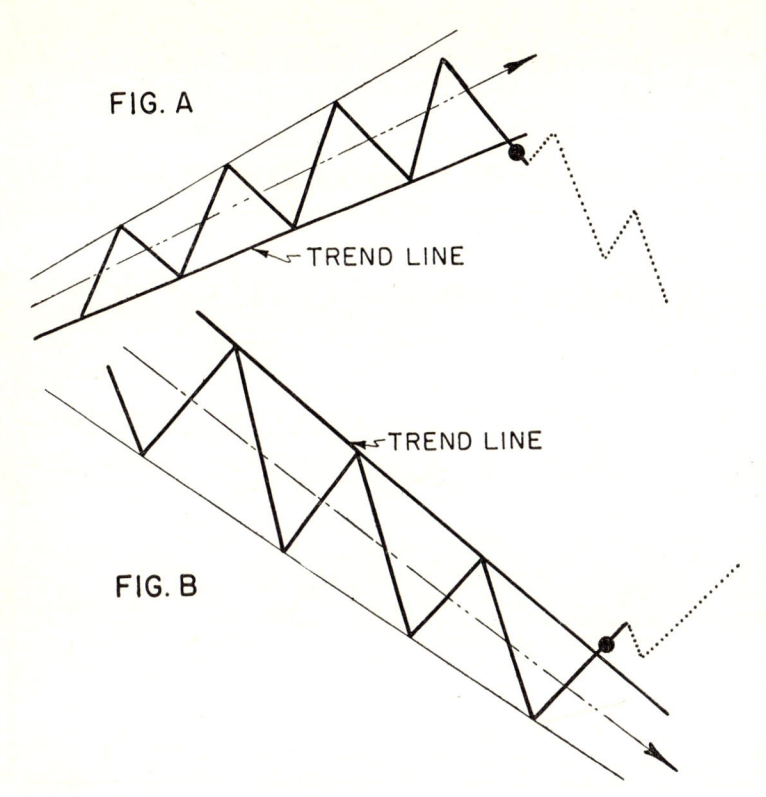

FIG. A — TREND LINE

FIG. B — TREND LINE

They *cannot* change direction cyclically "downwards" *without* quitting their old upward zig-zag track, i.e. breaking to the right of and below the lower parallel (i.e. the lower upward cyclical Trend-line). (See Figure A on Plate XII.)

And since it is somewhat *rare* for a share, or a commodity, or an index, to quit its cyclical track (i.e. break its cyclical Trend-line) *without* changing direction cyclically downwards, this second cyclical rule of "Track Breaking" is an excellent supplement to our former cyclical rule of breaking *below* the last of a series of rising conjunctural bottoms.

* * *

Thus, whereas the upper parallel in a rising market tells when a share is probably in *temporary* (conjunctural) or short-run danger, "quitting the track," and/or "breaking below the last rising bottom," suggests when it is probably in *long-run* or cyclical danger.

Transition from slump to boom.

The converse rule, of course, also holds good for a cyclical change of direction upwards after a cyclical slump, i.e. (1) Quitting the old track to the right of the *upper* falling parallel (see Figure B on Plate XII); and (2) Breaking *above* the last of the falling series of conjunctural *tops* (see Plate XI).

Survey.

Since it is only with rare exceptions that tracks are quitted, rising bottoms (or falling tops) broken, and parallels reached *without* the "normal" subsequent happenings subsequently happening, it is foolish to say that these three rough rules are not useful.

Inspection of share (and commodity) charts, for any business cycle, in any industry or country for the last 100 years, will convince any reader of the general soundness of this view. (See Plates XIII and XIV at end of this chapter.)

Sudden contradiction of recent indications.

In respect of Track-breaking, however, it is to be noted that although a fall in a (rising) graph to its lower parallel is "normally" a safety signal, a further fall to a position outside the lower parallel becomes a danger signal. Conversely, although a rise in a (falling) graph to its upper parallel is "normally" a danger signal, a further rise to outside the upper parallel (at the tail end of a falling market) becomes a favorable signal. Indeed, it may, on this principle, be right to sell a falling share on a recovery to its upper parallel, and to buy it back *higher up,* when it has quitted its recent falling track.

Similarly, after a prolonged rise, it may, on this principle, be right to buy on a reaction to the lower rising parallel, and to sell out *lower down* if the graph quits its recent upward track, especially if it has also broken below the last of its rising series of bottoms.

This is certainly a nerve-racking policy, but it is remarkable how often such behavior pays.

THE ART OF USING CHARTS

Foreign Industrial Common Stock Indices

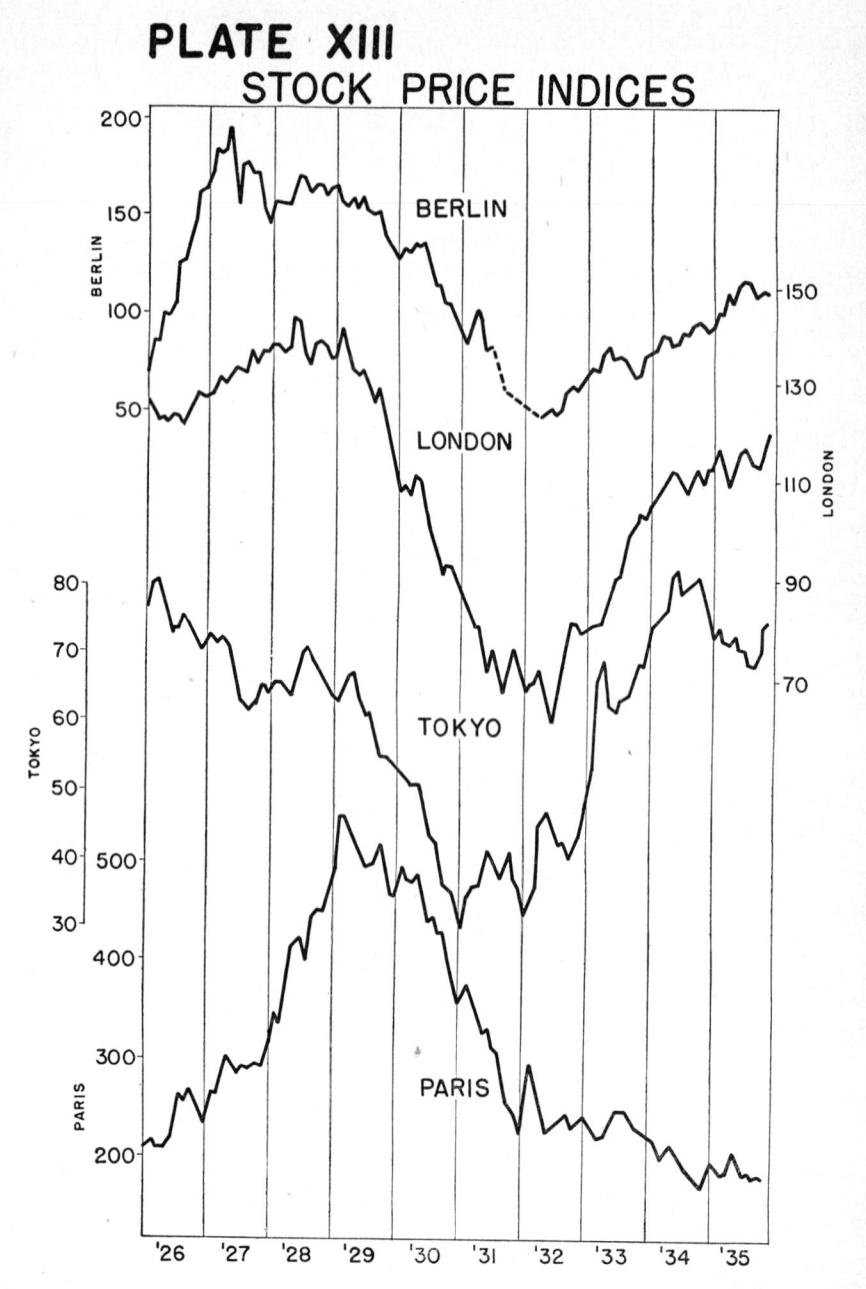

PLATE XIII
STOCK PRICE INDICES

THE ART OF USING CHARTS

FOREIGN INDUSTRIAL COMMON STOCK INDICES

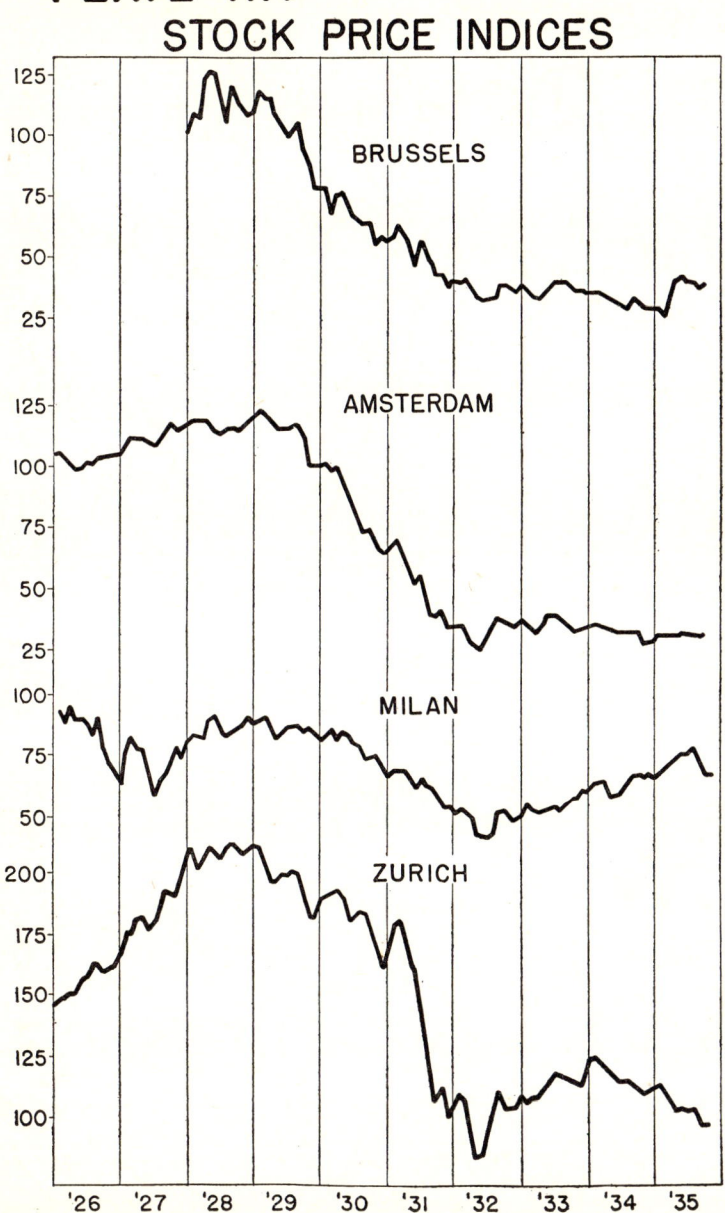

PLATE XIV
STOCK PRICE INDICES

CHAPTER XVIII

FINE POINTS IN CHART READING

Daily graphs as a guide to intermediate reactions.

Although the graphic rules laid down in the foregoing chapter have been described almost solely with reference to *cyclical* changes of direction in an index, or in a share, precisely the same principles apply to assessing a change of direction in an Intermediate swing.

Just as, cyclically speaking, a graph usually zig-zags (say upwards) astride a more or less straight rising mean, so, speaking from the point of view of the Intermediate swings, does each leg of the *Intermediate* swing follow a zig-zag upward or downward track—usually astride a more or less straight mean. (See Plate IX on page 108.)

Each of these Intermediate movements or legs (between the two *cyclical* parallels) has, as a rule, its *own* clearly defined upper and lower parallels, and its own succession of rising (or falling) bottoms and tops; so that *precisely the same* set of graphic rules for a change of direction can be applied just as much to these Intermediate movements as to the Cyclical movements.

Various refinements, however, should be mentioned to the three major rules for chart reading given in the last **chapter**—of (1) the higher and lower parallels; (2) the breaking below rising bottoms (and above falling tops); and (3) track-breaking.

Refinements to the three major rules.

Refinement 1. Sometimes a graph, instead of making zig-zags *astride* a rising mean, will rise *without* kinks in an almost straight line. (See Figure 1, Plate XV.) In such cases, to assess

FINE POINTS IN CHART READING

a change of direction, look not at the straight rising line just recently made, but at the new downward arm of the graph; wait till the new line has formed a zig-zag downwards and sell when the line breaks below the first of the nadirs or elbows in the new downward move.

For changes of direction upwards, reverse the argument. (See Figure 2.)

PLATE XV
MINOR INDICATIONS OF CHANGING DIRECTION

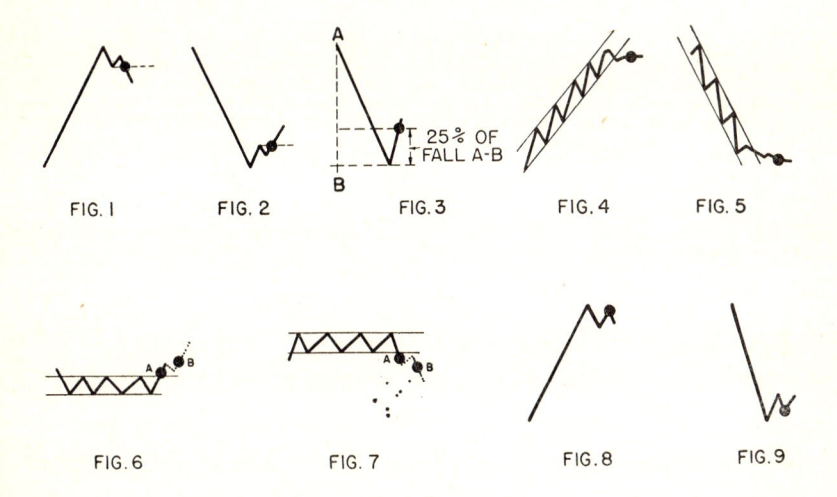

FIG. 1   FIG. 2   FIG. 3   FIG. 4   FIG. 5

FIG. 6   FIG. 7   FIG. 8   FIG. 9

Refinement 2. There may, however, be a new *straight* line move in the new upward direction (see Figure 3 on Plate XV) as well as a straight line movement in the old downward direction. In such cases it may be well to act when the new movement has equalled in length one-fourth of the length of the previous movement (unless this brings it to the higher parallel).

Refinement 3. Another test (to which we have already referred)—and an extremely valuable one—indicating a change of direction (downwards), is when the graph moves to the right of the previous apparent upward zig-zag track, i.e., outside its recent Trend-line or parallels. (See Figure 4.)

The same indication also holds good for upward changes after a fall. (See Figure 5.)

Refinement 4. If a curve is fluctuating between two *horizontal* parallels (see Figure 6), as distinct from between rising or falling parallels, be prepared to buy if it breaks *above* the horizontal, i.e., above the old line of tops at point A; particularly if the previous parallels were close together, so that one is not buying after a sharp rise.

In other words, when a graph quits a *horizontal* track which is *narrow,* it is normally right to go with the new trend. But if the horizontal track is wide (involving a spread of say 20%) it is normally right to wait for a reaction before buying, even though the old line of level tops has been broken.

* * *

Conversely be prepared to sell if a graph breaks below a horizontal lower parallel, particularly if the zone was narrow. (See Figure 7, Point A.)

Be particularly ready to act (especially if the previous zone was narrow) as soon as the graph in addition has made a

FINE POINTS IN CHART READING

further downward zig-zag of the nature indicated by Point B in Figure 7.

Likewise act when a graph, after quitting an upper horizontal, makes a zig-zag of the nature indicated by Point B in Figure 6.

Refinement 5. The fact that the second of two tops is lower than the first (see Figure 8), or that the second of two bottoms is higher than the first (Figure 9), indicates a probable change of direction.

Or, to restate this theorem in another way: Lower tops suggest subsequent lower bottoms (Point A on Plate XVI). Higher bottoms suggest subsequent higher tops (Point B).

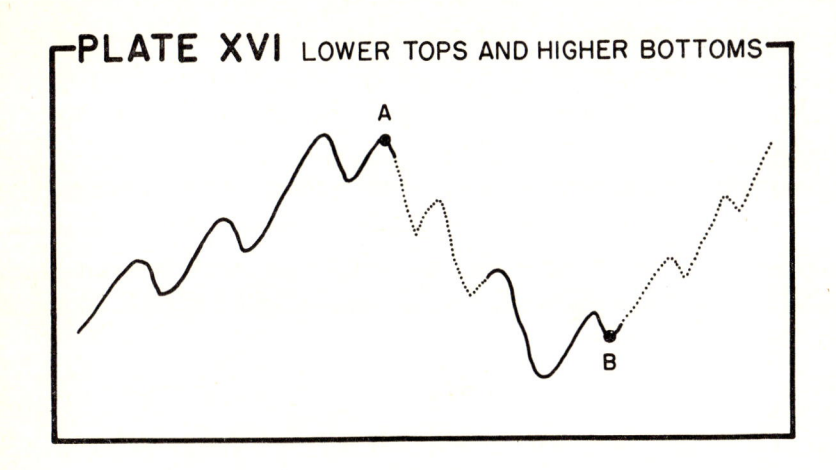

PLATE XVI LOWER TOPS AND HIGHER BOTTOMS

Mr. Rhea puts the matter, in his book on *The Dow Theory,* as follows:

"Successive rallies penetrating preceding high points, with ensuing declines terminating *above* preceding low points, offer a bullish indication. Conversely, failure of the rallies to penetrate previous high points, with ensuing declines carrying below former low points, is bearish."

Further notes on graph reading.

1. In respect of so-called parallels it should be realized that (on non-geometric paper) in a falling market they tend to converge towards the right (as will be seen from an inspection of the graphs on Plate XII); on the other hand, in a rising market they naturally tend to widen. (This, of course, refers to arithmetical scales; on geometric or ratio scales the so-called parallels keep more parallel.)

2. For cyclical changes of direction, examine *conjunctural* tops and bottoms. Monthly graphs will usually suffice.

3. For conjunctural changes of direction, *daily* (or weekly) graphs are essential.

N.B.—The same general rules, however, for assessing prospective changes of direction, hold good in both cases (i.e., for cyclical reversals, and intermediate reversals).

4. N.B.—Of course, as time progresses and old trend lines (apparently) become obsolete, a chartist has to re-draw his parallels and trend lines. (See Plates XIII and XIV.)

5. These rules can be applied not only to shares and share indices, but also to commodities.

Graphs as a guide to the probable duration and extent of movements.

Successive conjunctural angles of ascent, and angles of descent on a graph tend to be approximately parallel, i.e., at the same angle. (See Chart IX.) A graph thus often suggests (by means of its past angles) how far a movement is likely to go *within a certain time,* if the same previous angle of rise (or fall) is repeated. The parallels suggest when it will terminate.

Graphs as a guide to selling and buying limits.

For those who trade the market freely, graphs are an excellent guide to stop-loss orders.

To place a stop (or profit-conservation order) just *below* the last of a series of rising bottoms is usually sound policy.

To sell when a share which has been rising quits its conjunctural-track to the right, i.e., its short-term trend line is usually sound policy, particularly if already near the higher *cyclical* parallel.

To buy near the lower cyclical parallel, when a share has saucered out, with a stop perhaps 10% below the lower parallel (i.e., one's buying price) is, on the whole, a fairly sound system.

If wider stops are required, place them just below the last conjunctural bottom.

* * *

When a share has swung up to above its upper *cyclical* parallel it is often right to switch to something else at once, particularly if the shape of the graph suggests a delay of many months before it is likely to reach its lower cyclical parallel again—either by moving sideways or reacting.

I might add that in England there is usually a tendency for a market which is firm for three days running to react on the fourth. On the other hand, three days of weakness are often followed by one of revival.

In falling markets there are usually (not invariably) three weak days on end, and then one strong. The reverse is often true for rising markets.

FINE POINTS IN CHART READING

In England, if the first half of a so-called Stock Exchange Account period is strong, the second half is often weak. And vice versa.

In America I have noticed a tendency for day-to-day movements to reverse themselves more frequently than in England.

Incidentally, if a market becomes *wild* near or outside the upper parallel, and if several successive days of plus signs (i.e., sharp rises) are shown in the daily papers—it often pays to sell at the market on the first day that a few minus signs begin to appear in the papers. This indication rather suggests that the market is wavering, and often marks the beginning of a long reaction.

Action better (or worse) than the averages.

Some successful speculators quite rightly attach considerable importance to a group of shares like oils, or steels, beginning to act better than the (Dow Jones) Averages. When this begins to occur, as portrayed by graphs on *geometric* paper (as supplied by Investographs, Inc., and by H. M. Gartley, Inc., of 76 William St., N. Y. C.) there is *usually* a tendency for the better-than-average action of the group to continue for some months. Thus even if the speculator is one month late in his buying he *usually* has a two or three months profitable run for his money.

* * *

The converse is true for bearish behavior. Indeed one speculator whom I know is highly successful on both the bull and bear tack simultaneously in different groups—a policy which does *not* normally appeal to me individually. (I personally do not like bucking the *general* cyclical or intermediate trend, i.e., being a bull in a bear market, and vice versa.)

FINE POINTS IN CHART READING

Volume of shares dealt in.

Graphs of volume are also well worth keeping.

Increasing volume on a declining market (after a rise) is usually a sign of a nervous and over-bought market, and that the fall will probably gather momentum.

On the other hand, declining volume on a declining trend, is usually a sign that selling is drying up and that a rally will soon occur.

Increasing volume on a rise suggests a further rise; and declining volume on a rise, a tired condition which may portend an early fall.

The phenomenon of buying and selling climaxes should, however, be noted.

When a market has *already* gathered considerable momentum on gradually rising volume, the movement usually ends with a wild further movement on huge volume, representing an excited over-bought (or over-sold) condition.

Such situations, especially when they have lasted several days and are attracting attention on the front pages of the newspapers, usually indicate an early sharp reversal.

More often than not the right time to act (after a rise) is when a few minus signs begin to appear in the newspapers, after several days of somewhat violent plus signs.

Conversely, after a fall and a selling climax, buy as soon as a few plus signs appear. Rarely buy, however, in a selling climax unless the graph is near its lower cyclical parallel.

* * *

Broadly speaking, the significance of changes in Volume is, as Mr. Rhea puts it, usually as follows:

A market which has been over-bought becomes dull on rallies and develops activity on declines; conversely, when a market is over-sold, the tendency is to become dull on declines and active on rallies. Bull markets usually terminate in a period of excessive activity and begin with comparatively light transactions.

Miscellaneous theories.

Although the foregoing rough methods are those which I *personally* find most useful in telling when a single share, or group of shares, or a commodity is changing direction market-wise; there are numerous other graphic methods about which numerous books have been written, particularly in America.

All of these theories are true part of the time; none of them, all the time. They are, therefore, dangerous, though sometimes useful.

*Chart reading theories.**

In this work I am not prepared to deal in great detail with the fine points of chart reading, partly owing to lack of space, and partly to there not being available (as yet) in England a Service which purveys adequate charts to the public.

The student, however, who wishes to study the matter further cannot (I think) do better than subscribe:

(a) To the "Instruction Course" entitled "Profits in the Stock Market," supplied by Mr. H. M. Gartley of 76 William Street, New York City (price $40).
This fascinating piece of work covers not only chart reading but also the general problem of trading in stocks.

(b) To the "Instruction Course" of the Schabacker Institute (price $50, obtainable from *Graphic Market Statistics, Inc.*) wherein the principles laid down by the late

---

* Charts, daily, weekly and monthly, on every issue listed on the New York Stock Exchange and Curb can be obtained from *Graphic Market Statistics, Inc.,* 11 Stone Street, N. Y. C.

FINE POINTS IN CHART READING

W. Schabacker in his *Stock Market Theory and Practice* are elaborated in considerable detail; and

(c) *The Dow Theory* by Robert Rhea, published by the author at Colorado Springs, Colorado. Price 50 cents.

* * *

Broadly speaking, the lessons in these chart reading courses divide themselves up as follows:

(1) Formations suggesting a continuation of the recent trend.
(2) Formations suggesting a reversal.
(3) Trend-lines, and their significance when cut.
(4) Probable support and resistance levels.
(5) The significance of Gaps appearing on a daily chart.
(6) The significance of Triangles, etc.
(7) The significance of Volume when considered in relation to price trends; and
(8) False moves.

The Dow Theory.

Concerning the Dow Theory, which is, as I write, so popular in America: This theory is more or less bound to work from the cyclical or major-swing point of view. Wherefore it must be studied.

From the Intermediate point of view I rather mistrust it. The idea that the movement in the Rail Index must confirm (in direction, at all events) the movement of the industrial index, is to me unconvincing.

Mr. Rhea enunciates this theorem as follows:

"*Both Averages Must Confirm:* The movements of both the railroad and industrial stock averages should always be considered together. The movement of one price average must be confirmed by the other before reliable inferences may be drawn. Conclusions based upon the movement of one average, unconfirmed by the other, are almost certain to prove misleading."

It is true that the rails, being a highly representative industry (like Telephones or Chemicals) will "normally" move in the same general direction as the composite industrial index—both for economic and general sentimental reasons. But I personally regard the rail stocks as an individual group which is just as much subject to intermittent sectional activity or Market Fashion (or unpopularity) as any other group (like, say, oils, automobiles, chemicals, etc.); and there is little more reason why the rails (rather than, say, the chemicals) should be singled out, as regards the intermediate swings, to move with the industrials. They need *not* move with the industrials any more than the oils need move with the automobiles.

They "often" do so, but it is *not* inevitable; and since the rails may be subjected to special political, economic, sentimental and market influences *peculiar to themselves,* it seems to me rather far fetched to insist that purchases in the industrial group, i.e., in stocks in general, should be delayed "Till the rails have confirmed, in direction at all events." The idea is sound "cyclically" but not "intermediately."

* * *

Another tenet in the Dow Theory that I personally mistrust is the assertion that "The Averages Discount Everything!" To quote Mr. Rhea:

"The fluctuations of the daily closing prices of the Dow-Jones rail and industrial averages afford a complete index of all the hopes, disappointments, and knowledge of everyone who knows anything of financial matters, and for that reason the effects of coming events (excluding acts of God) are *always* properly anticipated in their movement. The averages quickly appraise such calamities as fires and earthquakes."

I may be guilty of misunderstanding the above tenet, but my own experience is that the Market as a whole is quite often wrong, and the effects of coming events are often *not* "properly anticipated."

* * *

Everyone, however, should learn the Dow Theory (and read Mr. Rhea), for many of its lessons are peculiarly useful. I prefer, however, the graphic principles which I have explained in these two chapters, and which largely embody the teachings of Rhea and Dow.

My personal experience.

My personal opinion of charts is as follows:

(1) They are invaluable in telling you *When* to buy, and *When* to sell—both from a cyclical and intermediate point of view.

(2) They often "suggest" *What* to buy, although purchases should not be made unless the trend is favorable from an economic point of view.

(3) They are useful in suggesting the wisest points at which to place selling limits and stop-loss orders.

(4) They often suggest how far a swing may go.

(5) They are much more reliable than economics in *Intermediate* Trading.

(6) They are slightly more reliable than economics in *cyclical* trading. (And I say this although I am an ardent supporter of the application of economic theory to market operations, both short term *and* long term.)

(7) The chart reader, however, should not be a fanatic. Charts are merely *one* aid, out of many, in making decisions. And obviously, not all chart-reading methods (or chart readers) are equally efficient.

Conclusion.

Our conclusion is that the share-chart system which we have advocated is reasonably sound and would probably prove successful even if operated quite regardless of the internal economics of given industries or of the Stock Exchange. If, however, a study of industrial and Stock Exchange economics is also brought to bear on the subject, the investor will have a *dual* chance of success.

No graphic rules, like no economic rules, are 100% right. Judgment will always be called for in practice. There are, however, certain "graphic rules of probability," which should not be disobeyed; and the wise investor is one who pursues only a general course of action which is "normally" right, and avoids acts or policies which are cartographically wrong.

First decide, by economic analysis, what industries and companies are promising. Then apply your graphic rules.

The share-chart system is an excellent *supplement* to actual business forecasting, especially if economic forecasts are not acted upon until share-charts give favorable confirmation.

* * *

All the rules outlined above can be applied not only to stocks, but also to deals in raw commodities.

CHAPTER XIX

GENERAL PLAN OF CAMPAIGN

This chapter attempts to synthesize the lessons of previous chapters

The policy advised.

We have already suggested (in Chapter XIV) that the *best* (though of course not the only) method of operating for a rise in ordinary shares is to adopt a compromise between long run and short run speculation, and to follow a system *initially* envisaging a lock-up definitely shorter than the complete industrial cycle of say four years, yet something longer, *if necessary,* than the normal conjunctural period of about four months (say eighteen months)—with, however, the preconceived intention of taking good profits if, in the meantime, public fashion, or conjunctural factors, or manipulation, should cause the shares to rise until they look over-valued on prospects.

Alternative systems of investment.

There are, however, various other (perhaps less preferable) systems of investment:

Some investors hold permanently, regardless of cyclical fluctuations in trade; others change their holdings every few years, in accordance with trade cycle principles; others, again, job in and out of the market, looking to short-term bouts of market activity, or to longer conjunctural movements, to afford them profit. A further difference lies in the time of buying; some buy only when the market is asleep, others wait until it is active.

Some investors will buy any security that happens to take their temporary fancy; others adhere to definite categories, for instance, the well-known Market Leaders, or the "Best shares in the most depressed markets."

In certain cases investors specialize only in particular types of industries, for instance:

(1) Industries which fluctuate violently with general trade and whose range of movement is therefore likely to offer great scope for cyclical profits (e.g., constructional engineering, and the raw material and luxury trades); or by contrast—

(2) Industries producing the necessities of life (e.g., bakeries, soap, margarine), whose earnings are not likely to be greatly affected by general trade fluctuations, and whose dividends are therefore likely to be stable.

(3) Established industries and financially strong companies with good past records; or alternatively—

(4) Infant industries of great promise (e.g., aircraft construction).

(5) New industries which have passed the infant stage, but which still have excellent prospects (e.g., artificial silk).

(6) Industries enjoying exceptional prosperity.

(7) Industries in the troughs of slumps.

Risk is inevitable.

Regardless, however, of what particular system, if any, is preferred and adopted, the first fact which must be borne in mind about investment is that *risk is inevitable.* This applies not only to ordinary shares, which are generally held to be the most speculative, but also to the gilt-edged securities in the Trustee list: Consols, for example, fell from 60 in 1919 to 44 in 1920—a fall of 26%.

The investor's problem is largely the elimination of risk. This end, it is true, is never completely attainable, but much progress can be made towards it by systematic and careful work. The problem resolves itself into: (a) Avoiding industries and companies (and bonds) which are in a dangerous economic position; and (b) Avoiding shares which are in a dangerous technical position, either because they are priced too high or because Stock Exchange conditions are generally unfavorable.

Narrowing down chances.

As already stated there are five main groups of factors which affect the prices of ordinary shares, namely:

INTERNAL FACTORS

1. Trade cycle factors and the trend of the cognate industry.
2. Finances, management, earnings and prospects of the particular company.

EXTERNAL FACTORS

3. Short-run external "conjunctural" factors affecting the Stock Exchange as a whole.
4. Long-run cyclical *external* factors which affect all share prices simultaneously, e.g., market rates of interest. (See Chapter VII.)
5. Manipulation by Pools and Insiders. (Chapter XXXVIII.)

Theoretically, in order to narrow down risks, the careful investor should only buy shares when the following five conditions are fulfilled:

    A. If long-run cyclical Stock Exchange influences are favorable. (See Chapter V.)

    B. If short-run conjunctural factors are favorable.

    C. If the trend of the single industry is upwards. (See Appendix A.)

    D. If the company itself is increasing its earnings, and

    E. If the shares themselves are quoted reasonably low in the market.

    F. If the graphic position is sound.

The investor's aim should, in fact, be *to narrow down economic chances* until he has eliminated most of the adverse risks and built up a favorable sequence of probabilities. This question is of paramount importance. Before making any purchases internal and external factors (both of short-run and long-run nature) should *all* be simultaneously propitious.

The art of investment is not merely to find prosperous companies in prospering industries, but also to buy their shares only when they are cheap and when Market Conditions are favorable.

"Quality" alone is not enough: "Price" and the current "Conditions of the Market" must also be considered.

System of investment advocated.

This being so the system of investment which we think most advisable may be summarized as follows:

1. Only to buy ordinary shares when one is convinced that the general *cyclical* trend of domestic trade (and preferably of world trade as well) is upwards.*

2. Only to buy into industries where one is convinced that the profit trend is upwards. (N.B.—Single industries are, however, capable of moving for some years on end counter to the general trend of industry in general.)

3. Only to buy into companies where management is good; where profits are believed to be improving and which show (or are likely to show next year) a reasonable estimated earnings yield (say 8 per cent or over) on current market price.

4. Only to buy in general Intermediate (conjunctural) market depressions, when prices are considerably lower than their recent highest.

5. Not to buy actually during falling markets, but to wait till the graph of the conjuncture as a whole, and of the share in particular, has saucered out or begun turning upwards.

6. To give stop-loss orders of approximately 20 per cent, so

* The exceptions are gold shares (and perhaps the equity shares in fixed interest holding companies; and an occasional infant industry).

that if one's prognostications occasionally go wrong, the losses on one or two operations will not wipe out the whole of the profits made on many others.

7. To decide how much one will lose on each share in advance, and to fix stakes and stop-loss orders accordingly.

Routine.

In other words:

(i) First, be an economist and say what ought to happen.

(ii) Secondly, be a chart reader and refuse to act on one's own economic theories until the public as a whole is showing signs of behaving in the way you have decided that they ought to. Don't go in or out too soon; irrational overswings are common on the Stock Exchange. Therefore, read your graphs carefully and wait until the *Market Gives Its Own Signal.*

Never, in fact, pursue a course of behavior which is "normally" unsafe and wrong; that is to say, beware of buying in the region of higher parallels; do not be a bear in a bull market; and so on.

(iii) Thirdly, having decided as above, how and when to act, become, as soon as you have made your purchase, a mathematical automaton. Place stop-loss orders on your shares without either hope or fear; let them be sold if they fail to justify what you regarded as rational expectations. Let them be sold even though their further fall has made them, in *your* view, cheaper and more promising. Realize that occasionally you are bound to be wrong in this despite all your confidence. Wherefore become an automaton.

The method here advocated will meet with general success. Do not expect to be right every time: cut your losses when necessary and get in cash for another operation when once again conditions appear favorable (in accordance with Numbers (i) and (ii) above).

Have the imagination to believe that such conditions will once more mature and recur again and again.

Be clear-headed concerning your time-factor.

Finally remember this. When an investor buys a security he should determine whether he is buying it for the Cyclical, Intermediate, or Minor swing.

It does not much matter if a long-run investor buys shares at the top of an Intermediate boomlet, but the short-run investor must beware of such action.

Moreover, whereas the long-run operator aims mainly at making profits out of the long-run cyclical swings in *industrial profits,* the intermediate or short-run operator is more concerned with the minor fluctuations which occur in shares astride their long-run cyclical means for technical *market* reasons. His chief mental occupation must therefore be very different from that of the long-run buyer. His aim must be to forecast short-run *external* influences rather than *internal* factors such as long-run industrial earnings.

Different securities suit different plans.

Then again it is important for investors to realize how far any share which attracts them is suitable for their short- or long-term purposes.

Take, for instance, the intermediate movements: Some shares habitually move by a large percentage (20% to 50%) as between successive conjunctural boomlets and depressions, whereas others as a rule only move by a relatively small percentage (say 5% to 15%). The latter are rather unsuitable for short-run speculation in view of "expenses"; the former are more suitable.

Again, within the same industrial group (say motors), since different shares habitually move in the short-run by greatly different percentages, the short-run investor should sort out those which habitually swing sufficiently wildly to give an attractive short-run profit. A long-run investor, whose ultimate success depends on a change in industrial *earnings,* might, however, be much better off with a higher grade company.

Personally, I do not like being asked "what I think of a particular security," unless my questioner informs me of the time-period which he is considering. Many shares may be promising as a four-year lock-up but most unpromising for the Intermediate or Minor swing.

Indeed investors, insofar as they do not confine their operations to the more or less long-term principles prescribed in this book, should divide their purchases into three categories, according as they are bought, for:

1. A lock-up of several years.
2. For an Intermediate up-swing, or
3. Merely as a short-run gamble.

Separate stop-loss order systems should be instituted in each case; and investors are advised to enter their purchases, according to their different time-objectives, on separate sheets of paper in their portfolios. They might also write down, at the time of each purchase, their mental reason for buying each stock; and their pre-conceived intention as regards future sale. Few faults are more common than lack of clear headedness as to whether one is buying and holding for the short- or long-pull.

If a pre-conceived plan unexpectedly goes wrong, clear out of the market and cut your losses.

PAGE FOR NOTES

CHAPTER XX

THE MIND OF THE BROKER

If you want good service from your broker, do not give him cause to believe that if, on a sale being made, he does not urge you to re-invest at once, he will lose business to another of your broker friends, who may in the meantime give you a hot "tip."

A sane broker will frequently encourage his clients to keep out of the market for a month or two on end. His clients should try to foster this sanity by not making the broker feel that your business is sure, in the meantime, to go elsewhere.

* * *

Incidentally, any broker who has watched the operations of his clients, or of the investment trusts, over a period of years will be fully aware that just at those moments when it is most desirable to buy, few of his clients will have any money (or any nerve).

This is because they have become and remained fully invested, probably at some previous top in the market. Or, even if they have a little money available, they are so frightened, owing to a series of recent losses, that they have not the nerve to go in and buy. They are anxious to wait "until conditions look more certain."

Profits on the Stock Exchange come, however, in the main, to those who have not only the humility to study the nature of markets, but also the conceit to expect the crowd to be wrong; to those, in fact, who will sell in the boomlets so as to have cash available to exploit the slumps; to those, in fact, who do not mind missing the intermediate tops in the certain knowledge that there will always be attractive situations later on which will again provide them with opportunities.

Against this, of course, it is often argued that one's own short term judgment may be wrong and that selling in the short-run boomlets may involve buying back the same shares or others at higher levels, despite such shares having at last reacted during a subsequent Intermediate depression.

This, of course, is a possibility. But the clever short-run operator is, in my view, one who has trained himself not to care in the least at *what* level of the market he makes money, provided he makes it. Such an operator, if he knows his business properly, will always be eager to sell in wild markets when the public is probably over-optimistic, and eager to buy in slack markets on the downside when the public is probably over-pessimistic.

He will, in fact, ascetically discipline himself to follow such sound speculative rules as are "normally" right, and thereby avoid those speculative actions which are normally wrong.

He will realize that there is always an excuse *this time* for not following "normally sound rules" (but he will take no notice of the excuse).

The clever man is one who misses the Exceptions—and follows the Rules.

* * *

A broker's most successful clients are those who, in almost all instances, have money available to pounce upon exceptionally favorable opportunities when they mature, i.e., when shares have become exceptionally cheap owing either to a wave of general fear or to a temporary shortage of money in the Stock Exchange arena.

This involves selling in the boomlets, and keeping money idle for the slumps.

Many brokers think this reduces their annual turnover. But this is not so. The best way for a broker to keep his clients, and to get more, is to help *them* make money. This is done fastest by following the rules laid down in this book. Clients get and take their profits *more often*. Brokers thus get much quicker commissions (though few know it).

Moreover, actual turnover of clients' funds is usually faster —and therefore more profitable to the broker—if shares are bought at the right time than at the wrong.

The way that many brokers lose business is by bouncing their clients in and out of the market at the (theoretically and practically) *wrong* times, until their clients have lost all their money.

The point is this:

If, as a broker, you want to make money, you should plan to make your clients buy in the Intermediate slumps, with the intention, if necessary, of holding for two years. This sounds dull and unprofitable to yourself, but in practice you will find:

    (a) That your clients make more money;
    (b) That they will bring you more clients;
    (c) That they will stay with you longer; and
    (d) That the annual turnover per man will increase because the selling and the buying is *well-timed,* and you have fewer clingers to stocks showing losses.

Brokers in a greater hurry rarely make as much money.

CHAPTER XXI

PROSPEROUS VERSUS UNPROSPEROUS INDUSTRIES

How misguided caution fosters buying at the top.

Although to buy in the cyclical slumps and sell in the cyclical booms is an obvious form of long-run tactics, and although lip-service is always paid to this policy, few investors will follow it in practice.

The reason is that the average investor, in his natural desire to be both prudent and cautious, is inclined to prefer an industry which he knows is doing well; indeed most investors will only buy shares in companies already enjoying high prosperity, when everyone is applauding the high earnings in the industry.

This is often followed by disaster. As already said, high prosperity in any industry rapidly stimulates the influx of new capital and usually leads to early over-production. On principle, therefore, the long- as distinct from the short-run investor should rather avoid industries which look extremely healthy and have been prospering greatly for some years.

Except in the case of monopolies, a slump almost invariably follows soon after new plant has become effective.

The capture of bargaining power.

Admittedly this danger is (temporarily) reduced if an industry, after a period of depression and low profit margins, is just re-reaching full employment and a full forward order book, which, if stocks are low, implies that industrial bargaining power is now passing from the consumer to the producer. In such cases manufacturers are, for a while, able to mark up prices and competing middlemen and consumers will usually pay them in order to get quick delivery. The result may be that a 10% rise in prices may, if the previous profit margin was only

10%, lead to a 100% increase in profits. And such profits may continue for many months on end until either demand becomes saturated or until new plant has at last come into production. Indeed, if demand is persistent or if the so-called gestation period required to set up new plant* is long, the industry may enjoy several years of continuous boomtime prosperity.

Thus, in not all cases should a boom in an industry be an invariable cause for an immediate sale. Booms, however, are "normally" dangerous; and this "normal" good rule should be borne in mind.

[It should here be added, however, that in not all cases will makers mark up price whenever they can. In the rayon industry in England for instance early in 1934 the industry began to work at capacity, but the leading concern which dominated the industry, instead of exploiting consumers who had lost their bargaining power, and instead of marking up prices as soon as it was possible, declared it was going to keep its prices low, and enlarge factories rapidly, so as to stimulate long-run demand by a policy of continuous cheapness. A boom in profits, and the shares, which might have developed was thus prevented from speedily maturing. But this is the exception rather than the rule.]

Booming industries ought to show high yields.

Finally, in respect of booming companies, a special danger arises. Many investors are so averse to buying shares in unprosperous companies that they tell their brokers to select only the financially strongest and most prosperous companies. The brokers, therefore, seek out those companies that are working at capacity, have excellent management, have good finances and are making exceptional profits, i.e., booming companies.

* Seven years in the case of rubber trees. Only a few months in the case of the radio industry.

"One cannot find a more prosperous company," they say; therefore the client buys. Such shares, however, have often soared to a 3% or 4% earnings basis because everyone is buying and because the company "is prospering abnormally." Such rises frequently occur even though the company could not, without fresh capital, double either its present output or profits; yet this would be necessary if the inflated prices are ever to be justified by a 6% or 7% earnings basis—which is reasonable for speculative securities.

In other words, booming companies, when working overtime and yielding no more than 3% or 4%, often have a latent fall in their shares of 50%.

Probably no company, which is *already* fully employed and is working overtime, is worth a 3% earnings basis—except possibly in cases where demand is clearly far from satisfied, where new plant takes a year or more to erect, where no substitute-product exists, and where producers themselves are willing and able to mark up prices against consumers.

Exceptions to the rule against buying in booms.

Buying into already booming industries and companies is only a sound policy for long-run investors:

(a) If the company itself happens to be a virtual monopolist.

(b) If supply cannot possibly be increased for a year or two owing to the long gestation period of new plant.

(c) If demand is growing so fast that even new additions to plant will probably be incapable of satisfying requirements.

These conditions, however, are rarely fulfilled. The long-run investor, therefore, should normally beware of highly prosperous industries and companies—especially since, as a general rule, their shares will be over-valued on the stock market.

Abnormal success throughout an industry should be a warning, rather than an inducement to buy.

CHAPTER XXII

THE CASE FOR BUYING IN EARLY REVIVAL

Depression per se does not justify buying.

Although buying into prosperous industries which are booming is "normally" unsound, buying into unprosperous and slumping industries, is not necessarily advisable, just because they are depressed. There is a right time in each slump at which to buy, just as there is a time in each boom at which to sell.

Admittedly if a slump in an industry has lasted several years, and if various companies are already going bankrupt, and if the commodity produced is of a sort for which the public demand is permanent, it will probably prove a profitable long-term transaction to buy those companies whose costs are competitively low provided that their liquid resources are sufficiently sound to see them over several years more of depression.

But buying into industries just because they are depressed, or have been depressed for some time, is not of itself a sound good reason. Revival (except in dying industries) may, it is true, some day be relied on, and the strongest firms will doubtless survive, but in the meantime the depression may continue for many years. Meanwhile finances may be so weakened that the shares will fall to very low levels. Buying too soon, therefore, should be avoided.

* * *

Actually, in my personal view, the best time to buy during a depression is when the depression itself has already shown signs of terminating.

Preferably buy during early revival.

Experience, moreover, shows that single industries rarely turn round every calendar year, but that they usually prosper or slump for about four or more years in succession, depending on the gestation period of new plant, etc.

An excellent time, therefore, for long-run investors to take an interest in an industry is during early revival, i.e., at the beginning, as distinct from near the end of a long period of prosperity. If one does this one usually has a three or four years' run for one's money with a chance of capital appreciation of 200% or 300%.

To buy when annual profits first start rising (or when dividends are first raised) after a long period of depression is quite a useful long-run rule.

Incidentally there is another point in favor of buying into recuperating as distinct from into highly prosperous industries. Plant which is at present under-employed has a much greater chance of doubling or trebling its earnings (when share prices will follow suit) than plant which is already at maximum employment.

Furthermore a reviving company is no more likely to slump 50% than a booming company (indeed, less so!); consequently, since reviving companies are more capable of augmenting their profits, they are to be preferred to companies already booming.

In terms of averages, even if only two out of ten selected reviving shares treble in value (giving aggregate profits of 400 units), their rises will cover losses of 50% on eight others. Therefore prefer reviving companies to shares in booming industries.

What to seek for.

Probably the ideal course is to buy into depressed but reviving industries, carefully selecting strong and promising companies, *where yields and earnings are already high,* even though plant is still *under*-employed; thus, if revival continues there will be large scope for an expansion in profits, without the aid of new capital.

Admittedly, it needs good nerves to buy into depressed industries which of recent years have been showing falling profits and dividends; but this is undoubtedly a sounder long-run policy than buying during periods of great prosperity. Boom-time purchases are usually followed by early slumps, while slump-time purchases are normally followed by rises.

The second year of revival as shown both by a share chart, and by a flattening out of the loss curve, or a rise in the profit curve, is normally the safest time to buy.

Methods of testing revival.

The way to test revival in a company is to plot the curve of its annual profits and then to buy on the first annual upturn. Take little notice, however, of changes in profits unless they exceed 1% on total capital, or, say, a 10% change in the net profits of the preceding year.

If the profit curve should be puzzling, examine the profits of rival companies doing similar business. Also consider unemployment trends in the industry, price-movements in the product produced, and the trend of general trade and its probable influence on the particular industry. The profit curve is, however, usually the most reliable index of revival.

If, however, rises in the profits of a single company lag behind rises in similar companies, it is often a sign of relatively bad management, and such companies should be rather avoided. Especially avoid reviving companies if they only revive at the tail end of booms. It is usually a sign that they can only prosper under *exceptionally* favorable general circumstances.

THE CASE FOR BUYING IN EARLY REVIVAL

N.B.—A steady or rising dividend record is *not* always a sound recommendation. A steady dividend record may admittedly be a sign that an industry does not fluctuate much cyclically. A recently rising dividend record may, however, be a sign of latent danger. To buy on the *recent* record of a company is not necessarily a sound practical principle in long-run cyclical investment.

CHAPTER XXIII

SHARES TO CHOOSE

Introductory.

This book so far has been largely concerned with narrowing down industrial and Stock Market chances and showing when single industries and shares-in-general are in a safe or dangerous position.

This process can be further applied to particular companies; for the art of investment is not only to buy shares when their cognate industries and the Stock Market as a whole are in a healthy position, but also only when the shares themselves appear healthy and offer good value for money.

BUYING RULES

No buying rules can ever prove infallible; the following, however, are worthy of mention.

Avoid new ventures.

Leave shares in undeveloped properties, or in new processes, to experts to exploit.

Insist on high earnings on market price.

Actual yields on shares do not greatly matter provided that net earnings, after depreciation has been allowed for, are high: say 8% to 10% on market price. An 8% earnings basis may at first sight seem severely exacting, but the cautious investor should normally insist on it. He will then avoid the violent collapses which often assail shares on a low earnings basis.

The biggest profits are certainly made on shares possessing low yields; but so also are the biggest losses. Keep to a high-earnings basis.

Prospects alone rarely justify a purchase by the truly careful investor; if market sentiment suddenly changes, "prospect" shares, i.e., those which are not on a sound earnings basis, usually collapse quickly. "Prospect" shares can make much money when general market conditions are strong, but they can also give considerable losses. Remember that a sudden fall in a share from a 4% to a 6% earnings basis means a fall of 33⅓%. On principle, therefore, avoid these risks—especially as there is no need to run them, and alternative choices are *always* available. (If they are not, then the whole market is too high.)

If you aim at carefully conserving your capital, profits will usually look after themselves.

Beware, however, of shares with *unduly* high yields and earnings. These things by themselves suggest inside knowledge of the existence of hidden dangers. Shares whose preference shares or debentures offer abnormally high yields should also be distrusted.

The importance of free markets.

A free market is normally essential, particularly in the prosperity phases of the cycle. If anything goes wrong with a small company which is a bad market and insiders start getting out, the shares may slump 25% before there is a chance of effecting a sale, and even then dealers may refuse to deal except at much lower prices.

Little-known shares are quite good while the market is active. As soon, however, as their swing of prosperity changes the investor may lose 40% or more of his capital, all within a few weeks.

Prefer large companies.

Biggish companies are to be preferred, not only because their shares are usually freer markets than those of the small ones, but also because they can afford to have specialists in all departments, and can buy and sell, and advertise, in bulk more cheaply.

Insist on a good directorate.

Good management is, of course, desirable, though not *absolutely* essential if the economic trend is strongly upwards. Well-managed companies, however, may make profits even if the trend of the cognate industry is downwards. Badly-managed companies on the other hand may make losses even though the trend of the industry is upwards.

Directoral integrity is vitally important. Shareholders are entirely in the hands of their directors; few realize to what extent. Always, therefore, avoid shares in any company whose directors are connected with financial groups whom the City "does not like very much." Also be nervous of investing in companies whose directors are known to manipulate their shares.

Beware especially of directors with megalomania. More often than not grandiose schemes collapse. Do not regard rapid capital expansion and a bold forward policy as automatically synonymous with practical wisdom—especially during a boom.

Avoid low grade counters, except in the early stages of cyclical revival.

Low priced and low denomination shares have a curious fascination for many people just because with £100 a large holding can be bought at what look like option prices.

Usually, however, the jobbers' turn is so enormous that it eats up the major part of one's profit. Incidentally, if one wishes to sell, expenses may come to 20%. For instance, in shares quoted at 4s.-5s., a 10% fall in middle price often gives a 30% net loss, while a 30% rise usually gives only a 10% net profit—which, of course, is not good business.

Prefer shares with highly-geared equities.

If you are confident in the future of an industry prefer shares with geared equities; that is to say, shares in companies whose ordinary share capital (taken at *market* value) bears only a *small* ratio to total capital; and which will, therefore, after fixed charges have been paid, get the whole benefit of any increase in profits earned on capital as a whole.

Realize, however, that if your trade forecasts are wrong, your losses will be correspondingly magnified.

Insist on reasonably strong finances.

If you are boldly buying during a slump, before it has ended, choose only companies with good finances. There is always the danger that any slump may be indefinitely prolonged.

Weak companies find it almost impossible to raise new capital during slumps.

Examine the technical market position.

Hesitate to buy shares in which there is known to be a weak bull account, especially if the bulls have bought much lower down (and are likely soon to encash profits).

Beware also of shares in which a pool is known to be operating if they have just had a big rise. The pool may shortly start to liquidate. (See Chapter XXXVIII.)

Buying on fixed assets.

One may sometimes find a common stock, valued in the market at say, $50, but possessing balance sheet assets of say, $100. It is often a great temptation to buy on the basis of "indicated Asset Value."

It is, however, inadvisable to buy merely on fixed assets, even though they are undervalued from a replacement-cost point of view, unless the trend of profits in the company is already apparently upwards, with the implication that the assets will soon become more valuable from an earnings point of view.

As a general rule, fixed assets, no matter how much they originally cost, or how high they stand in the balance sheet, will only sell (despite their nominal balance-sheet break-up value) on the basis of what they are earning at the time of the public sale. Therefore, buying on fixed assets is usually only sound if the assets themselves have adequate *current* earning value, or at all events, high prospective earning value in the comparatively near future.

Goodwill.

Do not be frightened by a large amount of goodwill, providing the earnings of the company are high, and the outlook good. Goodwill is often more valuable than fixed assets.

N.B.—Just because one company, owning say several newspapers (in England) may show much goodwill; whereas another shows no goodwill, but has a large number of shares in subsidiaries, it does not follow that the latter is safer than the former. Realize that if the former company also floated off a portion of its businesses in the form of subsidiaries, and then held "shares" in the junior companies, it might "appear" to have eradicated the goodwill item from its balance sheet, and to have ample assets in the form of shares. But the goodwill would be there just the same (at one remove); and the second company (without goodwill) might be no better, from an asset point of view, than the first (before the new flotations). Goodwill, in fact, can often become camouflaged by means of "the holding company system."

* * *

Let us now summarize the mental processes which an investor should follow in the selection of shares for his portfolio.

The art of selection.

When selecting shares for the contents of a portfolio, one should ask oneself:

1. What are the most upward industries (e.g., those with deferred replacement demand, cyclical come-back, geometric characteristics, etc.)?
2. Which are the best-managed companies in these industries?
3. Which are the cheapest shares (among these best-managed companies in the most promising industries)?
4. Of these latter (see Section 3), Which are the best shares from a chart-reading point of view?

Then buy—if the conjunctural (and general cyclical) situation seems safe.

One should, however, hesitate to buy a common stock unless both prospective profits *and* the share chart look capable of rising say 15% within three months, or 30% within eighteen months.

CHAPTER XXIV

THE TIMING OF BUYING

Exploiting the laws of probability.

No buying rules, however sound, can be expected to prove invariably reliable. There are, however, certain forms of behavior which are normally safe, and certain forms of behavior which are normally dangerous. The prudent investor, therefore, will eschew the dangerous, and only act in a way which is "normally" sound.

The Laws of Probability will then, in the long run, operate in the prudent investor's favor; and his capital account will show steady accretion—provided his selling rules are *also* sound. (See next chapter.)

Rashly bucking the trend.

Speculative investors should, of course, as far as is possible, exploit slumps in single industries, unjustified slumps in single shares, and conjunctural slumps affecting shares as a whole.

The general principle, however, of buying in slumps, has given rise to the Stock Exchange saying: "Buy when the public is selling; and sell when the public is buying."

This rule, although it contains some elements of wisdom, is not entirely sound. Since industries move in major swings which usually last four or more years, to buy whenever the public starts to sell may be to load oneself up with shares which will not revive for several years and which may in the meantime drop 50%.

Similarly, to buy when shares first start falling at the end of a conjunctural boomlet may be to involve oneself in an immediate loss of 20%.

The use of periods.

One way of *partially* overcoming the danger of buying too soon is to delay one's purchases, both in industrial and conjunctural slumps, until a certain fixed period, based on the average lessons of history, has expired: say about three years in the case of industrial slumps, and about three months in the case of conjunctural slumps.

Such a policy, however, is far from adequate. Falls even of such lengths may gain cumulative momentum and be indefinitely prolonged. Therefore to buy just because a fall is occurring, or because it has lasted a given period, is not sound policy.

Success on the Stock Exchange comes, it is true, from buying in slumps *before* the public sees the wisdom of buying, and selling in booms *before* the public as a whole sees the wisdom of selling; but there is a world of difference between acting early and acting too soon: in fact, one of the best rules in Stock Exchange operations is never to run counter to a current trend but to wait until it shows signs of changing direction.

The use of graphs.

Long-run investors, for instance, instead of buying while the profits of an industry are falling, should wait till profits turn upwards after some years of depression, preferably choosing the second year of revival, as shown by a *share* chart. Similarly short-run investors, instead of buying while single shares are falling, should wait until share-curves flatten out or rise slightly.

It is true these upturns may prove to be only temporary and deceptive; but nevertheless the rule of not buying in fast falling markets is normally sound. Only one person in a thousand can hope to buy at the absolute bottom, and, since falls may become cumulative, it is much safer to wait until the fall is apparently over, and downward momentum appears, at all events temporarily, to have been lost, than to buy during the falls, when sellers still appear to out-number buyers.*

Act before the majority, but do not fight the current trend.

This same principle of not running counter to a current trend and of only buying on the upturns can be applied not only to the prices of single shares and to the long-run profit-curves of industries, but also to the short-run conjunctural fluctuations which occur in the indices of ordinary shares in general. Do not buy while the weekly conjunctural index curve is falling and while Market Sentiment is still clearly bad; hold off until either the Curve flattens out or until there is a minor upturn.

Summary of rules.

To summarize: the best buying procedure is:

(a) To aim at buying in depressions before the public as a whole has seen the wisdom of buying; but

(b) Not to buy during the actual falls, but rather to wait for minor upturns—buying, if possible, during the first quarter of the new anticipated movement.

To buy shares when they first turn upwards (according to our graphic rules in Chapter XVII after a period of depression is, in fact, the ideal policy. This rule applies equally to long-run investment and to short-run conjunctural speculations.

* We would add, however, that the rule of not buying in falling markets applies more to "prospect" shares which are clearly over-valued on actualities (and may therefore fall much lower if confidence in the future declines further) than to shares with good earnings and prospects which appear to be already under-valued.

CHAPTER XXV

RULES FOR SELLING

Sell on internal deterioration.

As regards selling shares: Shares can fall for both internal and external reasons. External factors are usually only temporary in their influence and can to some extent be disregarded by the long- (as distinct from the short-) run investor. Internal factors, however, are always important and usually demand immediate action.

A sound precept for all investors, both short-term and long-term, is to sell shares on the first sign of internal deterioration either in the industry or the company, and not to wait either for a minor revival or until the weekly financial journals have had time to analyze the position further and to bring about yet more public selling.

A useful rule for long-term investors who cannot afford the time to watch the internal economics of their holdings closely, is to sell whenever a dividend is lowered or whenever annual net profits are 10% less than those of the previous year.

N.B. 1—A cut in the interim or final dividend is usually a sign to sell *at once,* for it usually indicates that those who possess inside information are not happy about the state of the order-book or finances.

N.B. 2—If a (non-monopolistic) manufacturing company lowers the prices of its cars, paint, rayon, etc., and says it is due to a forward policy of mass-production, or to lower costs, etc., be sceptical. Companies rarely cut their prices purely from kindness of heart; it is usually a sign of an unfilled order-book and deteriorating conditions within the competitive industry. Think of selling the shares at once and of not buying back until the profit curve again turns upwards.

Conserving two-thirds of one's paper profits.

In the matter of profit-taking on the part of short- and long-run operators, investors should always cash any profits available immediately they observe signs of internal deterioration in either the industry or the company.

If, however, no internal deterioration is apparent, let profits run on until shares look over-valued. Then sell as soon as the market graph wavers or prices relapse, say, 5% from highest.

A third useful rule is never to let a profit of over 15% run into a loss. Give a sliding stop-loss order which will conserve you a half to two-thirds of your paper gain. If the paper profit continues to grow, slide your stop-loss order up accordingly.

Sell "prospect" shares in unfavorable conjunctures.

Short-term investors will usually be well advised to sell all their "prospect" shares, whenever the conjuncture becomes unfavorable after a recent rise, especially if the shares have risen sharply. The majority of "prospect" shares collapse 15% or more in each bad conjuncture. Therefore, when general sentiment declines and money becomes scarce, sell—if you are a short-run investor—*all* your prospect shares on principle.

Only retain shares with good earnings-yields to support them.

The question of stop-loss orders.

As regards loss taking: We have already suggested cutting all losses of 20%, but the question of taking losses deserves some further enlargement on cartographical principles.

Investors buying near the lower parallels of shares which are apparently fluctuating astride a *flat* mean should, as a rule, place their stop-loss orders slightly below the last previous bottom so as to give their shares a chance of wavering over what appears to be a likely range.

Similarly, if a share seems trending upwards, the stop-loss

order should be slightly below an imaginary continuation of the rising lower parallel, i.e., a stop which will only be caught if the share begins to quit its "track." See Chapter XVII.

Such a stop should be raised if the share rises higher.

Again, if you ever risk buying a share with a falling mean, **the stop should** be outside the apparent lower parallel, **or just** below the lowest point recently reached; but if this involves a loss of over 20%, refrain from buying the shares.

Rules for selling shares with which one is encumbered.

One other point ought here be mentioned in connection with the problem of selling.

Although detailed rules have been given for taking profits and placing stop-loss orders on newly made purchases, a reader taking up this book for the first time may, especially if he has just come into an inheritance, during a period of slump, have in his portfolio a number of old holdings on which he has considerable losses, and which he does not know whether to keep.

A good rule on these occasions—assuming the shares are fairly salable—is to sell, if you would not invest new money in the same list of shares, even if the price were slightly lower so as to cover expenses. Willing sellers make good investors; beware, therefore, of ever becoming a clinger to bad stocks.

Above all, do not argue that because your shares are now down you cannot sell—*because the loss would be too great!* The loss, in fact, is already there.

Look, therefore, at your stocks at market price—regardless of price once paid—and regard them merely as receptacles for money which ought no longer to be used if any better receptacle can be found. To find something better to switch to immediately is a good way of overcoming one's natural repugnance to taking losses on one's own old holdings.

Some further notes on this important subject appear in Chapter XL.

Selling to raise cash.

If it is ever necessary to raise ready money, always sell the *worst* and least promising shares in your list first. Resist the powerful though capital-destroying temptation to sell the best shares with the freest markets first—in the hope that the others, which are either difficult to sell at the moment or which look under-valued on actualities, will revive later.

Shares with declining profit trends are almost always bad markets and are almost always under-valued on *actualities,* and remain so for several years on end on account of people discounting the future. Therefore throw them out at once, even though they look cheap on *actualities;* and abandon the folly of waiting for upturns, which may not occur until after a further big fall.

A very difficult lesson, this!—One of the tests of strong character in investment.

Basic selling rules.

Basically, then, our selling rules are as follows:

1. Sell *immediately* on internal deterioration.
2. Cut losses of 20%.
3. Never let good profits run off into losses. Conserve two-thirds of your paper gains.
4. Always sell prospect shares at the apex (or downturn) of a conjunctural boomlet.
5. Consider the wisdom of selling single shares whenever they reach their higher parallels.

CHAPTER XXVI

RECAPITULATION

At this point let us briefly re-enumerate the chief practical conclusions so far arrived at in the course of this book:—

1. Beware of booming industries. Prosperity normally breeds its own disintegration.

2. Endeavor to buy in early revival, when profits first start to rise.

3. Prefer geometric industries.

4. Aim at buying in conjunctural depressions when shares-in-general first turn upwards.

5. Shares should possess the following qualities:
    (i) High earnings on market price.
    (ii) A free market.
    (iii) Good management.
    (iv) Good finances.

6. Especial gains (and losses) can be made from companies whose shares have geared equities, or which are high-cost producers.

7. Always have a stop-loss order system compatible with your likely gains.

8. (i) Sell on a loss of 20%.
    (ii) Sell on internal deterioration.
    (iii) Sell prospect shares in bad conjunctures.
    (iv) Never let good profits run off into losses. Conserve two-thirds of your paper gains.

9. Never do things that are *normally* wrong.

10. Balance your stakes correctly.

CHAPTER XXVII

OCCASIONS FOR SPECIAL CAUTION

Having suggested some rules for buying and selling, we must now warn the investor against certain common eventualities, namely, being left with stock at the peaks of booms.

The five types of booms or boomlets to beware of are:—
1. Booms in single industries.
2. Booms in single shares.
3. "New issue" booms.
4. Trade cyclical booms, and
5. The Intermediate boomlets.

Booms in single industries.

To repeat a former statement, booms in single industries attract new capital, and when the gestation period is over there is normally a collapse; this affects not only the mushroom companies but also the market leaders.

A primary rule is not to buy shares for lock-up purposes in any industry which is enjoying a boom and where there is a share boom as well—especially if the gestation period of new plant is short, and if the shares themselves are on a low yield basis. The rise may be prolonged for a few months; eventually, however, a collapse is certain.

On principle, long-run investors should sell shares in booming industries as soon as they, or the share-index curve of their group, break below the last previous conjunctural bottom, or drop, say 20% from the recent highest. Such a fall is usually—though, of course, not always—a sign that public interest is waning and that a major collapse in the industry has begun.

Above all, do not buy over-valued shares on big falls in the hope of large recoveries. Once a collapse has set in, revival is unlikely for a period of years.

Sudden booms in single shares.

Turning now to single shares which happen to be booming: very often unscrupulous company directors advertise their shares scandalously and deceive the public with all sorts of rumors concerning current earnings, prospective profits, bonus issues, amalgamations and so on, their intention being to unload shares on a gullible public.

Beware, therefore, of shares that are being run up if they have doubtful directorates, or if groups are known to manipulate the shares. Even if directors are believed to be reliable, beware of shares which are run up to a low-earnings basis, if their prices are based solely on rumors of anticipated earnings three or four years ahead.

General new issue booms.

A third type of danger to avoid is the new issue boom.

Once or twice in every trade cycle savings and bank money become so plentiful that the public enjoys a glut of funds. Company promoters wait years for these conditions, and in the meantime collect in their files all manner of potential promotions. Schemes based on patents and new processes are usually the most popular bait.

Similarly, whenever a boom occurs in a single industry, company promoters try to make profits from it. They float all manner of mushroom companies whose prospectus estimates almost invariably seem absurd two years afterwards. The public nevertheless subscribes to them eagerly because established shares are now at such high prices. Indeed, the new issues themselves usually go to huge and inflated premiums.

Within eighteen months most of these mushroom companies collapse, and normally fall to half their issue prices or lower. Even the leading shares in the industry fall too, as soon as the new capital comes to fruition.

Beware, therefore, of new issue booms in which much rubbish is being absorbed. They always lead to much subsequent wreckage; even good shares in other industries become involved in the collapse, as a result of sales to finance losses on bad shares, or to meet called-in loans.

Beware of cyclical Stock Exchange booms.

Finally, beware of the normal cyclical Stock Exchange boom.

Near the end of each trade cycle, shares in general habitually rise to inflated levels prior to collapse. These collapses usually, though not always, begin gradually and then acquire cumulative momentum.

All that is needed is some unpropitious economic, monetary or political event to shake general confidence. Profit-taking then begins, and nervousness gradually spreads. Optimism gives way to pessimism; the more cautious cash profits at once. Speculators sell to pay off loans; and buyers tend simultaneously to withdraw. Certain prices fall in consequence and a good many stop-loss orders are caught. This means a flood of additional selling, and general sentiment is further upset. Nervousness spreads and gives rise to distrust; distrust gives rise to yet further sales. Prices, therefore, go on falling. Banks then probably call in loans because collateral values have shrunk. The calling in of loans means yet extra selling, and the fall thus gains more cumulative momentum, until at last—with only minor rebounds—a ridiculously low level of prices is reached, it being the sheer absurdity of the low level which alone brings in new buyers.

The point is that if people lose confidence and compete suddenly to encash paper profits, or to sell so as to pay off bank loans, they are attempting, in the aggregate, to take out of the Stock Exchange more money than is being put in (by new savers and bank borrowers). Even if the excess is no more than a few millions, it will lead to such a loading up of jobbers' stocks, and to such a decline in prices, that probably hundreds of millions of paper profits will suddenly disappear. (Read carefully Appendix F.)

Resist the lure of booming markets.

Looking, then, at booms as a whole, the investor must be ultra cautious. If people are making money in a share or group of shares, the normal man feels irresistibly tempted to rush in and acquire a holding. There is thus competition to buy and share prices soar to absurdly high levels. The curious magnetic attraction of booms breaks down the most sober resolutions of even experienced investors.

If, however, any investor would meet with success, he must recognize these temptations, and continually be on guard against them. A collapse *always* follows a boom (usually within eighteen months); and the collapse itself is always violent, and always steeper than the rise (as a result of industrial profits virtually disappearing, whereas they were probably reasonable before the over-investment commenced).

Investors, therefore, *must* learn to stand clear of shares in a dangerous economic or technical position. They may regret doing so for some months on end. Eventually, however, they will always realize the prudence of their policy.

A wise precept is never to be drawn wildly into the vortex of a booming market; if the market is entered deliberately, or if shares are already held, give rigid stop-loss orders and do not think of cancelling them.

If the shares go on rising, raise your stops. Conserve two-thirds of your paper profits.

Intermediate boomlets.

The more an Intermediate boomlet advances, the greater the caution that should be shown by short-run investors. Usually, as was said on page 78, the Intermediate upswing commences with increased activity, and with rises, in the market Leaders. This is followed about half-way up the Intermediate swing by activity in low-grade counters; and later with a decline in relative activity in the leaders, but with violent majority-activity in the "cats and dogs." Such activity itself is a normal sign of danger.

Nevertheless in each Intermediate swing there is certainly more money to be made by operating in the "cats and dogs" than in the Leaders; the fault, however, that most people make is as follows: To sell their Leaders as soon as they show good profits; and then, since other Leaders have risen so far as to look too dear to buy, to fill their portfolios with cats and dogs somewhere near the top of the Intermediate movement.

One may, it is true, if one is lucky, reap sharp, short-run profits in "rubbish" at the tail end of an Intermediate boomlet. But my own preference is, as soon as the graph for the general index is reaching the region of the upper parallel, to prefer *high yielding* shares with free markets to the cats and dogs. The cats and dogs will certainly fall more rapidly than high-class stocks with high earnings (as soon as the Intermediate fall begins), and the cats and dogs will become almost unsaleable, so that you will not be able to get out of them into cash, so as to have ready money in reserve for the next Intermediate slump.

In other words, as the Intermediate boomlet progresses prefer (instead of augmenting one's holdings of "dogs"), to get into higher and higher grade issues of a less-and-less "prospect" character.

On the other hand when an Intermediate slump has occurred, and when the tide turns, and the dealers begin to saucer out and rise, a percentage of "dogs" may well be bought for sale in the next Intermediate boomlet.

Majority activity in "dogs" is usually a sign that an Intermediate boomlet is approaching its Termination. Majority-activity in Leaders, on a mildly rising market, *after* an Intermediate slump, is normally a sign that the reaction is ending.

* * *

And the same thing is more or less true taking the business cycle as a whole, from a long-term investment standpoint.

An increase in the number of issues dealt in, out of all those quoted, is also a "normal" sign of danger. (A graph might well be kept of these fluctuating "numbers.")

CHAPTER XXVIII

CYCLICAL STOCK EXCHANGE SLUMPS

Cyclical collapses.

Once in every trade cycle there habitually occurs a serious Stock Exchange collapse. What usually happens is as follows:—

Shares having soared (despite a high market rate of interest) to a low yield basis, say, of 4% or under, naturally need continuously good prospects to keep them up. If, however, prospects change (owing, say, to a decline in national profits, or to a political crisis, or to an increase in the volume of unemployment, or to tension in the banks), and if future industrial earnings are thereby threatened, the supporting influence of "optimistic opinion" at once disappears. Ordinary shares are hurriedly sold by nervous holders, prices are lowered, stop-loss orders are caught, and prices fall furiously. The banks then probably call in loans because collateral values have shrunk. The selling thus becomes cumulative and usually goes on, with only minor pauses, until at last shares have fallen to a fair yield basis, say, of about 6%.

Now a collapse in shares from a 4% to a 6% yield basis means a fall of 33⅓%, and a further drop to a 7% yield basis means a total fall of 47%. On occasions such as these many investors lose the whole savings of a lifetime, especially if they have been operating with borrowed money. An important duty of the investor, therefore, is to avoid getting caught in these "normal" cyclical collapses.

Watch the national profits curve.

These collapses usually occur near the end of each cycle, but theoretically they can also occur at any other time as well. All that is needed is a sudden change in Market Sentiment at a time when ordinary shares are selling on a low yield basis.

In connection with confidence suddenly disappearing, a highly important factor to watch is the curve of national profits.

If after some years of expansion the curve for national profits begins to flatten out, or worse still to decline, while at the same time shares in general are on a low yield basis, confidence may suddenly disappear and people may rush to sell their ordinary shares. This rush to sell may bring about a collapse from a 4% to a 6% yield basis.

The investor, therefore, should watch the national profit curve exceptionally carefully, and be prepared to sell when it begins to show signs of wavering.

Incidentally, he should also keep curves indicating the volume of trade (i.e. unemployment, imports, bank clearings, pig iron production, railway traffics and so on), and he should be particularly nervous if any of these curves decline. Volume, however, is rarely so reliable or early an index of changes in the long-run trend of Stock Exchange prices as are Aggregate Profits, since volume often stays large in a mass-production world although general profits are rapidly declining—and, obviously, it is industrial profits which mainly govern Stock Exchange Sentiment and prices.

Concentrate, therefore, on watching the general profit curve of the country, and be careful if it flattens or changes direction.

Watch the level of the bank rate.

In addition to the national profit curve two other factors deserve close attention whenever the yield on ordinary shares has become abnormally low; these are the general banking position, and the bank rate in relation to the yield on ordinary shares.

Millions of pounds (the normal appears to be about fifty millions in England) are habitually borrowed from the banks by speculators and financial companies to buy Stock Exchange securities. If the bank borrowing rate is below the yield on most ordinary shares, speculators will be quite willing to borrow freely provided they see fair chances of capital appreciation. If, however, the bank rate rises high above the yield on ordinary shares, or if ordinary shares rise until their yield is far below the bank rate,* few people will continue borrowing unless appreciation prospects are still amazingly favorable.

If, therefore, the bank rate is raised high, while the yield on ordinary shares is low, the investor should regard the cyclical danger phase as having been definitely† reached. He should henceforward be ultra-careful not to get caught in an avalanche.

[We would say, incidentally, that a rise in the bank rate to $5\frac{1}{2}\%$ and over, when shares in general are already on a low yield basis, is as a rule (unless currency inflation is taking place) a sound sign to sell *all* one's ordinary shares at once, unless it is absolutely clear that trade itself is still improving. On such occasions it is normally right to sell on the same day that the bank rate is raised. Share prices, it is true, will be marked down fiercely on that day, but it is normally bad policy to wait hopefully for recoveries. More often than not, if one waits, and if

---

* Or, more strictly speaking, whenever the borrowing rate, i.e., bank rate, plus, say, $\frac{1}{2}\%$, is higher than the net yield on ordinary shares *after* paying income tax. (The ordinary share yield can be reasonably assessed by taking the average yield on the first 100 shares in the *Investor's Monthly Manual,* whose issued ordinary capital is over £1,000,000.)

† There are two possible exceptions to this rule: (i) if the bank rate has been raised purely for temporary gold-protection and foreign exchange reasons; and (ii) if it has been raised by the Managers of the Currency to put the brake (temporarily) on an inflationary tendency—without actually intending to cause positive deflation—as distinct from mere anti-inflation.

other people are given time to analyze the position, selling will increase and prices will fall to still lower levels. Therefore, on principle, risk missing the top of the market, and be one of the first to get out. Do not wait for a further drop of 10% or more in all your securities.]

The ordinary share yield in relation to the bond yield.

A third factor to watch from a cyclical standpoint is the yield on bonds in relation to the yield on ordinary shares.

If ordinary shares are on a lower yield basis than bonds at a time when cautious investors might justifiably become nervous about the future of industry, the tendency will be to switch over from ordinary shares into bonds, i.e. from those securities where dividends are low and where capital values are uncertain, into bonds where the return is actually higher and where capital values are probably more secure.*

Survey.

To recapitulate. The three main Cyclical Dangers confronting investors are:—

1. Ordinary shares rising to a low yield basis, especially one lower than bonds.
2. The bank rate rising above the yield on ordinary shares.
3. A decline in national profits.

* Of course, a nation-wide switch from ordinaries to bonds is, strictly speaking, a theoretical impossibility, for the simple reason that each sale involves a purchase and somebody must own the ordinary shares sold. The attempt to switch, however, involves the offering down of ordinaries and the bidding up of bonds, with the result that mutual competition to get clear of ordinaries leads to a violent marking down of their prices. Bonds will usually simultaneously rise unless the funds received from the sale of ordinaries are hoarded or used for private expenditure, or used for paying off bank loans, or are diverted into new issues. (See Appendix F.)

If any of these conditions are reached, the investor must be especially careful. In the case of 1 and 2 happening, there is usually no need to sell all ordinary shares immediately, for there is frequently no general reaction in shares for about twelve to eighteen months. Nevertheless, despite this possible delay, the prudent man will, as soon as one or more of the above three danger phases has been entered, be careful to take in rein as a precaution against a sudden collapse. He should not borrow at these periods and should stand clear of shares on a "prospect" basis. If he does speculate he should be very rigid in applying his stop-loss orders.

The difficulty of predicting cyclical changes in Market Sentiment.

Of course, the main problem confronting investors on these occasions is to differentiate between what are going to be merely intermediate conjunctural reactions and what are the actual beginnings of a major cyclical slump. This is a very difficult problem.

We have already insisted that when once a Danger Phase has been reached from the economic point of view, it is primarily Sentiment that brings about the collapse in share values.

Sentiment, however, is psychological, and charts and statistics are of little use in determining exactly when, and to what extent, the minds of men will react adversely to various economic and political phenomena.

On some occasions, when shares have risen to a low yield basis, general confidence will still be maintained even though appreciable falls are taking place in national profits. On other occasions confidence may suddenly decline even though general profits are still rising and employment is still good. The question is thus to some extent one of unpredictable mass psychology.

A good practical rule, therefore, is first to recognize economic Danger Phases as soon as they are entered; and, secondly, to decide that, whenever any relapse takes place in the general share index of more than the normal conjunctural amount (say 7% near the top of a cycle), one will take it that the cyclical tide has turned at last—even though one may not have expected it so soon; and that, therefore, one will at all costs ensure oneself against getting caught in a major drop of 30% to 50%.

On these occasions a good rule is to sell *all* one's shares that are on a "prospect" or non-yield basis, and to put small stop-loss orders on the remainder.

What, in fact, we advise is the contemplation of the national index of ordinary shares in the grand cyclical manner, with the decision that as soon as it begins to turn downwards (after an economic Danger Phase has been entered) by more than the normal conjunctural amount,* that one will sell the majority of one's ordinary shares on cyclical index "downturn" principles.

This may appear rather a bold and sweeping policy at first sight, but in reality it is a form of Napoleonic strategy that will save the investor from the enormous losses which investors in ordinary shares habitually sustain at the end of *every* trade cycle.

Adherence to this policy needs great resolution, and at the moment of execution may appear to be unwise. Six to twelve months afterwards the investor, however, will realize that his adamant policy of scientifically standing clear of the top-heavy market was one of great discretion.

Expect to lose slightly (and perhaps to miss profits) at the top of each major cycle.

* Or if the index reaches a lower conjunctural bottom than the one preceding it. (See Chapter XVII.)

EXCURSUS

Should ordinary shares be entirely deserted at the peak of each cycle?

At this point an answer should perhaps be given to an objection which might be raised to the policy advocated earlier on in this book (Chapter IV), of disposing of virtually *all* one's ordinary shares at the peak of each cycle.

If our statement (in Chapter VIII) is correct, that in almost all trade cycles there are some industries which move in an opposite direction to the majority of industries, and enjoy large profits during general trade slumps, it might at first sight be thought wrong to carry out a wholesale switch from ordinary shares to bonds at the peak of each cycle (after waiting till the first credit-crisis is apparently over).

This objection appears at first sight reasonable, but the following points should be borne in mind:

First—although a decline in interest rates eventually stimulates building and municipal expenditure—it is very difficult to pick out those few industries which, although they may appear to be about to do well, will not start slumping if a general trade slump occurs.

Secondly, even if one were successful in picking out the few industries that would actually go on prospering, the probability would always be that, although earnings might increase, share prices in the market would not do justice to actual earnings.

During every cyclical trade slump ordinary shares earn for themselves a great reputation for insecurity and investors become much keener on avoiding losses than on making profits; so that, even though profits in certain industries may go on rising, investors with new savings will keep mainly to bonds and will try to stand clear of ordinary shares altogether. The chances therefore are that the ordinary shares in question, although they are prospering, will not* rise appreciably even though earnings rise considerably.

The following chart depicts the influence of trade cyclical factors on these exceptional industries.

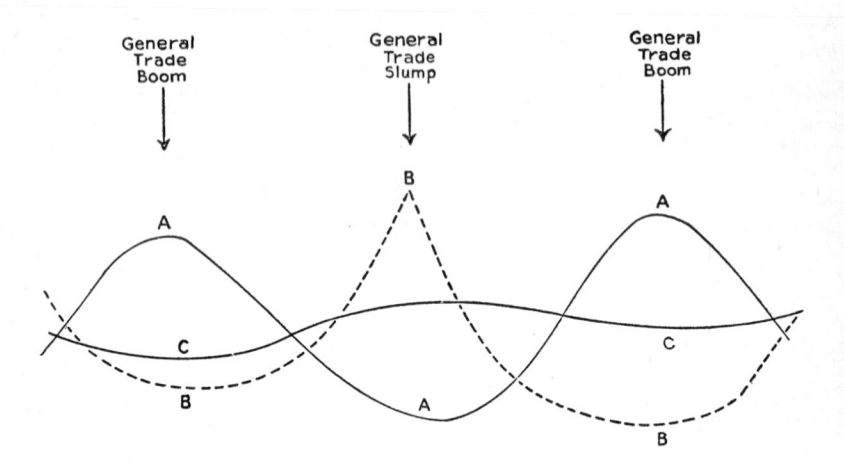

Curve A = The course of ordinary shares in general.

Curve B = The course that the shares of a few industries should, other things being equal, follow, because of their profits.

Curve C = The course that they actually do follow because of general Stock Exchange influences of a cyclical nature.

On principle, therefore, the cautious investor will at the peak of each cycle usually profit most by switching wholly into bonds†—after the first credit crisis is over and as soon as the bond index itself makes a small turn upwards—rather than by

* With the possible exception of gold shares, and a few new infant industries.

† With the possible exception of gold shares, where costs usually fall during trade slumps although output and selling prices remain unaffected.

trying to pick out those few industries which will move against the main tide.

When to re-buy common stocks.

Investors should, we think, postpone buying ordinary shares—
(a) Until a crash in the majority of securities has occurred.
(b) Until the bank rate has again fallen below the yield on both ordinary shares *and* bonds, say to 4%; and
(c) If investors wish to be ultra careful they should, in theory, wait until the national profit curve again turns upwards after an intermediate slump. It will usually suffice, however, to act (as regards a portion of one's capital) before this happens, provided that the ordinary share index has again turned upwards and, in addition, made a higher conjunctural top and bottom (see Chapter XVII); for in most trade cycles shares start to revive nine months to a year in advance of published industrial profits.

Avoid trying to hit cyclical bottoms.

We must, however, warn the reader against trying to hit the absolute bottom either of the market in general or of a single security. If one has lost money by not selling in time, or even if one has cleverly sold at the top of the boom, there is a great temptation to try to bring off a brilliant coup by buying near the bottom during the panic, say after six months of slump. Such attempted brilliance is normally disastrous, and is theoretically unsound.

Certainly ordinary shares will look attractively cheap when compared with prices some months previously, and certainly their earnings-yields will be high on the basis of last year's profits.

Have the strength of mind to realize, however, that you have run into a new and depressing kind of market, where ordinary shares will show greatly reduced earnings over the next two years (although there may be few outward signs of it at present, and although hope of *early* revival will be the general tone of politicians and the Press).

Realize that bonds alone will steadily rise; for every time that ordinary shares appreciate, they will encounter heavy selling by insiders (who know the worsening state of order-books) to drive them back. Ordinary shares will thus fluctuate in a downward zig-zag, the only buyers being foolish people who lack knowledge of the normal length of industrial slumps and whose sole motive for buying is the "recent" earnings-record of the company or the fact that the shares now "look" cheap compared with previous prices.

Be big-minded, however, and avoid trying to hit cyclical bottoms; the risks are much too great. In fact, deliberately aim at missing all cyclical bottoms; wait till the national index of ordinary shares has saucered out and turned upwards. Even then only buy in conformity with the rules given in the last section: that is to say, wait till the profits of selected companies are apparently reviving (or their losses falling), and until their shares (and the national conjunctural index) have both made the requisite upturns as explained in our chapter on Charts.

Trying to hit cyclical bottoms before twenty months of slump have elapsed, before wreckage sales have been eliminated, and before confidence in the industry and in ordinary shares in general has once more revived, is a petty and greedy unscientific policy unworthy of broad-viewed long-term investors. It constitutes a course of behavior which is *normally* wrong.

Cultivate ability to "wait"—until short-run and long-run internal and external factors are *all* once more simultaneously favorable.

The second year of revival is the safest time to buy. Avoid

buying too soon in declining industries after only a few months of slump.

The use of a moving average.

I might add that a 200-day moving average, of say the Dow-Jones Industrial Index, is usually a valuable graph to keep from a long-run investment point of view.

When, on the conditions described in the two following sections being fulfilled, the daily figure (on the graph) moves, after its cyclical rise, *below* the 200-day moving average, it is usually right to sell.

Conversely when, after a cyclical fall, it moves to the right of and *above* the line for the 200-day moving average, it is usually right to buy.

SUMMARY

Cyclical conditions to fear.

1. Ordinary share yield below bond yield; and a downturn in the general index of ordinary shares of over say 7% from highest, until at last the previous conjunctural bottom has been broken through.

2. A downturn or flattening in national quarterly profits.

3. Bank Rate above the yield on Ordinary shares and on Bonds.

Conditions to wait for at the end of slumps before re-investing in ordinaries.

1. Ordinary share yield above bond yield.

2. A bank rate below the yield on both ordinary shares *and* bonds.

    [N.B.—This condition encourages borrowing from the banks to buy bonds; and extra funds consequently flow into the Stock Exchange and gradually flow on to the higher class ordinaries, thus setting in motion an upward movement in the shares of those industries where prospects are no longer too bad.* (*Read the footnote.*)]

3. An upturn in the national index figure of ordinary shares from lowest by something exceeding the normal conjunctural amount (say 10% at the bottom of the cycle), thus indicating that general sentiment in favor of ordinaries is at last beginning to return. (Successively higher conjunctural bottoms, and tops; and the "quitting of the cyclical down-track" are also normally a useful indication. See Chapter XVII.)

4. An upturn in national profits and employment.

---

* We would point out that not only does a lowering of the bank rate encourage borrowing for speculation in ordinaries, but the simultaneous lowering of the deposit-rate (to a point well below the bond yield) pushes money off deposit into the higher yielding bonds; and this influx of extra money into the Stock Exchange exerts an important influence on stock market revival.

CHAPTER XXIX

PANICS

Panics are of three sorts:

   i Stock Exchange.
  ii Banking.
 iii Industrial.

Stock Exchange panics.

Stock Exchange panics can occur at any stage of the cycle. They can be brought about either by banking panics, industrial panics, calling in of bank loans, or merely by Fear.

Selling increases, buying dries up, stop-loss orders are caught, and loans are called in. The market cracks perhaps 25% within a few days.

The third day of *wild* selling is usually (though not always) a good time to buy.

There is normally a recovery of one-third of the fall. Then later the market *usually* sinks to still lower levels.

Stock Exchange panics occur most frequently at the end of a long and wild bull market, when some unexpected piece of news suddenly re-orients general sentiment, and causes shares to fall from a low to a high yield basis.

Banking panics.

Banking panics usually occur at the bottom of a trade slump, when bad trade and a decline in market values has so weakened the asset position of the banks, that the public starts a "run."

Banking panics could, however, occur at other stages of the trade cycle as a result (i) of a sudden loss of gold abroad (due, say, to a war scare); (ii) of adverse legislation, such as a tax on bank deposits, or a high tax on the use of checks; or (iii) as a result of a general belief that the banks were over-speculating in a boom, and were becoming unsound.

The government will usually intervene in a banking panic, and either supply the banks with more legal tender paper money, or will guarantee deposits.

Banking panics usually last only a few days; although the stock market may remain shaken for many months.

Usually the Stock Exchange is kept closed for longer than the banks.

Industrial panics.

Industrial panics are rare. They are due to a wave of Fear (economic or political) causing consumers to stop buying, and producers and middlemen to cancel their orders. The circulation of money dries up, velocity falls, and business comes to a standstill.

The Stock Exchange will slump, and will normally be closed until the industrial panic has been over for some weeks.

* * *

Buying in panics often pays, but no definite rules for such buying can be laid down, except that the securities bought should be cheap on actualities; and also market leaders—unless one is buying for the long pull.

CHAPTER XXX

AVERAGING

Buying on a scale.

The system of investment which we have advocated in this book relies on the investor being right more often than wrong. Theoretically, however, it is also possible to make money, provided one augments one's stakes progressively, even if one is less than 50% right in one's selections. This implies keeping large reserves of cash.

Every investor has doubtless pondered the possibility of superimposing upon his scientific methods of forecasting a mathematical system of raising stakes progressively in order to recoup past losses (either by averaging down in the *same* share, or by increasing the size of the next purchase of *another* share).

Certainly such a system would be attractive—

(a) If one had enough capital.

(b) If one could rely on the required rises or rebounds in price occurring.

(c) If one could be sure of neatly timing and hitting off these rebounds.

(d) If there was no danger of one's dealings ever becoming too big for the market.

(e) If one did not have to wait too long for the requisite rebounds.

Die-hard averaging.

Averaging down in shares (as distinct from commodities) is a dangerous business.

Averaging downwards may be all very well on occasions when market leaders in healthy industries look cheap in nervous markets, if, and only if, after careful thought, one buys, say, half one's requirements at the current price and the remainder on a 15% or 20% drop, and then institutes stop-loss orders if any further fall takes place. But it is highly dangerous to average downwards systematically, at given mathematical intervals, in the hope of striking an eventual rebound and getting out at a profit.

Upward rebounds of much over 10% net, after expenses have been paid (say 15% gross), cannot normally be relied on. And even if one were to rely somewhat rashly on progressively bigger percentage recoveries, the fund which one would require would be huge. Three thousand units would often be needed to make a profit of only ten! Take, for instance, the following hypothetical case:

At the price of £	Number of Shares to buy	Cost £	Price at which to sell all purchases £	Profit on whole Transaction £
10	10	100	11	10
9	11	99	10	10
8	20	160	9	10
7	41	287	8	10
6	82	492	7	10
5	165	825	6	10
4	328	1,312	5	10

Total spent on 60% fall = £3,275 to yield a profit of £10 only.

Thus we see that a policy of averaging, pursued rigorously, requires a vast capital. One may need idle funds of thirty times one's original stake—implying that with a capital of £10,000 one could only operate in three shares simultaneously, even if one's initial investment in each was to be only £100.

AVERAGING

Limited averaging.

Nor is it prudent to try to avoid the mathematical implications of continuously-pursued averaging by deciding never to average for more than, say, three successive falls.

If one stops short in the above table on a drop to £7, and eventual recovery, after a further fall, only occurs to £6, total losses on the four successive purchases will be £(40 + 33 + 40 + 41) = £154, which would require no less than fifteen consecutive successful *unabandoned* averaging operations, each winning £10, to recoup one's losses!

* * *

It has been said of mathematical averaging that only millionaires can afford it, and that they are not such fools.

What usually happens. (Missing the turns.)

Perhaps, however, the most damning argument against averaging is that although ample recoveries may eventually occur, one may unluckily miss them.

Take, for instance, a man who is averaging downwards at 20% intervals. He may buy twice in succession, i.e., at minus 20% and at minus 40%, with the intention of buying again at minus 60%. If, however, the shares only fall to minus 59% and then recover 19 points to minus 40%, he will get a 19-point recovery (which, on the lowest point touched, i.e., minus 59%, will mean a recovery of over 30%), but he will not get any benefit from it at all. His bad luck (a) in his selected intervals, and (b) in the run of the short-run nadirs and peaks will—despite a 30% recovery—cause the failure of his system.

Incidentally if one's own broker either lacks diligence or is unlucky, he may not actually deal even if the price does fall temporarily to minus 60%.

And yet despite these indisputable facts the system of averaging is rigorously supported by many writers on the fallacious theory that it helps you to buy big at the bottom of the market.

Our conclusion, however, is that although at first sight averaging appears a policy which one ought to study, in practice it has few merits. Firstly, things cannot eventually go right every time; while, secondly, it is foolish to pour money into a security unless one still regards it as the best in all the market.

Averaging to get one's own back.

Beware, incidentally, of the normal temptation which invariably besets all investors with losses. When a share which they own has fallen they cannot help feeling that "now it is really cheap." They therefore argue: "I am not actually averaging: I am merely buying more of a sound security on its prospects." But this is how gamblers always feel. They habitually excuse themselves into what is virtually averaging downwards. A much better system is to cut losses early and not to buy more at all. Averaging is the policy of obstinate persons who hope to be right every time—people, in fact, who have not the strength of mind *ever* to admit themselves wrong, and who cannot resist the temptation of "trying to get their own back." on any share which has failed them.

Averaging downwards is probably only a sound policy in the raw commodity (as distinct from share) markets when products are already selling well below marginal costs, and costs cannot easily be reduced. Under these conditions *eventual* recovery is likely, although it may take some years.

Rational averaging.

If, however, a broker has a client who insists on averaging in shares, he should train in him the proper way; namely, only to begin to do so:

(1) At the nadirs of conjunctural slumps.
(2) When shares are well below recent highest.

(3) Only if the shares are clearly undervalued in view of existing earnings. (Always avoid averaging in shares with low earnings-yields.)

(4) Keep to industries which are clearly improving.

(5) Never start, or continue, an averaging campaign when the most recent fall is due to internal deterioration, as distinct from purely external market factors. In the former case abandon the averaging system at once: do not throw good money after bad.

(6) The riskier a share the greater should be the intervals at which successive purchases are made. Ten per cent intervals may be good for high-class investment shares, especially if they are first purchased after a big drop. Twenty per cent intervals should be the smallest in the case of highly risky shares, especially if the jobber's turn is wide. Smaller gaps than 20% tend to land one in too heavy a downward progression of stakes, and also to make sensible stop-loss order-giving difficult. Bigger gaps, however, tend to cause one to miss the market, even if there are recoveries of 30% or more from bottom.

(7) Some people advocate secondary purchases, not according to some pre-arranged scale (which may involve fighting the current trend of a fast falling market), but on a basis of economic judgment. These speculators prefer to wait until the last fall is apparently over; they buy only when the shares appear to have grounded, and perhaps made a slight turn upwards, thus showing that selling no longer exceeds buying. This policy certainly departs from the realm of pure mathematics into that of economic judgment; and certainly it involves a risk of missing the market nadirs on account of ordinary bad luck. We think, however, that on the whole a system of using one's judgment in averaging is, despite its mathematical faults,

less risky than a system of blind mathematics, where, if luck happens to be out, losses become enormous.

(8) Averaging as a bear is not advisable even though shares which rise usually become easier and easier markets. As a bull, falls cannot exceed 100%; as a bear, rises may be indefinite.

CHAPTER XXXI

PYRAMIDING

Pyramiding profits.

In sharp distinction to averaging downwards is the policy of pyramiding upwards. Pyramiding consists of augmenting stakes if one's selections turn out to be fortunate.

The successive augmentations can be effected in either declining, increasing, or in equal numbers of shares; in declining, increasing or equal sums of money; and/or at declining, increasing or equal intervals.

Pyramiding, to be successful, must always be combined with rigid stop-loss orders.

A popular method of pyramiding is to lower stakes to start with—on the principle that the risk of a set-back becomes greater on each successive rise—(though later gradually to increase them in value).

See next page.

PYRAMIDING

A much-favored scale is:—100 shares, 50 shares, 25 shares, and repeat, with stops placed at the prices of the penultimate purchases. For example:

Purchase No.	At $	Buy Shares	Cost $	Stop at $	Result when stop is caught $		$
1	40	100	4,000	35	− 500	= −	500
2	45	50	2,250	40	− 250	= −	250
3	50	25	1,250	45	+ 500 − 125	= +	375
4	55	25	1,375	50	+ 1,000 + 250 − 125	= +	1,125
5	60	25	1,500	55	+ 1,500 + 500 + 125 − 125	= +	2,000
6	65	25	1,625	60			
			12,220				

Total risked (on stop) = $500
Profit made = $2,000
Profit ratio to risk = 400%
Capital employed = $12,220
Profit ratio to capital = 16½%
Total rise in shares = 62½%
Expenses are omitted.

According to the above table one could afford to be *completely* unsuccessful four times running if the rise went to a sixth purchase, i.e. 62½%; but only twice running if the rise ceased at the fifth purchase, i.e. 50%.—Not a very attractive programme!

* * *

190

PYRAMIDING

Another method.

If one pyramids in equal successive *numbers of shares* or in equal successive *stakes,* perhaps the best rule to follow (both as regards the scale of stakes, the intervals at which to pyramid, and the stop-loss orders to give) is that one should *never allow any unsuccessful secondary purchase to wipe out the whole of the profits on the previous purchase.* In following this procedure one should, of course, be careful to consider the nature of one's shares and the freeness of the market so as to arrive at reasonable stop-loss orders in each case.

If this method is adhered to, handsome profits can often be made from pyramiding, both in investment over long periods, and in short-run fast-moving markets.

It should be borne in mind, however, that unless intervals are very wide (e.g. 20% and over) it is difficult to construct an upward scale in conformity with the foregoing italicized rule, for if intervals are narrow it will be difficult to give sensible stop-loss orders. It must further be added that in most pyramiding schemes it is difficult to make a net profit until after the *third* purchase, i.e. until after shares have risen about 30%! And since *short-run* rises of 30% are rare, pyramiding, except in violent booms, belongs more to long-run investment on successive *reactions,* when shares have reacted to their lower rising parallels (see fig. 1 on page 59), than to short-run *continuous* rises.

Take, for instance, the case of a rise from £5 to £7=40%.

At price of £	Number of shares to buy	Cost of new purchase £	Sell all purchases at £	Net result £
5	100	500	4	— 100
6	100	600	5½	nil (less expenses)
7	100	700	6½	+ 150 (less expenses)
[8	100	800	7½	+ 400 (less expenses)]

Result = no profit if stops get caught, until the third purchase.

191

Pyramiding in equal amounts.

Or, to give another example based on pyramiding in (approximately) equal amounts, as distinct from in rising, *amounts*:

Purchase No.	Price £	Invest £	Number of shares	Sell all at £	Net result £
1.	5	100	20	4	−20
2.	6	102	17	5½	+ 1½ (less expenses)
3.	7	98	14	6½	+ 31½ (less expenses)

Rise from £5 to £7 = 40%.

* * *

Personally we do not greatly advocate pyramiding. To double up when you are winning, however, is only to risk profits. Doubling down when you have losses, i.e. to average, is to risk losing all.

Pyramiding is usually only worth while when rises of over 30% are envisaged. Such occasions are rare; therefore hesitate to pyramid.

Pyramiding against the whole of a margin.

Pyramiding against a margin is also possible. For instance, a man may decide to risk £200 in buying 1,000 shares costing 20s. each, on contango.

If the price rises 10% he will have another £100, on paper, to play with. He can therefore buy and carry over, say, 500 more shares (assuming his broker is satisfied with a 20% margin), and yet another 500 if the price rises further, his intention being never to lose more than his original margin of £200 (and to give stop-loss orders accordingly), but to go on risking the major part of it until he has had a gigantic win.

This system is to be distinguished from progressively increasing commitments and at the same time gradually *reducing* risks, i.e. always conserving a *part* of any paper profit shown.

PYRAMIDING

For instance:

At price of	Number of Shares to buy	Cost £	Sell all at	Loss in shillings	Loss in pounds	Profit if transaction is closed at next higher price Shillings	Pounds
20/-	1,000	1,000	16/-	—4,000	—200	+ 2,000	100
22/-	500	550	18/-	{—2,000 —2,000}	—200	{+ 4,000 + 1,000}	350
24/-	500	600	20/-	{—2,000 —1,000}	—150	{+ 6,000 + 2,000 + 1,000}	450
26/-	500	650	22/-	{—2,000 —1,000 +2,000}	— 50	{+ 8,000 + 3,000 + 2,000 + 1,000}	700
28/- (30/-)	500	700	24/-	{—2,000 —1,000 +1,000 +4,000}	+100	{+10,000 + 4,000 + 3,000 + 2,000 + 1,000}	1,000

Result:
Profit   = £1,000
Risked   = £200
Ratio   = 5 : 1
Rise in Shares = 50%

Speculators following the above routine must, of course, be very strict with their stop-loss orders, and they should stop pyramiding immediately the conjuncture becomes unfavorable.

Pyramiding can be effected with advantage on the bear tack in slumps.

Options.

Options are normally a gross waste of money.

Options for three months, with expenses added, usually cost

15% to 20% on market price. A 30% to 40% movement in share prices is therefore necessary, within three months, to give a profit equalling the total cost of the option. The odds against this are enormous, although one's likely gain is only 1 : 1.

The sole merit of options is that they limit your losses, but since this can usually be equally well achieved without additional expense by giving stop-loss orders, it is normally foolish to waste money on buying options.

CHAPTER XXXII

OPERATING ON BORROWED MONEY

Scope of profits.

If one operates only with one's own capital, the amount of money that can be made on the Stock Exchange over a period of years is somewhat limited. Take for instance what can be done in ten years.

If you make 30% every year cumulatively for ten years, you only raise your original stake 14 times. If you make 50% cumulatively every year for ten years you only turn one unit into 57; and if you make 100% every year for ten years you can make just over a thousand units out of one unit. I, personally, regard making 30% cumulatively every year as good, and yet that is only turning one unit into 14 in ten years. And yet that is about as much money as can be made in practice *unless* borrowed money is used.

If borrowed money is used successfully to the tune of, say, 50% of one's own capital, much better results can naturally ensue. For instance, if there occurs a 30% cumulative accretion every year for 10 years, and if only 50% of one's own (growing) capital is borrowed at the beginning of each year, one unit will (after paying off all loans) rise to 55 units, i.e., five times as much as if no borrowed money were used.

All this, of course, sounds very tempting; and it is a temptation to which most foolish, and all greedy, persons fall prone.

What happens to them, however, is normally as follows: After perhaps a measure of success they run into a series of mistakes and misfortunes, and make the following form of losses:

For instance, if a man, who has £1,000 of his own, goes the whole hog and borrows, say, another £1,000 from his bank or his broker to buy shares, a 30% fall in his £2,000 worth of securities will mean a loss of £600, or 60% of his *own* capital. Losses, in fact, will be accentuated in exact proportion to the extent to which one is borrowing.

And since in the course of 10 years every investor will almost inevitably run into a period where he sustains an average loss of 30%, the operator on borrowed money may be ruined.

Indeed, if he is borrowing to the tune of 200% of his capital, he will lose the whole of his capital. And this is what happens again and again to thousands of people in every trade cycle.

When borrowing is particularly dangerous.

The two stages of the trade cycle at which these disasters most usually happen are:

1. At the top of each boom;
2. Near the end of each slump.

At the top of each boom there is always a galaxy of investors who, having gained confidence in their own ability to make money with the aid of borrowed funds, go bigger and bigger near the top. General sentiment then suddenly changes, and the share market which has become over-valued on prospects in anticipation a further rise in earnings suddenly swings down until a decrease, rather than an increase, in earnings becomes discounted.

If this sharp fall (usually of 30%) does not wipe out the speculator entirely, he is probably so disappointed and has become so unbalanced mentally, that he will probably decide to make a sudden final throw in order to get his money back quickly. He will, in fact, borrow up to the hilt and add to his holdings in the hope of a quick recovery.

If, however, his luck is "normal," his hoped-for recovery

will not occur; and another 15% fall in the share market will lead to calls for more margin which he cannot put up; and thus his speculative position will be sold out by his brokers.

This is the ruin which "normally" faces every speculator on borrowed money, whose success in the upward swing of the cycle has made him go too big at the top.

* * *

The second stage of the cycle during which a great many investors are normally wiped out is when the slump has lasted perhaps for two years, when shares look cheap on actualities, because of their high earnings-yields, and when the investor feels, as distinct from reasons, that the slump has already gone far enough.

Then, disappointed with his series of losses over the past two years, he will go to his bankers or brokers pledging everything he has got, so as to take one final fling at the market.

If the market falls another 15% or 20%, more margin will be called for, and his position will probably be sold out just at a time when he ought to be buying.

Moreover, even if he has any money left, his nerve, and his belief in his own luck, will probably be so disastrously shaken, that he will never dare venture into the common stock market again until perhaps near the top of the next business cycle when fury at having missed the rise, will induce him to go in once more, again on borrowed money—probably once more unfortunately.

This is how the foolish speculator loses his money. This is the history of the stock exchange gambler.

The moral of the story is: DON'T.

The best times to borrow.

But although unscientific borrowing is foolish, prudent borrowing may be highly profitable.

The best times to borrow are those at which it is psychologically most difficult.

The easiest time, psychologically, is when one has just made a considerable profit on one's own capital in a rising market. One then feels that one can safely afford to gamble with one's profits, and to run into debt accordingly.

Nemesis, however, has sadistically arranged that highly profitable upswings in the market are usually followed by reactions and falls. Thus, it normally happens that the gambler, who only borrows when he has just made profits, habitually goes in on borrowed money near a temporary top, and suffers the chagrin of seeing his recent profits, made on his own capital, evaporate because he is now on borrowed money.

Such behavior by the masses is "normal." The scientific investor should avoid all such folly.

In fact, the right time to borrow, if at all, is when one psychologically feels that one is least justified in doing so. One should, in fact, as a rule only borrow in the conjunctural slumps, early revival stages of the cycle, when the market has been weak for some time, and when the falling graph is just beginning to saucer out—according to the rules laid down in Chapter XVII.

Scientific short-run borrowing.

To borrow in the Intermediate slumps, and then gradually to reduce one's holdings in the Intermediate boomlets, until at last one has a large proportion of idle cash is, in theory, a rational practice.

To borrow near the peaks of the Intermediate boomlets, and to get sold out in the Intermediate slumps is foolish—though normal.

A cyclical borrowing policy.

Cyclically speaking, to borrow, not too heavily, early on in the second year of revival (preferably during an Intermediate slump); and to pay off one's loans in the third or fourth years of revival, preferably during an Intermediate boomlet is rational.

The scale of one's borrowing must, however, never be so great that an Intermediate re-action of, say, 30% can endanger more than 50% of one's capital.

Indeed, owing to the fact that a 20% borrowed position will lead to a 25% loss of personal capital, if a 33% Intermediate fall in the market occurs, I strongly advise against any long-run cyclical borrower becoming much more than 20% borrowed.

Greed is what kills the majority of investors; therefore, of course, don't be greedy.

In any case, if you must go and borrow, never borrow and buy without stop-loss orders.

Borrowing during inflation.

Only in one case is borrowing really justified and scientific, and that is if inflation is definitely occurring and if it seems, as yet, virtually impossible for the government to stop it. Then, to be a debtor is good, whereas to be a creditor is dangerous.

CHAPTER XXXIII

LIVING ON INCOME

The need for realism.

It is often regarded as a moral and economic tenet that a person should not live on his capital; but only on his income.

Clearly, however, in cases where capital is depreciating faster than income, i.e., when a man is becoming poorer, a policy of living up to one's income (just because it is stationary) without setting aside some income against the depreciation of capital is economically unsound.

My personal preference in fact is that an investor, before deciding year by year upon his scale of living, should look at his combined capital and income account; for it is only by this method that he may accurately assess whether or not he is *in toto* better or worse off, and whether he can afford to adhere to the same standard of living as previously.

If, however, this principle is adopted, it virtually requires acceptance of the principle that investment (and one's scale of living) should be conducted more with an eye on security and capital appreciation than on income. Indeed, since capital values often fluctuate much more rapidly than the income derived from such capital, the justifiable standard of living should be assessed more on capital fluctuations than on income fluctuations.

Perhaps the safest and most practical attitude to adopt is to ask oneself what the average rate of earnings is on a capital fund, divided, say, equally between first class bonds and first class stocks; and then, having arrived at this nominal current rate of yield, to value one's own portfolio at current prices; and then to live only on this "apparent" rate of "current market yield."

What standard of living can be afforded?

The point is this: If a man's capital fund is invested at 6% and remains stationary throughout the year, he is 6 points better off at the end of the year.

Similarly, if income is only 3%, but if capital appreciation is 3%, he is likewise 6 points better off.

On the other hand, if his income remains at 6% and his securities slump from 100 to 80, he is 14 points worse off; and yet he is popularly regarded as living "wisely" provided he is living "within his income."

Conversely, if his capital fund rises 50%, although his income stays at only 3%, then, if he spends 6 units, he is living (imprudently?) beyond his income.

A rational policy.

A man (without an "earned" income) must live on something, *even if* he is getting poorer. The right amount (I think) to spend annually is that approximate per cent of his capital, valued at *current* values, that money as a whole is *currently* earning, i.e., 5% at one stage of the trade cycle and say 3% at others.

Or alternatively, though not quite so soundly, a man might decide always to live on say 4% (or 5%) of his pooled income and capital account.

This would insure that he spent less when he became really poorer, and more when he was really richer, and could therefore afford more. (This is what I personally encourage.)

* * *

Income self-deception is dangerous in investment, particularly in the case of Trustee accounts. Beneficiaries should be regularly informed of the total value of the capital fund, and should try to live accordingly—on the downside, at all events—saving and investing the residue of their income privately.

CHAPTER XXXIV

THE HUMAN FACTOR

Cultivate keenness to sell.

Most books on investment treat the art of buying as the major problem. In this book an attempt has been made to show that selling is equally important.

The general bias of investors is towards a rash and dangerous optimism; consequently the profit-seeker, who takes his investments seriously, should strive to counter-balance this natural tendency. It is possible, as experience shows many times a year, for even the market leaders to fall 50% and not recover. Preparedness to sell, therefore, and to take unexpected losses early, must be a vital part of the investor's equipment. There is no more futile hope than that of being right in every instance. Some selections are bound to go wrong; for this reason, however hopeful you may be of a share's future, stop-loss orders should be given.

Losses, when they occur, should be taken in a philosophic spirit; it is a waste of time to resent them, and a waste of money to let them run on. Keen sellers make good investors, and nobody loses so much money as the man whose optimism makes him a "clinger" to falling stocks. Stop-loss orders should be given *in advance*—preferably at the time of buying, so as to avoid the human temptation not to give them later. Stop-loss orders should never be cancelled. The only time when a stop-loss order should be revised is after a rise, when it should be varied to conserve about two-thirds of any appreciable paper profit.

Mistrust your optimism; trust your pessimism.

A successful operator once gave his son this advice: "Human nature being what it is, you are far more likely to be hopeful than despairing. So follow your pessimism, and distrust your optimism."

On this principle the investor should be forever trying to pick holes in his securities, and looking out for others to which he can more profitably turn. He must learn to change his plans as conditions change; and, when internal conditions deteriorate, he must be ready to sell *before* the financial Press induces other holders to sell also. Above all, he must not hold in the hope that his adverse forecasts may turn out to be wrong. To cut losses early, particularly if internal deterioration is scented, is the part of a skilled operator, and should be a genuine source of pride—even if it turns out to be wrong.

Typical faults.

The chief faults to which most investors are prone may be summarized as follows:

Increasing stakes in fancied shares *pro rata* with one's optimism, i.e., not adhering to sound staking rules.

Overtrading in booming markets, and at the same time failing to give stop-loss orders.

Thinking depressed shares cannot fall any further and therefore cancelling stop-loss orders when they are nearly caught.

Thinking that rises are likely to continue, and that reactions will be negligible, and therefore failing to give sliding stops.

Averaging shares because they look cheap, and thereby breaking sound staking rules.

Buying shares which you know look too high, merely because you cannot find anything better. (Keep out of the market till something looks cheap.)

Not being able to wait.

Failing to resist the lure of booming markets, even though shares are already obviously too high and do not give value for money.

Buying low-grade shares in active groups because you have missed the market in the leaders.

Reaching for shares on a rapid rise just because you feel you ought *originally* to have had some.

Not being able to realize that equally attractive opportunities are sure to crop up later, even though you do not happen to see quite how, at the moment.

Not being able to wait with funds idle after taking profits, although this may be necessary for months on end as part of the ordinary routine of short-run investment.

Buying shares regardless of price just because the companies are excellent (or because general markets are rising).

Slap-dash buying on tips and rumors without previous analysis of:

(a) The industry.
(b) The company.
(c) The price curve of the share.

Not being able to say "No" to a tip, especially if given by a man of "personality."

Buying on intuition.

Selling good shares instead of bad, when it is necessary to raise ready money.

Relying on unlikely happenings to save you from further losses.

Letting hope outweigh reason.

Trying to get your own back quickly by recklessly increasing your stakes; and by borrowing.

Wavering as to a course of action—just because other people are wavering—when you have a sound set of rules to guide you.

* * *

The correct procedure in investment is usually the most difficult. Be prepared to inflict on yourself the mental anguish temporarily entailed by scientific daring and self-control.

Character.

Character is the rock upon which most investment schemes are eventually wrecked. It is one thing to define a set of rules and another to apply them. This often implies vigorous self-discipline, the combating of one's natural optimism, and determination to trust the theory rather than the impulse. When you are considering whether to sell, you will frequently desire to hold; you will very easily allow the wish to become father to the act. Perhaps half the losses in investment are due to this; for humanity is slow to recognize that disinclination to sell has no more than an emotional basis. If you think your loss-cutting rules sound, do not break them.

It is not difficult to learn a sound set of economic principles; in the long run, indeed, one would almost certainly make money if one had the self-control to obey, continuously and rigorously, the following few rules:

1. Never to buy into a company whose last published profits showed a decline.

2. Never to buy into an industry whose profits had been rising for more than four years.

3. Only to buy when the Stock Exchange was slack, and when shares in general had been falling for say ten weeks (i.e., during conjunctural depressions).

4. Never to buy during Stock Exchange booms, and never to buy into booming industries.

5. Never to buy unless current earnings were 8% on market price.

6. Never to buy an ordinary share if the bank rate was over 5%.

7. Never to buy an ordinary share during a fall in national profits.

8. To cut all losses of 20%.

9. To conserve two-thirds of all paper profits over, say, 20%.

10. To buy low-rate-of-interest long-term bonds if the above conditions were not fulfilled.

Any investor who went abroad for twenty years, and instructed his agent not to break these rules except under serious penalty to himself, would almost certainly reap large profits in the course of a very few years. To stay at home and attentively manage one's own affairs is, however, an entirely different matter. An investor working for himself does not mind the responsibility of occasionally taking unscientific risks. He makes exceptions to his known good rules, and therefore often loses.

Investment psychology.

(i) BE FASTIDIOUS—AND PATIENT

The only way to make money consistently is to wait until almost unimpeachable opportunities have matured, i.e., until short and long-term conditions, internal and external, are simultaneously favorable; and until shares, although possessing free markets, are clearly cheap.

Opportunities such as we have described mature, at most, only two or three times a year. To invest scientifically, therefore, it is often necessary to wait with money *uninvested* for many months on end. The active investor must realize this; he must learn to be *inactive*.

(ii) BE COOL—AND PESSIMISTIC

When ideal opportunities do not exist, and prices are high in relation to prospects, it is often necessary to wait until after an adverse sequence of price-movements has occurred. When, however, markets are rising, it is difficult for human optimism to envisage an early collapse. Despite past experience of the unwisdom of buying in booming markets, it is easy to feel that, at the present juncture, things are somehow different. Many investors, therefore, in the fear of missing the market, place their funds at once; they buy what seems to them "best at the moment"—even if "the moment does not seem the best," and even if prices are high. They concentrate too much on what to buy, and forget the importance of buying only at the right moment and at the right price. This psychological inability to foresee a future relapse is an important stumbling block to success.

If ideal investment opportunities do not exist at the moment, it is usually impossible to see precisely how they will mature later on; consequently to wait for such eventualities requires enormous faith—only to be acquired by a prolonged study of the economics of the Stock Market. Nevertheless waiting, possibly with funds idle and uninvested for six or more months on end, is often the only road to success in speculative investment. Few investors realize this, and anxiety to keep all funds invested all the time is one of the commonest causes of loss.

First be fastidious about your buying; secondly, have faith and patience to wait till shares have fallen sufficiently to make them cheap. Be pessimistic enough to believe that the future holds big reactions in store. A difficult lesson.

(iii) DO NOT BE SWAYED BY THE CROWD

Crowd buying is most infectious. Inoculate your mind against the disease.

It is fatal to buy shares simply because they are being bought, or because they are rising. The test of value must always be rigidly applied, and shares should be allowed to go by if they appear too high. Value for money and favorable Market Conditions are the important criteria. Let a boom in a group of shares be a warning rather than an inducement to buy.

(iv) REFRAIN FROM PURELY SHORT-RUN PLANS

Short-run economic forecasts usually rely too greatly on luck, even though much is to be gained by a careful study of conjunctural conditions. The only truly reliable economic forecasts are "long-run" forecasts requiring, perhaps, two years to come to fruition. The scientific investor, therefore, must be fundamentally a long-run investor. He must be prepared to wait for some years, *if necessary,* for his results, even though skilful conjunctural timing and good fortune will probably give him his profits much earlier.

To adopt long-range plans, however, is what weak-willed speculators seem never able to do. Shortage of funds, or ambition to make money quickly, usually induces them to base their plans on doubtful short-run happenings which must always be uncertain. This is usually fatal. Small investors should imitate rich trust companies and be prepared to make their money slowly.

The long-run factors working on the market are often well-nigh certain in their incidence; if, therefore, risks are spread, and the moment well chosen, profits are tolerably certain. The only quick way of making money is never to be in a hurry.

(v) RESIST CONTINUOUS DABBLING

To invest scientifically the investor must watch the market day by day: he cannot hope to recognize his opportunities without a continuous study of detail. Many people, watching thus studiously, find it impossible to resist the lure of day-by-day dealing, even in unfavorable circumstances; they cannot keep their hands off the market. Buying, however, for excitement's sake, or merely because one has funds idle, is a cardinal sin.

(vi) BE WILLING TO TURN FROM THE EXCITING TO THE DULL

A common fault among investors is the inability to leave given markets alone after they have made money out of them. The capacity to stand clear of a market, despite its having proved benevolent, must be carefully cultivated.

At the peak of each rise the investor must be prepared ungraciously to stand clear of the shares that have graciously profited him—probably for a considerably period.

After conjunctural rises and a period of conjunctural excitement, one has usually to stand clear for ten weeks or more—most dull! Similarly, after booms in any single industry, it is normally correct to shun that industry for from four to seven years. Likewise, after cyclical prosperity, one has normally to stand clear of ordinary shares and invest in dull bonds for perhaps two years on end.

This ability to turn stoically from the exciting to the dull, and to desert old friends, is one of the most exacting tests of self-control in investment, especially as it is "human" superstitiously to believe that fortune favors one particularly in certain shares or markets.

(vii) DO NOT BE CARRIED AWAY BY SUCCESS

Although to make money on the Stock Exchange is at times far easier than making money in business, to do so continuously is much more difficult.

Success impels most people to lack of caution. It should impel them to extra care. Luck and prices move in cycles.

Time needed.

The question arises, Can the private investor carry out the instructions prescribed in this book?

The long-term cyclical investor can probably do so, with the assistance of a well-trained broker or Investment Counselor. But if attempts are to be made to hit off the Intermediate swings, or to trade for even shorter periods, a considerable amount of apparatus in the shape of graphs, statistical services, etc., is necessary; and several hours each day must be devoted to the market.

As in other walks of life, professional assistance is probably required; for a study of the market is a full-time occupation.

Few private investors have the knowledge or experience to manage their own affairs satisfactorily; and even though the financial Press and the statistical services contain an admirable quantity of information, to read what they write requires much time, which few individuals are able to afford.

There is, in fact, no quick and simple way of making a success in the investment field. Professional advice of the highest quality only is desirable.

The majority of forecasting services (in America) try to follow the principles laid down in this book and the average investor would perhaps not be unwise to subscribe to one or two of them. They are, for the most part, honestly conducted, and reasonably imaginative, although showing a tendency to be somewhat late on the market. Their quality, however, tends to improve, and the investor, out of touch with the market as a whole, might keep in touch with their general conclusions.

CHAPTER XXXV

QUALITIES REQUIRED

The simple view.

Remember that most people lose on the Stock Exchange; as a rule it is only brokers who gain. That is because the economic forces which are really powerful in Stock Exchange affairs move almost imperceptibly, like the hour hands of a clock. The mental focus of the average investor, however, is usually riveted on the short-run excitements receiving attention in the daily Press. The movements of these latter are fast and sudden—and easily perceptible—like the second hand on a clock. Or to change the simile, the human mind focuses on the eddies rather than on the tides.

The result is that the tides are usually missed, because the eye does not see the imperceptible, though continuous, change.

The wise investor is one who concentrates his attention on the invisibly moving economic hour hands, rather than on the second hands which tell him, virtually, nothing.

* * *

It is interesting to note that to present-day students of military strategy, the successful operations of Napoleon always appear so simple as to have been necessarily obvious at the time of his campaigns, and requiring no great wisdom nor intelligence for their execution.

Similarly today, the causes of all major cyclical changes of direction in industry in the past are always, to the economic student, obvious—after the event.

At the time of their occurrence, however, the majority of stock brokers, investors and trust companies missed the market because they failed, at the time, to appreciate the dominant, though almost invisible *tidal* forces then at work within the economic arena.

What one wants, therefore, is the mind of a Napoleon—The Baby Mind—which is capable of seeing the obvious (and important) at the time, while lesser minds and less *simple* minds, are exciting themselves about the unimportant.

Study the tides rather than the eddies: the hour hands rather than the second hands.

Be simple. Take the grand view.

Essential qualities.

The chief qualifications of an investor seem to be as follows:

1. A knowledge of the business cycle, both in single industries and in industry as a whole.

2. A knowledge of the economics of the Stock Exchange (conjunctures).

3. A knowledge of the simple mathematics of staking, and of compatible loss- and profit-taking systems.

4. A knowledge of crowd psychology.

5. A good judgment of men (managerial honesty) as well as of investments.

6. Patience, and self-control.

7. Total lack of inordinate optimism, or greed.

8. Willingness to change one's mind, and admit that one was wrong.

9. Willingness to cut losses early.

10. A curious mixture of courage and caution: of scientific theory and speculative technique.

11. Extreme fastidiousness in selecting shares.

12. Ability to adhere to a general plan.

13. The nerve to follow rules which experience and analysis have clearly shown to be sound.

CHAPTER XXXVI

BEAR OPERATIONS

Over a period of years stocks decline nearly as many points as they advance, so that the trader who cannot bring himself to sell short misses about half the opportunities for profit.

Points in favor of the bear tack.

There are various points in favor of bear operations, as follows:

1. Booms in single industries are more certain to be followed by slumps than slumps by booms. In fact, in non-monopolistic industry booms are invariably followed by early slumps.

2. To fail in business is easier than to succeed; and a bad time comes to every company eventually. The bear almost always "eventually" comes into his own—particularly if he confines his operations to the first and second years of cyclical depression in an industry, after a previous boom.

3. Businesses can collapse faster than they can be built up.

4. Unforeseen happenings such as fire, strikes and wars are more in favor of bears than bulls.

5. The public are 90% bullish; consequently shares more often become clearly over-valued on actualities and prospects than clearly under-valued. Counters deserving a fall are therefore easier to find than counters deserving a rise.

6. Bears (in England) usually receive backwardation money for their efforts, whereas bulls usually have to pay.

7. Falls in shares, once they begin, are usually much faster and more continuous than rises, because during rises there is

always profit taking; whereas during falls buyers often stand temporarily clear of the market altogether.

8. A strained conjunctural position is more certain to lead to short-run falls in securities than a healthy position to lead to rises; since even if the technical position is healthy a flood of new issues may quickly eat up any surplus funds available and prevent appreciable rises occurring.

Objections to being a bear.

1. Over a period of years there is, in most industries, a considerable bias in favor of the "bull," partly due to the tendency of trade in general to expand and partly due to the compound interest factor working in favor of ordinary shares in any companies which regularly put back a large proportion of profits to reserve. This, however, is transcyclical rather than cyclical in its effects, and is therefore, perhaps, of little practical importance.

2. Theoretically a bear may be cornered if bulls buy up all the floating stock and then suddenly refuse continuation (loaning) facilities.

3. A bear may not get a long enough run owing to continuation facilities being refused.

4. It is difficult to bear the most suitable shares, i.e., those in small, declining, and inefficiently managed companies. As a rule it is impossible to "take in," i.e., borrow, shares unless they are market leaders in which there is an open bull account; it is also very rare that one can arrange to deal in small counters for delivery three or six months ahead. Consequently one is usually prevented from bearing those shares which are normally the most suitable for attack.

5. A share can only fall 100%; it can rise 500% or more.

BEAR OPERATIONS

Best conditions for bearing shares.

The ideal conditions for bearing shares are as follows:

I. INTERNAL

1. The particular industry declining after a long rise (its profits falling and its unemployment growing).
2. The company doing badly—worse than its fellows, with very few orders on hand.
3. Bad news likely to be published soon by the company.

II. EXTERNAL

4. Shares in general on a low yield basis.
5. The bank rate likely to be raised.
6. A political crisis imminent.
7. General trade declining, unemployment growing, and national profits falling.
8. The general conjuncture about to wane.
9. Jobbers with too much stock on their books.
10. A large bull account in the shares either (a) "hidden" on borrowed bank money, or (b) "open" on contango at very high rates.
11. Current price based mainly on prospects as distinct from earnings and assets.
12. Share prices near their higher cartographical parallels.
13. The shares well "distributed" among the public as distinct from closely held by insiders.
14. A free market in the shares.

When all these conditions are fulfilled bear operations are very safe. Usually, however, some factors are absent and one has to be content with less ideal conditions.

* * *

Beware of bearing shares when the floating supply has largely been accumulated by insiders or pools, lest perchance Manipulators may now be about to force up prices, and may refuse continuation facilities.

Similarly, beware of bearing shares which you know are being bought for control. If a group has bought 48% of the capital of a company at a reasonable price, it does not greatly mind what it pays for the odd 3% required for control. The market price may therefore suddenly double as a result of high-pressure marginal purchases.

* * *

Long range (two or three-year) bear operations in overvalued securities in industries which have been rising for four or five years, and which have already boomed for one year, are probably one of the most certain methods of making money on the Stock Exchange. The shares, however, should have been well "distributed" among the public, the conjunctural position should be shaky at the time of the bear sale, and internal deterioration should now be apparent.

CHAPTER XXXVII

INTERNATIONAL INVESTMENT

Under the gold standard.

Under a fixed gold standard international investment is the same in principle as domestic investment.

A flow of gold into a foreign country tends to increase its bank reserves; to lower its interest rates; to foster credit expansion, and better internal trade; and to cause both bonds and stocks to rise.

The loss of gold has opposite effects. The movements of gold can, in fact, give momentum to, or check, the internal business cycle of a foreign country.

Under the paper standard.

But if the fixed gold standard has been abandoned, and the foreign exchanges have become unpegged, the principles of international investment are more complex.

On the rough principle that a foreign paper money is worth, in terms of another foreign money, what it will buy in the form of commodities, there has grown up what economists call the Theory of Purchasing Power Parity. That is to say, if Country A's internal prices double while those of Country B remain stationary, A-money should become worth only about half what it was previously worth in terms of B-money.

Admittedly numerous different factors can drive current market quotation away from purchasing power parity as measured by index numbers,* but there is certainly a rough tendency for exchange rates to fluctuate with internal prices.

* See my "Problems of the Foreign Exchanges," Knopf, in U. S. A., and Macmillan in United Kingdom.

Operations in foreign common stocks under paper.

Insofar then as inflation in a foreign country tends to force up the prices, not only of its own common stocks but also of its commodities, so will its exchange rates tend to depreciate externally, *pari passu* with the internal appreciation of its common stocks.

A foreigner, therefore, who wishes to exploit the booming common stock market, within the inflationary country, must protect himself against exchange losses by selling the foreign currency forward; for otherwise part of his stock market profits will be wiped out by the loss on exchange, incurred when he collects them.

Conversely, if a foreign country is deflating, and one wishes to exploit the deflation by bear operations in the common stocks of the deflating country, one must buy the foreign currency forward, for otherwise its interim appreciation will wipe out, in terms of one's own currency, one's bear profits abroad, owing to one's own currency having depreciated relatively in the interim.

So much for international operations in Common Stocks. In both bull and bear deals the exchanges should be covered.

Operations in foreign bonds under paper.

As regards international operations in Bonds and other fixed interest bearing securities: these latter usually tend, as was shown in Chapter IV, to appreciate during deflation abroad and to depreciate during inflation, i.e., to move the same way as the currency.

If, therefore, one wishes to buy bonds within a foreign country which is deflating, one need *not* cover the exchange, because the exchange will appreciate *pari passu* with the foreign market prices of the bonds abroad.

Conversely, if one wishes to bear bonds in a foreign country while it is inflating, one need not cover the exchanges forward as the foreign currency will slump *pari passu* with the bonds.*

Survey.

Or to summarize: international operations in common stocks, under an unpegged system of foreign exchanges, normally require that the exchange risk should be covered by forward transactions. Whereas in the case of operations in bonds no such covering is normally necessary.

In practice, of course, frequent short-run exceptions will occur to this broad, general rule, but it reflects the major principles at issue.

* * *

There are, of course, inflations and deflations of different degree, and it is really only when rapid internal commodity price movements are expected, that the broad rule of purchasing power parity becomes reliable. If only mild movements in the commodity price market are expected it is probably not worth while covering the exchange.

Moreover, the paper exchanges, and common stocks, often fluctuate, temporarily, in an opposite direction to internal prices.

*One might, however, sell the foreign currency forward to the extent that one has to put up a margin *abroad* (as distinct from at home); and also perhaps to the extent of one's anticipated (guessed) profit abroad.

N.B.—It is sometimes possible to operate a margin account abroad, against a *domestic* margin, pledged to one's foreign correspondent.

CHAPTER XXXVIII

MANIPULATION

Reasons for manipulation.

Manipulation is sometimes an important influence on Stock Exchange prices. This consists of moving a share either up or down, or of keeping it stationary.

The reasons for manipulation are manifold.

Manipulation of information.

In some companies directors are active speculators in their own shares. They are fully conscious that adverse information will depress the market while favorable reports will raise it. They may, therefore, withhold information until they have made their own dispositions; either buying if the news is to be good, or selling if it is to be bad. They may also divulge information only when they are fully covered to benefit by it; sometimes they even issue false preliminary information. This is not a general practice; but it is a force to be reckoned with in certain companies.

There are, however, other reasons for manipulation.

Price pegging.

Powerful interests may wish to hold prices up so as to induce stockholders to exercise their rights to subscribe to new shares at a premium; alternatively, they may wish to hold prices down for a while so as to induce shareholders to exchange their holdings on a low basis for cash, or for the shares of some other company. Or again, an underwriting syndicate (or pool) may wish to force prices up after being allotted (or after having accumulated) a long line of shares, so as to dispose of them at a profit.

The technique of manipulation.

It is well known how company promoters and underwriters, by high-pressure salesmanship, can stimulate a large public demand for their shares: they are, as a rule, indifferent as to whether it is a bona fide investment demand or merely a short-run part-payment speculative demand financed with bank money borrowed by "stags." Not everyone realizes, however, that similar methods can be used to stimulate bona fide and speculative demands for existing securities. This is, nevertheless, frequently done by cunning and ingenious methods.

Shares can be advertised by letters to the Press, by first-hand and second-hand directors' tips, by newspaper articles, by the distribution of pamphlets, by market slips, by brokers' circulars, and above all by ostentatious large scale buying in the market through brokers known to be connected with the company. Indeed, one of the best advertisements a share can have is large scale buying from supposedly well-informed quarters leading to a rise in price. A share can be made to advertise itself by heavy dealings at rising prices. This is generally followed by comment in the City columns of the popular press, which, in its turn, is almost certain to lead to new support being given. A share rarely becomes popular with the public until people have actually made money out of it. The best way to whet the public's appetite is to bring about a rise.

The control exerted on share prices by insiders.

One of the first things to realize in connection with manipulation is the nature of the personnel from whom emanates the demand for and supply of shares.

These persons fall into the following categories:

I. *Insiders.*

The company's directors, executive officers, bankers, auditors, solicitors and brokers—and the people to whom they may give tips.

II. *Professionals.*

Investment companies and so-called shops (who may possibly be in receipt of inside information). Professional operators. Pools.

III. *The general public.*

An important point to note is that it is difficult for shares to move very far in any direction unless insiders think the movement is right. Admittedly shares can move without the approval of insiders as a result of sales, say, of deceased estates, but such movements are unlikely to be of great magnitude or length. The reason is that if insiders think the price too low they will buy for themselves or tell their friends that "a few shares will not hurt them": whereas if they think the price too high they may sell bears themselves, and will tell their friends that there is "no hurry to buy."

Incidentally, insiders are watched carefully in the market. Brokers who act for directors often pass on the information that "directors are buying" (or selling), and other people watch these dealings and say that the buying is good, or bad. The result is that the City soon learns whether or not inside interests are confident or otherwise about their shares, and the news spreads.

Insiders thus tend to set the pace of the market, and indirectly largely control it in the end. Insiders may not, it is true, be good judges of the absolute worth of their shares, or of their relative values compared with other shares; but they are, from their knowledge of current earnings, contracts, amalgamation proposals, and so on, excellent judges of whether the internal position is positively improving or deteriorating; these internal changes are the principal factor determining the movements in shares, apart, of course, from factors of a purely "external" or Market nature.

We repeat that no movement in shares is likely to go far unless insiders think the trend is right; and it is inside knowledge which, in the main, propels large advances and falls (except in the relatively rare cases of general Stock Exchange booms and collapses).

The marginal floating supply.

In considering the manipulation of shares, an important question to ask is, Who holds the shares?

The distribution of shares in any company may be somewhat as follows:

Half (or less, in the case of well-distributed shares) may be strongly held for purposes of control by people particularly interested in the company; 25%, perhaps, are locked away for permanent investment by the outside public; the remaining 25% of the total may constitute the marginal or floating supply dabbled in by speculators.

This floating supply is very important. Obviously, if anyone can buy up the major portion thereof, while the remainder of the capital is strongly held, only a little high-pressure buying is necessary to denude jobbers' stocks and force up the price considerably—with the result that the public may be aroused and induced to buy as well.

Conversely, if heavy selling takes place and the floating supply is suddenly increased, jobbers will become overloaded with stock and prices will rapidly fall: the public will then become

MANIPULATION

very frightened and start selling too, in the belief that something is wrong internally and that the shares ought to be sold. Indeed, only a little extra selling is usually needed to force prices down considerably—unless insiders disagree with the movement and give the shares their support.

The result is that unless insiders lend or withdraw support, one man or a pool can quite easily manipulate a market first by cornering, and then later on by unloading, the major portion of the floating supply.

If manipulators and insiders work hand in hand, remarkable results may ensue.

Manipulation by insiders.

What usually happens in the case of a market manipulated by insiders—as distinct from by outside pools—is as follows:

First, there is a period of dull published earnings during which the shares gradually decline or remain stationary.

Later on earnings expand, but the directors do not deem fit to show them; they thus keep their shareholders and the Press in ignorance, and very little public buying takes place. Meanwhile, the directors unostentatiously buy up any shares that are offered, and gradually accumulate a considerable holding. This is known among manipulators as the Period of Accumulation.

When the floating supply of shares has been virtually absorbed, and the remainder appear to be strongly held by permanent investors, the manipulators will wait till Stock Exchange markets as a whole appear confident and then ostentatiously buy heavily for themselves and at the same time publish excellent news about earnings, contracts, negotiations, and so on.

The public are thus induced to buy with a rush, partly because of the good news and partly because insiders are believed to be buying. Since, however, the floating supply is small, prices will bound up fiercely. This is known among manipulators as "Putting up the shares," or the "Mark-up."

When the rise has gone far enough, the manipulators unload; but if on doing so they find the market tires, they often support it themselves and at the same time issue yet more favorable information. This makes the shares again a good market, and then the manipulator again goes on with his unloading and "Distribution."

Eventually, when insiders have unloaded their holdings, they cease concerning themselves with the market and allow it to collapse. They may even turn from the bull to the bear tack, and at the same time spread unfavorable rumors, reduce dividends and so on, in order to depress the shares.

At last when the shares have fallen sufficiently, they may cover their bear operations and then perhaps repeat the whole bull process once more.

Manipulation by outsiders as distinct from insiders.

The foregoing remarks have referred solely to manipulation initiated or assisted by insiders. Sometimes, however, manipulation occurs without the assistance or connivance of directors. Pools, for instance, may start working a share—especially if they know that the directors are by nature reticent and conservative, and do not regard it as their business to contradict or confirm market rumors. In this case outside manipulators, by spreading rumors once or twice, and by simultaneously buying aggressively, may make the public eventually believe in the reliability of rumors emanating from a certain source. Hence, when the public has been "prepared" in this way and taught to follow a given lead, the manipulator can usually start an upward movement at will.

We would here add that directors rarely object to their shares being put up 20% or 30% by bull pools, especially if the movement engineered is justified by the internal economic position. Directors, as a rule, only run counter to outside pools if the latter are attempting a bear raid.

If a bull pool is working without the aid of directors, the internal economic condition of the company and its cognate industry must, however, be clearly favorable, for otherwise the directors may unload, and defeat the pool. The external or conjunctural position should also be propitious if maximum success is to be achieved.

Characteristics of a pool.

A pool is a syndicate of financiers who join together to make money out of shares; their main object is to buy cheap and sell dear; or alternatively to sell short and then depress the market.

Some pools are of the long-run lock-up type with a buying and selling programme spread over two to three years. These pools usually aim at profits of 100% or more. Others are short-run pools (three to six months) which aim at rises of only about 30%.

Since a pool will usually be operating in a very large number of shares, it cannot hope to do all its buying and selling at the bottom and top of the market. It can only aim at a low and high *average* price. Nor can it effect its Accumulation or Distribution in a day; this will probably be spread over several weeks or months.

The object of a bull pool is to buy up almost the whole of the floating supply; to cause a rise; then to unload.

In Wall Street, for instance, to effect this programme it is usual for a pool manager to be appointed and given a very free hand. He is either paid a lump sum in cash or more usually paid in kind, and given the call of, say, 10,000 shares at three different prices, the last of which is somewhat *above* the price at which the pool itself hopes to unload, thus enabling the Manager to make a private profit if he can force the shares up and sell them in the market above his call-option prices. A portion of these calls is sometimes handed on to brokers and others whose assistance is considered desirable.

The syndicate usually arranges the calls with big outside holders, possibly directors, who are sometimes only too glad to grant the options for a purely nominal fee in the hope of seeing their shares put up to the higher prices.

In New York a skilled pool manager can sometimes make five hundred thousand dollars in six months. In London the pool system is not yet much practiced—but is, unfortunately, spreading.

The first qualification of a pool manager is an accurate knowledge of market psychology—especially if he happens to be acting without the assistance or connivance of directors. He must also have a good knowledge of market conditions and of the general theory of short-run general market tendencies (i.e. conjunctures). A knowledge of market psychology is, however, the most important qualification; and it is therefore here desirable briefly to indicate those features of crowd psychology on which manipulative tactics are mainly based.

The tenets of crowd psychology.

1. A share which remains stationary is not attractive to the majority of speculators. If, therefore, a manipulator can hold a share at around a fixed price (by selling at, say, one figure and buying at another), speculative holders can usually be induced to tire of their shares and eventually to unload. The manipulator can thus often acquire a long line of shares, and accumulate most of the floating supply.

2. The general public are normally 90% bullish and usually

MANIPULATION

operate only on the buying side. Professionals alone are likely to sell short, and even professionals will hesitate to do so if they believe the stock is closely held and controlled by manipulators. They are afraid of taking-in facilities for continuing a short position being suddenly refused; consequently bull pools in control of shares have little to fear from bears (as distinct from bona fide sellers), even if the price looks abnormally high.

3. The crowd will follow any inside or outside lead when once they have learned to regard it as good. They will almost always buy if they believe insiders are buying, on the ground that "If insiders think it is right to buy, that is good enough for me."

4. A booming market has magnetic attractions for the majority of speculators. Everyone wants to take a hand. One buyer thus makes many others.

5. The individuals composing a crowd always believe firmly in the general wisdom of the crowd. For instance, if everyone else is buying, individuals buy too—in the unconceited belief that it is quite impossible for so many people to be wrong about a share simultaneously. Thus if a rise can once be started and the public can be induced to buy, confidence breeds confidence in a rising spiral, and this gives momentum to the upward movement.

Conversely, if everyone is selling, nervousness spreads and others rush to sell. The belief gains ground that the only right thing is to sell at once at best. Thus astute selling, coupled with several adverse rumors, can often cause the crowd to sell too; it quickly becomes fashionable to unload.

This phenomenon of imitative behavior is one of the most important psychological factors upon which manipulators rely.

6. Another characteristic of the crowd is that it tends to

believe that what has been recently happening will go on happening. Thus when a short- or long-run trend has once been established, and a share has acquired a reputation for being an upward (or downward) mover, and as being either a sound or an unsound purchase, that reputation dies slowly. Believers require strong and indisputable proof that any change in economic direction has actually occurred. Rises and falls therefore usually go too far, and the public are usually well behindhand in both their selling and their buying.

This holds good both as regards short-run conjunctural movements and as regards long-run cyclical swings. Astute pools, therefore, can often acquire long lines of shares when they are clearly too low. Conversely, they can often sell in large volume, even though the price is clearly too high—solely because of the slowness of the public to change its economic views about shares with established reputations.

7. When a share is low there is little public interest. Interest increases as prices advance, and is greatest when prices are at the top, i.e., when shares have had much advertisement in the Press. A stock, therefore, must be made active to attract large scale public buying. A good rise on increasing volume is the best advertisement of all, for on such occasions all news purveyors make it their business to satisfy the public demand for plausible explanations of the rise; and although such explanations may only refer to, and only justify, the rises which have *already* taken place, the public, being especially careless as regards the Time-factor, apply the old reasons to present conditions; and using the arguments a second time, conclude that, since the *causes* mentioned have not yet ceased to operate, the shares should still go on rising; they ignore the fact that current price already discounts the favorable forces daily being discussed by the Press! The result is that further buying takes place and a further rise occurs, until at last the shares become

grossly over-valued. During these rises pools can unload, despite prices being too high.

8. When once a share has become really active, a speculative following is attracted towards it. The fact that a rise is going on suggests to some minds that it is capable of continuing. Short-run speculators therefore rush in and buy, probably on margin with borrowed bank money, in the hope of snatching scalping profits before the relapse eventually occurs.

9. Finally, if the manipulators have cunningly caused their shares to break into new high ground after each relapse, they may thereby have earned for the shares a reputation of being a good purchase on every reaction, until at last the public buys heavily on any appreciable fall.

This is a state of mind which the manipulators desire to engender with a view eventually to unloading their purchases high up in the market.

The process of accumulation.

In order to buy cheaply the pool manager often sells a large block of shares through the company's own broker or the brokers of the directors—so as to give the semblance of well-informed selling—and at the same time buys in driblets through provincial brokers entirely unconnected with the company, hoping to acquire more shares than he actually sells. He never buys heavily when others are buying; indeed he will often sell out what he has carefully accumulated as so to quash any unwanted incipient rise, for, as already said, if a share starts rising rapidly it usually attracts a speculative following, and this is not what the accumulator wants yet.

The mark up.

When the pool manager has at last accumulated all the shares he requires or thinks he can obtain without causing an appreciable rise in prices [i.e., when he has acquired most of the floating supply—preferably in the form of carried-over stock, so that when he takes it up and pays for it (when he wishes the price to rise) the corresponding bears will be refused taking-in facilities and be forced to cover and buy in the market at best] his next step will be to spread exaggerated rumors (founded, however, slightly on fact, so that they cannot easily be contradicted by directors) and buy fiercely himself with a view to exciting the general public and bringing them (and the bears, if any) into the market with a rush.

If the public are sluggish in responding to the rumors, "wash sales" and "matched orders" may be resorted to in order further to mislead the public by market appearances. Members of the pool will arrange between themselves to sell to and buy from each other a large number of shares at fictitiously high prices. The public will thus most probably be deceived by the "increased activity at rising prices," and may enter the market as avid buyers because they think that the shares are "now on the move" and also because they hear it rumored that a pool is going to put up the shares.

If it is a short-run pool it will more often than not unload on the rise and distribute as far as possible during the course of the rise, letting out, say, 10,000 shares at a time, so as to keep the market a free one.

Quite often, however, a pool manager, especially if it is a long-run pool, will deliberately aim at causing a zig-zag upward movement in his shares, his object being to make the public believe that buying on reactions is a suitable policy.

Phase three. Distribution.

When, however, the share has reached a level which the manipulator thinks sufficiently high, he starts selling in enormous volume.* This usually causes a reaction in price. If, however, the fall goes very far, he himself will probably support the market. He will again try to give the price an upward turn, and this will usually bring in more buyers who have been trained to buy on reactions. Indeed, it is amazing in what large volume the public will buy a popular share on a fall if it has had a long series of rises.

The manipulator may also support the share every time it falls to some given figure with a view to inculcating in the public a new belief that insiders will always support it whenever it falls to this particular figure. The public can then be trained to buy at the figure (a) because the Big Interests apparently think the shares worth it; and (b) because there seems little chance of a fall. The pool can thus later exploit this habit and unload at the chosen figure.

This process of supporting the market whenever necessary, and unloading whenever a chance occurs, may go on for weeks or months according to the volume of shares to be unloaded and according to the way in which the public respond.

---

*We might here add that pool liquidation is often commenced under the guise of scattered bear sales effected by numerous small brokers unconnected with the company, which not only clear the market of loanable stock, and thus prevent other people from selling bears, but which also give jobbers the impression that equal repurchases will have to be made later on (by these ill-informed people) so that they do not mark prices down greatly.

Later on the pool manager can either close his bears and possibly make a profit, or, if he deems fit, he can eventually deliver the stock and "distribute" out of his original accumulations.

Another, though expensive, method of unloading in a shaky market is to buy call options to *twice* the amount intended for sale. It is the practice of sellers of options to cover half their commitments. Thus buying is stimulated to balance the selling.

Phase four. Collapse.

Eventually when the business of distribution is complete, the pool manager no longer concerns himself with the market. Favorable rumors cease to be spread; and the share is no longer supported. It is allowed to break through what have recently come to be known as its "lower resistance levels." It thus leaves its recent high zone and usually falls precipitately, for the floating supply of shares will have grown enormously owing to the pool having liquidated its stocks, and sold them probably to weak speculative holders—who may incidentally be squeezed by their bankers (or asked for more margin by their brokers) as soon as the shares start falling in value. Professional bears, moreover, will start to operate as soon as pool support is known to be withdrawn.

Beware, therefore, whenever a share is pushed up rapidly from a low zone to a high zone and then fails to rise further despite the continued emission of *unexpected* (as distinct from *expected*) favorable information. It often indicates the presence of "leadership" in the market, and investors should be nervous, especially if the share itself appears to be over-valued on actualities.

On principle, only buy shares which are fluctuating in a low zone or appear to be under-valued on actualities. The latter are the most likely counters to be taken in hand and marked up by pools.

Cartographical conclusions to be drawn concerning manipulation.

The aim of the active investor should be to exploit, rather than to fight, the activities of powerful groups. The following points are worth considering:

1. Beware of tips from insiders about shares in a high zone; they may be given with an ulterior motive.

2. If a share which is depressed, but sound, has been held almost stationary in a low zone for some while, and then suddenly breaks its old series of highs and enters new high ground, it is often a sign that a rise (usually of over 30%) is about to be engendered. It is therefore not unwise for speculators to consider going with the new tide (even though they may have just sold out at the previous level of old highs). A big zone changing movement may just now be commencing.

3. If a share which has been making successively higher conjunctural bottoms and tops fails eventually to advance any further despite the issue of unexpected good news, it is often an indication that distribution is occurring and that the shares may soon collapse.

4. If a share which has been fluctuating astride a flat mean in a high zone breaks below its old series of bottoms, it often means that pools or insiders have now withdrawn support. In such a case it is often sound, even though one may have only just bought at the old lower parallels, to turn with the tide and go bear.

5. Or again, if a share which has for some years made successively higher conjunctural bottoms and tops breaks below its last conjunctural bottom, it often suggests that this particular share has commenced a long-run change of direction—especially if shares-in-general as represented by any reliable index of shares-in-general have not also made a lower conjunctural bottom.

CHAPTER XXXIX

SHARP PRACTICES

This book is written on the assumption that directors are honest and efficient. Sometimes, however, honesty is combined with inefficiency, and efficiency with dishonesty.

By rights, a director should regard himself as the employee of his company, and should not divulge information to his friends, nor take advantage of it himself, prior to communicating such information to his shareholders. Many directors, however, are exceptions to this rule.

1. Information is often used by insiders, and their friends, before their shareholders are given an equal opportunity in the market. Kindness is sometimes the guiding motive; sometimes baser motives operate.

2. Since published profits may be manipulated by variations in depreciation, in valuation of assets, and so on, the scope for dishonesty among directors is infinite. They can show low profits; buy the shares; then show high profits; then unload; then sell short; then show low profits; and repeat.

3. Sometimes directors show low profits for a period of years; sell the company to another concern at too low a price; and receive large personal compensation for loss of office on the part of the grateful buyers.

4. At other times they show high profits and get themselves voted exceptional salaries by their grateful shareholders.

5. Sometimes a directorate will wreck its own company by giving orders for equipment, etc., to some second company in which they are shareholders, causing the first company to be grossly overcharged, and the second to make exceptional profits.

Later they can reverse the operation, and reverse their share operations accordingly.

6. A big (motor) company can give its contracts, one year to one accessory company, another to another. The directors can buy or sell the acccessory shares accordingly.

7. Directors of one company can sell its assets to another at an abnormally low price, themselves buying shares in the second company.

8. Cases have occurred of a company selling parts, etc., to a foreign subsidiary to be assembled in the foreign country, the charge for these parts being unduly low. The foreign company thus shows good profits; the directors, meanwhile, help themselves to the foreign shares, eventually unloading these shares on the foreign public. Then subsequently they sell parts to the foreign subsidiary at a reasonable price. Meanwhile, they personally exploit the ups and downs in the two stock markets concerned.

9. The directors of a hotel company can form a small wine and cigar company of their own and give this profitable part of the hotel business to their own private company.

10. Triangular holding companies, with interlocking directorates or nominees, are another common form of swindle. Company A holds the shares of B; B holds those of C; and C holds those of A.

A buys the shares of C in the market and puts up their price. B's total holding is now worth more on paper. A's holding of B-shares are then sold to the public at a profit to A.

These profits are shown, and since Company C holds A-shares, it too looks worth more.

The A-Company then sells its artificially inflated C-shares to the public.

Then C can sell some of its other assets to A at a ridiculously *low* price. Losses can then be shown by the C-Company. Then A can buy back its C-shares cheaply.

These mutual manipulations by interlocking directorates or "associated interests" can go on until this form of dishonesty seems unsafe to pursue any longer.

11. The interlocking directors may also use the funds of each of the three companies to buy each other's shares, force them higher and higher in the market until at last options granted to the directors in the early days of the formation of the companies can be exercised at a huge profit to the directors.

12. These manipulations can often be successfully hidden by the directors themselves having a fourth Holding Company which shall operate in the shares of the first three, for the benefit of the directors.

13. Realize that a private company can sell, for several years running, articles of small value (say, old newspaper cuttings) to "friendly interests" at an exorbitant price. These profits can be shown on paper, and the business then sold to the public capitalized at fifteen times the false profits.

Thus, although the friendly interests may make a loss on the almost worthless articles which they buy, they may be compensated ten or more times over when the inflated securities in which they are interested have been foisted on the unsuspecting public.

14. Some accountants have the gift of becoming blind to these ruses, for an adequate fee.

15. Birds of a feather flock together. Some directors are already known to be tricky. Beware therefore of companies having directors who sit on the same boards as those who already enjoy doubtful reputations.

16. Avoid new issues sponsored by second class houses. And be careful to find out if any of the prospectus profits shown for

any one year represent non-recurring items, like the sale of old investments.

17. To define a business profit is virtually impossible. Profits can be manipulated without infringing the law.

CHAPTER XL

THE TREATMENT OF

OLD HOLDINGS SHOWING LOSSES

(In the *falling* half of the cycle)

A difficult problem.

Almost every investor has in his portfolio a number of securities bought at high levels, which now show heavy losses. This applies particularly in the *falling half* of the business cycle, when investors in common stocks who have failed to sell out at the top become confronted with a series of losses on paper, which they probably "feel" are too big to take.

Such securities are the result of his own plans, or those of other people, going unexpectedly wrong, and of stop-loss orders not having been placed on the securities when purchased. In the collapse stage of each business cycle the number of such securities habitually grows.

The treatment of unsatisfactory lists of this nature is one of the most difficult problems in finance. I am therefore going to discuss it at some length, at the risk of wearying the reader.

Psychological difficulties.

The chief fault of the average investor, when reading through the rubbishy part of his list, is to close his eyes and give up thinking, for the simple reason that the mere inspection of such a list is painful and humiliating. And yet, the treatment of depreciated holdings in periods of depression, is one of the most important problems in investment. It is often worth diverting one's attention from ninety-nine good shares to rescue one that has strayed.

Cost prices are irrelevant.

The first thing to realize about depreciated securities is that the original cost-price is entirely irrelevant. Whether a man has bought 20% above, or 20% below, the present market price does not in any way affect the correct policy as regard holding. If a loss is now showing it should never be argued that one cannot sell now "because the loss would be too great"; the loss in fact is already there, and to sell is merely to clinch it.

Look therefore at your securities at market price regardless of the prices once paid, and regard them merely as "receptacles for money" which ought on no account to be used if anything theoretically is wrong with them.

Various alternative policies.

Depreciated securities, however, may be of several sorts:

(1) Shares still possessing good markets, perhaps in high-grade companies.

(2) Shares in second-grade companies with difficult markets.

(3) Almost unsaleable rubbish.

Several alternative policies present themselves concerning the treatment of shares showing losses:

(1) To average now, or on a further fall.

(2) To switch to some other more promising security.

(3) To place stop-loss orders immediately, which will limit further losses.

(4) To sell all, or half, at once, and either:
   (i) To hold the proceeds in the hope of exploiting some temporary semi-panic condition in the market at a **later date.**

(ii) To sell and put the money on deposit, or into gilt-edged stocks, until trade in general has clearly turned upwards, when a purchase might again be made of ordinary shares on sound cyclical principles.

(iii) To use the proceeds of immediate sales as a margin for future bear operations.

(5) To hold, with the intention of selling on the next intermediate recovery.

(6) Alternatively, if the investor thinks that the bottom of the trade slump had nearly been reached, and that the general index of ordinary shares is now likely to turn permanently upwards, to hold all, or part of, his depreciated holdings and to make definite, and scientific, plans for taking future profits, and losses.

Industrial trend is the chief criterion.

Whether or not, however, any share in any industry should be held depends, partly of course on the management of the company, and on the price of the share in relation to its current earnings and assets; but mainly on the trend of the cognate industry.

In the cases of some securities which show losses, the profits of the cognate industries may be stationary; in others they may be declining or likely soon to decline; in others they may be showing incipient signs of revival. The general trend of the cognate industry is, in fact, the crucial factor to consider when determining whether or not to hold.

Theoretically, if a cyclical upturn is not yet apparent, and if the investor would not buy with new money such shares as he already possesses—he ought not to hold.

This principle should, I think, be adhered to in the case of all the *existing* shares in one's list, regardless of whether they show profits or losses. Sales should be made of the unsuitable holdings, as determined by this principle, and the proceeds either invested in what are theoretically more promising "receptacles," or kept idle.

The investor might even pretend to himself that he has got a 30% profit, instead of a loss, and consider whether he ought to take this (imaginary) profit.

The policy of stop-loss orders.

The above procedure, however, will often prove psychologically too difficult for the average investor. He will feel such action *might* be wrong, and might result in selling at the bottom; and in any case he may be reluctant to act lest he should buy yet other securities which may also fall.

A simple rule under these conditions is, in theory, to decide at once how much *more* money one is prepared to lose in each of one's depreciated holdings; and then immediately to give stop-loss orders to one's broker.

But in practice, many of the depreciated shares in one's portfolio will be such bad markets as not to be suitable for stop-loss orders at all.

In such cases the only thing to do is either to sell at once at best; or alternatively to continue to hold, at all events, part of one's holding.

Selling half at once is, if one is in doubt, often an excellent and easy half-measure policy.

This question of one's "doubts" must, however, be analyzed.

*Shares with declining industrial trends
    habitually remain undervalued.*

Whether or not a share is worth holding depends not only on its economic prospects, but also, to some extent, on whether or not the current price discounts these prospects, if they are adverse;—for it is conceivable that a share with bad immediate economic prospects might stand so low in the market as nevertheless to be cheap.

The following point, however, must be noticed:

In the second and third years of depression, many depreciated shares will, on an analysis being made of last year's published figures, appear to be already so heavily *under*-valued on actualities, as to suggest that, other things equal, they might soon enjoy a recovery.

What is not always realized, however, is that shares in industries or companies, with declining profit trends, due either to cyclical forces or to bad management, tend to remain habitually undervalued throughout the whole of their period of cyclical declension. At no time during the cyclical fall are they likely *ever* to be reasonably valued "on actualities," for the market habitually discounts the future; and, until there is an apparent change of direction in profits upwards, the shares must be expected to remain undervalued.

The folly of waiting for recoveries.

This being the case, it is little use waiting and hoping for recoveries to "reasonable" price levels with the intention of then unloading. In fact, if the trend of the trade, or of the company's profits, is not yet *definitely* upwards, and *may* possibly still be downwards, it is a good rule to sell unattractive shares *at once* at best *despite* their apparent undervaluation.

It is, moreover, little use waiting for *minor* revivals, for, even though a 15% recovery may some day occur (for technical market or conjunctural reasons) there will just as often as not be a further 15% fall first. Indeed if you are not willing deliberately to add to your holding now (or to advise your friends to buy the shares), it is *usually* wise to sell at once, almost regardless of the price. In nine cases out of ten you will be able to buy back more cheaply lower down.

TREATMENT OF OLD HOLDINGS SHOWING LOSSES

I admit, of course, that sometimes a share may have fallen to such a ridiculously low figure (based on earnings as distinct from past quotations) that to hold is better than to sell. In most cases, however, it proves correct to sell shares in declining industries at once, at best—and to wait until the earnings-trend begins to show a recovery.

Selling policy depends partially on the time factor at issue.

Here, however, an additional factor protrudes itself into our problem, namely the Time Factor. Some securities, although possibly unsuitable as short-term holdings, may be quite suitable to hold for say a three-year lock-up. The investor, therefore, when revising his old lists must make up his mind for how long he is prepared to hold.

It must, however, be realized that cyclical collapses in national industry usually last three years, while cyclical collapses in single industries often last much longer.

If, therefore, a share has slumped for a period of only two years, and still looks risky, it is highly probable that the share will not *permanently* turn upwards for at least another year. There is little use therefore holding any such share (about whose industrial health one is still doubtful), even if one is prepared to lock up *some part* of one's capital for as much as three or four years. A 50% fall may well occur first before the shares eventually start turning upwards.

A test of undervaluation.

In fact, on general principle, no one should hold a share in any trade which is not yet clearly reviving, unless:

    (A) Even after allowing for a further 50% fall in profits over the next year, the shares, at the present price, would still show a 10% earnings-yield; or

(B) Unless the asset value of the shares reckoned conservatively is at least double their present market value; or
(C) Unless liquid finances are sufficiently strong to see the company comfortably through at least four years of successive losses of say 10% on total capital.

Indeed, in respect of this last point, the financial strength of companies whose shares have recently collapsed is one of the first criteria in considering whether one should go on holding. A long lock-up in a declining industry, is, unless finances are particularly strong, almost always an expensive and foolish policy.

Depreciated shares which have recently fallen 50% or 60% always *look* capable of suddenly rallying 20% or 30%, but experience shows that shares of this type are just as often capable of falling a similar amount. To sell at once is therefore usually right, and it is little use holding merely because of assets, or in the hope of technical recoveries.

Since the market will go on discounting the future, recoveries to levels which *current* actualities would "appear" to justify, are rare.

"Hoping" for recoveries.

At this point a word must be said concerning the *psychology* of "Hoping for early recoveries." Every investor holding bad securities is almost automatically obsessed with the idea that any recent big fall will soon be followed by a partial recovery and that he will then, when the time arrives, be able to unload at all events part of his holding. Such resolutions, however, are rarely kept, since, as soon as the shares begin to recover, the rise re-inspires the holder with confidence that the cyclical revival has at last begun, and he therefore continues to hold.

Greed, moreover, may prevent him selling out on the plan that he had originally laid down.

If, therefore, an investor is optimistic (or foolish) enough to hope that his bad shares will shortly recover, he should give his broker a selling limit higher up, or at all events institute sliding stop-loss orders, and raise them with any rise in the market, thus conserving to himself say two-thirds of any future paper gain above the present low price.

If the shares are such bad markets that stop-loss orders will not work, immediate sales are probably advisable.

I might add that one should particularly beware of regarding shares in companies where the capital structure possesses high leverage, as cheap, merely because they show abnormally high yields. A 10% further fall in net profits may wipe out the whole of the profits available for the common stock.

Policy of conserving resources till the second year of general revival.

One useful method of treating the doubtful shares in one's list is to realize that the easiest and safest time to make money on the Stock Exchange is during the Revival Stages of general business cycles, when trade has clearly been reviving for nearly twelve months and when the curve representing the ordinary share index of the nation as a whole has been moving upwards for about a year.

An important plank in every investment policy, therefore, over the course of a lifetime, must *always* be to have as large an amount of cash as possible on hand to exploit this *one particular period* of the business cycle.

Act therefore in "the grand manner," and do not be afraid to sell merely because you *might* happen to hit the lowest level of prices yet reached. To get in cash for a sound and scientific campaign *in the future* is the soundest of all investment policies. So do not be in the least distressed if you do happen unluckily to sell at the bottom.

Sell your theoretically unsound shares at once, and either place the money in unexciting gilt-edged securities, until the second year of general industrial revival, or use it on the bear tack (with close stop-loss orders).

Fear of "selling at the bottom" is one of the most capital-destroying diseases in investment.

Never rely on unlikely happenings and hang on in the hope of early revival.

Although the writer considers it best to sell and not to buy till the second year of revival, thus deliberately missing to bottom on the upside, it is fully realized that there are other investors who mentally prefer (so they say) to miss the bottom, not on the upside, but on the downside, i.e., to buy early.

Investors with this kind of temperament are, however, usually those who habitually suffer the largest losses. Such investors are almost invariably tempted to go on holding declining shares in declining companies and industries even though the profit trend appears to be still clearly downwards. They excuse what is really a weak-minded reluctance to take losses, by arguing that since only one man in a million can hope to hit the absolute bottom, that therefore one might just as well miss it on the downside as on the subsequent upside.

They argue further, that even if they do sell out at once, they will probably never have the courage to buy in again lower down *even if* a further big relapse eventuates. They therefore (logically, according to them) go on holding in the personal hope that "Public Hope" will soon cause an early and, so they pray, permanent recovery in their holdings.

Personally I do not agree with this policy. Cyclical downswings in single industries usually last *at least* four years. To buy, or to hold, therefore, in the second or even the third year of depression is *normally* unsound policy; it is usually better to sell boldly at once, and not to buy again until revival is clearly occurring, though *possibly* higher up. Be strong minded enough to pursue this course. It is one of the prime tests of strong character in investment. It does not matter at what level of the market you make money, so long as you make it—*for certain*. And the most "certain" time is during revival. The fear of selling at the bottom is the cause of *most* of the big losses in investment.

Accumulation of funds against panic conditions.

The question of selling, and waiting for a panic, should, however, be considered.

In every downward swing of the general cycle there is usually a Stock Market panic as the result either of the political crises which usually occur in every period of bad trade; or because of the failure of certain banking or stockbroking houses.

The investor, it is true, is unlikely to *foresee* these "normal" occurrences *in advance,* but he is perfectly justified in "relying" on them eventually happening before the bottom of the big bear market is reached. At such times when the market is wildly panicky, and when people are wildly selling to raise cash, to have a cash reserve for speculative purchases is extremely advantageous.

On such occasions, if after some weeks of continuous decline, followed by three or four days of virtual panic when no favorable features are visible, the investor buys the market leaders as soon as there appears some mild signs of steadiness, he is likely to get a very quick profit—especially if he only buys shares which have recently fallen 30% or so below recent highest.

In such cases if small stop-loss orders are given, and if the stop-loss orders are raised parallel with any future appreciation in paper values, paper gains will be conserved and losses will be small.

Have the courage therefore to sell out bad shares during cyclical depression, and to bide your time against future panic conditions.

That, again, is a test of fine character.

If no panic occurs, wait for definite revival.

Switching to the bear tack.

Another and even sounder method of treating unattractive holdings, during the falling half of the cycle, is to sell them immediately, almost regardless of price, and then to earmark the proceeds, not for bull operations during future panics, but for bear operations.

These bear operations (always with a stop-loss order) should be in leading shares (preferably with a highly leveraged capital structure and with a low earnings-yield), in those particular industries which habitually suffer most in the downward swing of each cycle, namely raw materials, luxuries and constructional engineering.

Such action of course needs mental courage, but theoretically, and in practice, it is advisable. Investors, in fact, should realize that for roughly two years out of every seven the bear tack is the only correct policy in ordinary shares.

The organization of a weak list of shares near the bottom of the cycle.

Although to sell and get in cash for a bear campaign, or for the second year of revival, is undoubtedly the *most* scientific method of treating the unattractive shares in one's list, it cannot be gainsaid that if general revival is *already* in sight; and if the economic conditions precedent to revival are *already* present (see page 27); and if one or two industries have already begun to turn upwards after a period when *all* industries have recently been declining, excellent recoveries may shortly mature even in depreciated "rubbish" holdings.

Here the major question at issue is, Is general trade revival *clearly* in sight or not? The test here to apply is, Are the five main indices of general trade, namely Railway Traffics, Bank Clearings, Unemployment, Commodity Prices, and Imports and Exports, yet showing signs of flattening out?

Is the bank rate below the current yield on bonds and common stocks?

Has the recovery in long term bonds already apparently begun?

Has revival commenced in several consumer-goods industries? And so on. (See Chapter V.)

If one is clearly *convinced,* as distinct from merely "hopeful," that such a change of trend is now occurring, it may be sound policy to regard the unsuccessful shares in one's list as a deliberately held speculative holding which one will in future treat on highly scientific lines.

On no account, however, should such a fund be allowed to exceed 25% of one's total capital. If the holding exceeds this ratio some shares should be sold to correct the balance.

✷ ✷ ✷

Secondly a definite profit- and loss-taking scheme should be thought out for these speculative shares *considered as a whole.*

What, however, most investors are inclined to do is to sell whatever few of their unattractive shares rise, as soon as they have risen a few per cent, and to hold on to the remainder, without stop-loss orders, in the hope that they too may rise later. This usually results in diminutive profits being snatched on a few holdings, while heavy losses are allowed to run on in others.

Such policy of course is ludicrous since profit- and loss-taking systems must be compatible. If small profits are snatched one also has to take small losses, and since this is difficult with "dogs" one ought to go out for *large* profits. To snatch small profits and let losses run on is one of the cardinal sins in investment.

Personally, in fact, I rather prefer the idea of treating all one's unwillingly held dogs *as a group*—and selling all or none.

* * *

I should say this, however.—In respect of the speculative portion of one's capital, the various "stakes" should be properly balanced. If, for instance, two or three unattractive holdings exceed in value, at present market prices, five or six other holdings of similar calibre, an adjustment ought to be made at once so that stakes in each shall be virtually equal. Otherwise a fall of 20% in one of the largest holdings may exceed a 50% rise in one of the others.

In all investment schemes, stakes, and loss- and profit-taking systems should all be mutually adjusted.

Conclusion.

To hold either first class or third class shares in the declining half of the business cycle is almost always an unsound policy, quite regardless of current prices.

Most of one's holdings will eventually depreciate heavily; therefore courageously to sell at once is normally correct. Willing sellers make good investors; beware, therefore, of ever becoming a clinger to bad stocks.

It is true that to find something better to switch to immediately is a good way of overcoming one's natural repugnance to taking losses; but normally it is an even better policy to sell all one's ordinary shares at once and use the proceeds for "bear" operations; or to keep the money in gilt-edged stocks, or on deposit, until general trade has *clearly* begun to revive; and the five main indices of trade have *all* turned upwards.

This policy it is true requires "ability to wait," but "Patience" is—in view of the existence of a general business cycle—one of the greatest mental gifts with which an investor can be endowed.

To do what is mentally difficult in investment is normally the proper procedure.

Summary of rules.

(1) Try invariably to follow sound investment strategy and refuse absolutely to hold any ordinary shares in any industry which is not definitely trending upwards.

(2) In the case of *first class* shares which show losses it is only right to wait for temporary technical recoveries if a general market recovery has *already* begun (according to the graph), after a month or two of general decline.

(3) Holding *third rate* shares in anticipation of (as distinct from during) technical conjunctural recoveries is rarely advisable since such shares are not usually influenced by technical conditions to the same extent as are the market leaders.

(4) Only continue to hold third rate shares:
  (i) If the cognate industry has *already* begun to revive; or
  (ii) If the conjuncture is clearly favorable and if the daily index curve of ordinary shares is still pointing upwards. (Then sell later).
  (iii) If the shares stand at option prices and are yet virtually unsaleable.
  (iv) If assets, on a conservative valuation exceed market price by 100% or if a 10% earnings-yield will still be shown after allowing for a 50% fall in profits.

(5) Prefer the bear tack, or waiting *patiently* (with your funds in dull long-term bonds) till the second year of revival.

PAGE FOR NOTES

PAGE FOR NOTES

CHAPTER XLI

BUILDING BALANCED PORTFOLIOS

The need for a plan.

Investors who balance their stakes scientifically; and who have an objective; and who follow a *Plan;* are those who make the most money. That is my own experience.

An inspection of most investment lists, however, shows that few investors balance their holdings scientifically.

Distribution as between countries, industries, and types of securities is usually unintelligent; and as a general rule, the investor is unable to state why his Distribution is what it is; nor why he is still holding some 30% of his securities.

I venture, therefore, to give a few lists of what will "probably" indicate sound Distribution at the various stages of *most* business cycles.

Admittedly in every trade cycle there will be changes in what are the most suitable groups during the successive phases of Collapse, Depression, Revival, Prosperity, and Boom; but broadly speaking the following tables of Suggested Distribution seem worth consideration.

Each table is divided into tenths. In certain cases an allocation of more than one-tenth of one's capital is prescribed for a single group.

TENTHS	LIST I Collapse Phase of the Cycle
1st	**High Grade Long-Term Government Bonds**
2nd	**Ditto**
3rd	**Ditto** (But possibly earmark this fund, and fund No. 10, for switching into common stocks in a Panic)
4th	**Impregnable Preferred Stocks** (Buy as soon as bank rate has started falling, but not before)
5th	**Long-Term Bear Operations** (with wide stop-loss orders) Prefer the constructional, luxury, and raw material industries; and shares with high leverage
6th	**Ditto**
7th	**Short-Term Bear Operations** (with small stop-loss orders) (But only according to graphic indications)
8th	**Ditto**
9th	**Gold Stocks** (But only buy when the gold-index graph has given the cyclical signal)
10th	**Idle Cash** (for special Panic opportunities)
NOTES ON POLICY	Do not go "bear" for more than your uninvested capital. If bear operations are impossible, buy miscellaneous high grade long-term bonds in the industries mentioned in List II. Avoid buying common stocks (except gold). Do not borrow at all.

TENTHS	**LIST II** **Transition Stage** (when cyclical trend still doubtful) Act as follows, when conditions on page 27 have matured; when bottom is believed reached; and when long-term speculative purchases of common stocks for a cyclical lockup seem justifiable
1st	**High Grade Long-Term Government Bonds**
2nd	Ditto
3rd	**Miscellaneous High Grade Long-Term Industrial Bonds** (In the industries mentioned in List III)
4th	Ditto
5th	**Gold Shares**
6th	Ditto
7th	**Utilities**
8th	**Semi-Necessities and Proprietary Articles**
9th	**Stores**
10th	**Miscellaneous Market Leaders** (With high earnings' yields)
NOTES ON POLICY	Keep to the high grade securities. The common stocks purchased must have a high yield, and a considerably higher earnings' yield. Cease bear operations; or at all events, give limits which will conserve the major part of your "bear" profits. The building industry may prove promising, if there is a housing shortage, or if a government-aided scheme is adopted. Do not borrow to buy yet.

TENTHS	**LIST III** **Early Revival** (Provided the curve of national profits has turned upwards, and the graph has given the upward cyclical signal)
1st	**High Grade Long-Term Government Bonds**
2nd	**Depressed Industrial Bonds** (In the industries mentioned hereunder)
3rd	**Stocks in Depressed Replacement-Demand Industries** (Paint, textiles, motors, etc. See Appendix A)
4th	Ditto
5th	**Five Miscellaneous Market Leaders**
6th	**Ultra-Promising (Geometric) Industries**
7th	**Depressed Preferred Stocks** (Possibly in the building industry)
8th	**Long-Shot Cyclical Come-Back Industries** (Raw material, luxury, and constructional industries)
9th	**High Leverage Stocks** (In most countries the rails, steels and utilities have particularly high leverage)
10th	**Well Known "Dogs"** (With a theoretical come-back)
NOTES ON POLICY	Show courage. Be bold. The second year of revival is the safest phase of all. But do not buy according to the above List, until profits have accrued on List II. Only buy into companies where the profit-curve is rising, or the loss-curve declining. Do not borrow more than 33%. Only commence borrowing in the Intermediate slumps, when y charts indicate a recovery.

TENTHS	LIST IV Prosperity Stage
1st	**Bank Stocks**
2nd	**Market Leaders** (in promising industries)
3rd	**Ditto**
4th	**Building Stocks** (Assuming the industry to be prosperous)
5th	**Raw Materials** (If other countries are beginning to boom also)
6th	**Luxuries**
7th	**Constructional Industries**
8th	**Geometric Industries** (and Vertical Combines)
9th	**Promising "Dogs"**
10th	**Ditto**
NOTES ON POLICY	Do not borrow more than 20%. (Reduce your loans as you augment your "dogs.") Beware of long-term bonds, and of the *deferred* replacement demand industries (see Appendix A). When buying the shares in any one group, have one or two "dogs" in addition to the Leaders. But be very attentive to stop-loss orders; and keep on sliding them up. The crash may come much sooner than you anticipate. Watch your "dogs" more carefully than the Leaders.

TENTHS	LIST V Boom Stage (When money rates are high)
1st	**10% in Cash** (on deposit) (And pay off all your bills and debts; double your life insurance; and pay three premiums thereon in advance.)
2nd	**Market Leaders**
3rd	**Ditto**
4th	**Rails, Communications and Chemicals** (If highly leveraged)
5th	**Raw Materials**
6th	**Luxuries**
7th	**Constructional Industries**
8th	**Geometric Industries** (and Vertical Combines)
9th	**Short-Term Speculations** (But only according to the Graph, and with close stops)
10th	**Ditto**
NOTES ON POLICY	Give your broker fixed stop-loss orders on Everything (and slide them up if the market rises). Expect many of your stops to be caught; i.e., to see some of your paper profits run off. Only hold shares with very free markets. No "dogs" at all. Be ultra-timid; not bold. But no "bear" operations yet—unless with very close stops (and then only in over-valued shares whose profit-curves are flattening, or falling). Pay abnormal attention to your charts, and to the Profit-curve of the country as a whole. Watch for a "flattening out."

Conclusion.

Although the above tables of suggestions will "normally" prove a profitable guide, conditions will vary from cycle to cycle, and there will be ample scope for the investor to use his own intelligence and to "weight" our suggestions according to conditions.

We would, however, emphasize that without a balanced list success is unlikely, and no investor should make the mistake of holding in his portfolio an undue proportion of any security, or group of securities.

One ought to be right "on the whole" with one's purchases; wherefore choose the five or ten most promising groups and distribute your stakes accordingly.

Then what might be called the Law of Average Rightness will work in your favor—though probably not otherwise, except by sheer chance.

* * *

If market movements distort a previously well-proportioned list, re-cast your Distribution. Such action is normally necessary every six or nine months.

Prefer to do your selling for the purposes of re-orientation in the Intermediate boomlets, with intention to re-cast in the following short-run slump.

Do not be afraid to be out of the market. To anticipate missing numerous gains is the right "state of mind" for the Rational Investor.

* * *

Geographical distribution may at times be advisable as an insurance against political disorders and currency dislocation.

PAGE FOR NOTES

CHAPTER XLII

DON'TS

Buying rules.

Don't buy in a hurry. One is almost always sorry next day.

Do not buy when excited. You have probably caught fever from the crowd.

Never operate unless you are sure of a "Cyclical" trend. If undecided, have the courage to have no position open at all.

Don't buy just because you have funds idle. Only buy because you think shares attractive.

If in doubt about buying, wait.

Never act unless you consider there are overwhelming *economic* reasons for taking a position.

Have no feelings; only reasons.

Study your company *before* you buy. If you haven't time for that, do not buy at all.

Never regret not having bought. Remember that *you* will remember only such of your past "hunches" as came off. (One always forgets one's own bad "past hunches.")

Take a long view and not a jobber's view.

Don't buy a share without first asking for an *adverse* opinion of it from your brokers.

DON'TS

Do not confuse your own long- and short-run investments. Separate them in your portfolio.

Do not fail to distinguish between what stocks are suitable and unsuitable for long- and short-run operations.

Never enter a market without studying its internal technical condition.

Don't trade large in unseasoned stocks.

Rarely trust a successful tipster. You will probably come in at the peak of *his* boom. Prefer to follow scientific students of the cycle.

Never buy in desperation. If you have missed an opportunity, resign yourself to it. Don't climb for stocks.

Beware of abnormally high yields, particularly if the prior charges are depressed. They may signify dangers known only to the directors.

But beware also of low yields unless prospects are abnormal, or earnings' yields are already quite high.

Selling rules.

Do not grab at small profits, and cling to your losses. Cut your losses; and let profits run on (till the graph says, Sell).

Never let a profit of over 15% run into a loss.

Sell and regret! Expect to be wrong three times out of ten. And always expect to miss best prices.

If in doubt about selling, sell half.

Bear operations.

Never be short of any market without a stop-loss order. More money can be lost by a bear than a bull.

Never be a bear of shares greater in value than your idle cash.

Never go bear unless you have arranged with your broker about continuation facilities.

Never buck the main trend. Don't be a bull in a bear market, or a bear in a bull market.

Do not be a bear and a bull of common stocks at the same time.

Graphic rules.

Do not buy without examining a five-year graph of the profit-curve of your company. (The Investograph Service of Rochester purveys them.)

Do not buy a share without looking at its individual graph (a) over the last 5 years (monthly); (b) over the last 15 weeks (daily or weekly).

Rely on your graphs. They prevent you being too "premature," and from locking up your capital uselessly.

If a graph does not show a change of trend yet . . . wait.

Do not buy if a graph says it is dangerous.

If you do not sell when the graph says sell, at all events give *close* stop-loss orders.

DON'TS

General behavior.

Try not to trade more than 12 times a year. Any broker will tell you that those who continuously job in and out always lose in the long run. (Although the most active traders at any given moment are those who are *temporarily* making money.)

Don't be afraid to be out of the Market. To anticipate missing numerous upswings is the correct "state of mind" for the Rational Investor.

Trust your pessimism; mistrust your optimism. (But expect to feel rather nervous when you buy.)

Don't fail to "re-balance" your portfolio repeatedly. Never let its Distribution become distorted.

Do not, at any time in your life, fail to have a *written* list of the dangers you see ahead in the general market within three months.

If a share fails you, punish it by selling.

Never average a "rubbishy" share. Do not throw good money after bad.

Don't over-trade, especially at the top (or bottom) of long moves. Stick to small quantities. Be conservative.

Habitually pay off your loans in the boomlets.

Only borrow in the Intermediate depressions.

Never go big in unholy gambles.

* * *

DON'TS

If you have margin losses with your broker, Settle up—or sell.

If ever a bank calls in an old loan, Sell out widely. It is probably a sign that the banks will soon be calling in loans all around, and that a general collapse will soon ensue.

Watch your rubbishy shares more carefully than the Leaders.

Try always to have cash in reserve.

Don't, in the falling half of the cycle, be anything but a "bear" of common stocks (except perhaps gold shares).

* * *

If you cannot follow sound rules *continuously,* do not speculate.

Never break a sound rule. (If you feel you are breaking one, reduce your commitment.)

The wise investor aims to succeed by following his Rules—not the Exceptions. (Although he will always "feel" that somehow things are different *this time,* he should not give way to these dangerous "feelings.")

Don't antagonize your broker. Always forgive him.

Never be meek. Be brave and conceited enough positively to expect the crowd to be wrong.

Sell when the world is full of hope. Buy when your own nerves are frayed.

Always beware of too much "company."

PAGE FOR NOTES

CHAPTER XLIII

SURVEY OF RULES FOR INVESTING IN ORDINARY SHARES

Let us now summarize the major points in our policy:

The ideal speculative investment.

For medium-run purposes probably the ideal speculative investment for capital appreciation is one which fulfills the following requirements:

I. COUNTRY TO CHOOSE

In a country where cyclical revival has begun.

Where long-term interest rates are falling.

Where the banking position is strong, and credit can easily be expanded; and where the bank rate is more likely to be lowered than raised.

Where the internal commodity price-level is apparently below that of the world outside, so that exports are likely to be large and imports small, with the result that gold is more likely to flow in than to flow out, and the general banking position to improve rather than to deteriorate.*

II. INDUSTRY TO CHOOSE

In a recently depressed but geometric industry where revival has already begun; or in promising industries whose products are still selling well below marginal costs (so that no further fall is likely).

* If you believe in the general future of a country, a reasonably representative interest can usually be acquired by buying shares in its banks, railways and electric supply companies.

III. SHARES TO CHOOSE

The share should be a free market, and should show high earnings on current market price. The company should be honestly managed.

IV. DESIRABLE EXTERNAL CONDITIONS

The conjuncture should have been depressed but should now be reviving.

V. DESIRABLE CONDITIONS CONCERNING GRAPHIC POSITION

The share curve itself, the conjunctural share-index curve, and the price of the commodity produced (in the case of, say, a raw material like tin) should be near their lower cartographical parallels; and all should be turning mildly upwards.

The share price should be below its recent highest. There should not have been a sharp recent rise.

* * *

If the above conditions are fulfilled most of the adverse risks in investment will have been eliminated, and a favorable sequence of internal and external, long-run and short-run, probabilities will have been built up.

Chief rules for buying and selling.

WHAT TO BUY

Only buy into companies and industries with rising profit-trends (or falling loss levels).

Prefer the second year of revival.

Prefer geometric industries.

Keep to the Market Leaders.

Prefer shares with highly geared equities.

Yields should be reasonably high; earnings considerably higher.

Management must be honest and good.

If an industry has not recently slumped there should be no signs of recent over-investment.

WHEN TO BUY

Buy only during conjunctural depressions, but wait for the share-index curve, as well as the curve of the share itself (if it has been falling), to saucer out and turn upwards.

But hesitate to buy shares on top of a recent rise of much over 10%.

Prefer shares standing 15% below their last high-points.

Rarely buy shares unless they are standing near their lower chart-parallels.

WHEN TO SELL

Always sell *at once* on internal deterioration in the industry or company.

Sell on a loss of 20%.

Think of selling whenever shares look over-valued and (or) if they are near their higher parallels. If, however, general markets are still good, consider letting profits run on till the general market itself begins to waver. (Use sliding stop-loss orders.)

Sell (if you are a short-run investor) all your "prospect" shares in a bad conjuncture when the graph gives the signal, or if the market becomes wild—especially if the shares themselves are near their higher parallels.

If the expectations on which you base short-run or long-run speculative purchases do not mature, sell your holdings at once. If shares will not go your way, go theirs. Never hold doggedly or aimlessly on.

If a paper profit of 15% or more is shown, short-run investors should institute a system of sliding stop-loss orders that will conserve them two-thirds of their paper gains.

Concerning investment dogma.

The reader will have noticed that throughout this book we have not hesitated to make dogmatic statements concerning:
   What losses to take,
   What paper profits to conserve,
   When to sell,
   When not to buy,
   How to read charts,
   And so on.

Anyone with professional experience will know the temerity of arbitrary dogma of this sort. Anyone without professional experience will have found difficulty in interpreting statements appearing in books on investment such as:

It is dangerous to buy after a "sharp" rise.

One should cut losses before they become "too" big.

If paper profits are shown one must not be "too greedy."

We have preferred, therefore, to be dogmatic and open to criticism (and, we trust, clear) rather than to be vague and cautious.

Our hope is that the reader will condone this policy, treating our somewhat definitive rules and figures not as indisputable dogma, but as a *normal* "state of mind" to be cultivated by the Rational Investor.

THE END

APPENDIX A

FORECASTING A CHANGE OF TREND IN THE PROFITS OF A SINGLE INDUSTRY

Introductory.

Since success in investment largely depends on accurate forecasts of changes of trend in single industries, the matter deserves the closest attention. In Chapter VIII something was said of the way in which prosperity bred depression as a result of the influx of new capital. And in Chapter XXII we suggested that since industries moved in cycles whose two halves were usually about four years in length, an upturn or downturn in an industry's profit-curve was often a sign of a new major trend, so that buying in the second year of revival was "usually" safe. Some further notes are, however, necessary.

Although an economist can usually say "what" will happen in a single industry, and what the "sequence" of future events will be, he can rarely say "when" the changes will occur or to what "degree" their influences will be felt. Forecasting dates and magnitudes can never be an exact and reliable science. Investors, nevertheless, have to forecast in order to determine net probabilities, so something must be said about the economic, as distinct from the graphic, methods to adopt—especially in determining when industries are in a dangerous position.

Main points to consider.

In forecasting single industries five main factors have to be considered:

    Prices being received,

    Future production, and competition, at different price levels,

Probable consumption at different levels of prices,
Bargaining power with consumers, and
Costs.

and it is by reference to these factors that changes of trend can alone be forecast.

Commercial bargaining power.

In connection with price movements, a rise in the selling price of a product usually means a more than proportional rise in profits (unless costs rise parallel). For, as was said in Chapter XXIII, if costs are, say, 100, and current selling-prices are 110, a rise in prices of 10% may mean a 100% increase in profits.

And *vice versa* as regards falls in prices.

When forecasting price movements the primary thing to consider is Bargaining Power as between producers and consumers.

If stocks are large and plant is only partially employed, the balance of bargaining power lies with consumers. They can play off sellers against each other and make them cut prices fraction by fraction down to, or below, prime costs so as to secure orders—even though, in the long run, true costs (which should theoretically include an allowance for depreciation and amortization) may be much higher than current market prices.

On the other hand, if stocks become small and factories receive more orders than they can immediately meet, the balance of bargaining power shifts to producers, and the competition of consumers for immediately available stocks enables producers to raise their prices.

Incidentally, when prices start rising and goods become scarce, middlemen try to increase their own stocks, so as to ensure being able to give immediate delivery, or so as to make extra money if prices go on rising still further. Thus a rise in prices, when once begun, often stimulates extra orders and gives producers the double benefit of more orders at higher prices. Profits may then become enormous; and they may possibly be added to by the overhead economies frequently secured by working at maximum output.

On the other hand if Bargaining Power shifts back to consumers, and prices start to fall, consumers at once cease buying in the hope of buying cheaper later on. Middlemen also let their stocks run off for fear prices may fall still further. This is the Law of the Falling Market, namely that *prospective* falls in prices check market demand (as distinct from actual use in final consumption), and tend to cause temporary stagnation.

What the investor must do, therefore, is always to watch carefully in each industry for any fluctuation in either Demand (due to fashion, saturation, attrition, and so on) or Supply (due to foreign competition, rival industries growing up, or new plant coming to fruition), such as will alter the Balance of Bargaining Power as between producer and consumer—(as evidenced usually by a change in stocks and/or a change in prices, or a change in the scale of employment in factories).

The investor should stand clear, or take a hand, according as the tactical initiative in bargaining power shifts from one side to the other.

Again, it is often possible for combinations of producers or consumers to tilt bargaining power from one side to the other by artificial means. A policy, for instance, of temporarily postponing consumption may so frighten producers and middlemen that they may start cutting prices competitively with a view to clearing existing stocks and booking forward orders with their customers before any further still greater fall in prices takes place. The result may be that prices will become low; and, even though demand and supply in the future may remain exactly equal, the market price may remain depressed for several years on end, solely because it was pushed down to a low level *"initially."*

The theory of "initial price."

This question of "initial price" at the beginning of an era wherein Demand and Supply remain about equal is one of the most important factors in investment.

The condition for price-stability over a period is that Demand should be approximately equal to Supply. "Initial price," however, at the beginning of such a period, is highly important, especially in those cases where demand is inelastic.

The point is this: In most *industries* (as distinct from in single competing *companies*) the total volume of Demand is not appreciably choked off by high prices; for it is only in the luxury trades, and in industries where there are alternative products, that price largely influences aggregate demand.

Hence in eras where demand and supply are likely to remain approximately equal, prosperity depends mainly on the price at the beginning of the period, i.e., on the *original* balance of bargaining power between producer and consumer.

If the tactical initiative has been lost in the first place, i.e., at the beginning of the period wherein inelastic demand and supply remain equal, the profits of the industry may remain depressed for years on end, even though consumers *might* all the while have been able and willing, if only bargaining power had been captured from them, to have paid much higher prices (and yet not have reduced their scale of consumption at all). Rubber, tin and oil provide examples of highly inelastic demand.

Bargaining power is thus one of the most important factors to consider as regards all industries, when forecasting. It is one of the major phenomena which investors must habitually watch.

APPENDIX A

Beware when goods sell high above costs.

Investors must be able to detect the signs which indicate that an industry is in a dangerous position. In this connection it should be noted that there is always considerable latent danger when price is high above costs. An apt example of this is furnished by the tin market. If average mining costs are about £70, and if marginal costs, i.e., the costs of the most expensive producers, are about £100, then if tin is selling at £200 the slightest change in Bargaining Power, due, say, to only a 5% surplus in production over consumption, can switch the tactical initiative over to consumers.

Rival producers may then be induced to cut prices fraction by fraction so as to dispose of all that they have produced; the price may thus fall in a very short while from £200 down to £100. And yet, although the price may be falling, not one single extra ton of tin may be consumed. Indeed, purchases may *temporarily* fall off owing to the Law of the Falling Market.

Simultaneously, not one single ton of production may be knocked off as a result of the falling prices, because the price is still above prime costs.

In some cases producers may even try to *increase* their production so as to gain through larger turnover, and perhaps lower costs per ton, what they lose in price. Thus despite the *long-run* economic Law that lower prices check production and stimulate consumption, exactly opposite results may ensue in the short-run. Stocks may rise and production may increase and demand may fall off *as a result* of the lower prices.

Investors, therefore, must especially beware of industries where products are selling high above costs, lest bargaining power should suddenly be lost. In the first place, new capital is bound to flow in; secondly, when the new plant comes to fruition, and as soon as Bargaining Power is lost, prices will slump down to at least the prime costs of the most expensive producers. This may mean a fall of 60% or more in a great many share prices, since shares usually slump considerably faster than cognate commodity prices.

All this, we repeat, often happens in the course of a year or nine months.

Beware, therefore, of any change in Bargaining Power in any industry where products are selling high above costs. Get out early on the very first sign of this internal deterioration. The shares are no longer a medium for bulls, but only for bears.

Industries approaching saturation.

Another danger point in any industry is the probable approach of saturation of demand—especially if the recent rate of total growth has been rapid.

In the lorry and motor-bus industry, for instance, it is conceivable that total national demand could increase 20% in a year, but that when this somewhat special expansion demand was satisfied the only future demand would be for normal replacement which, if it took vehicles seven years to wear out, would equal roughly 15% per year of the total registrations.

The industrial result of quickly satisfying an expansion demand of the foregoing nature might be that whereas in the big expansion year roughly 35 chassis would be bought for every previous 100 existing registrations, i.e., roughly 15 for replacement and 20 for expansion, in the following year only 15 (or slightly over) would be needed, because the only demand would be a replacement demand. The consequence would be a decline in production from 35 to 15 units, i.e., $57\frac{1}{7}\%$, which would mean a violent slump in profits, and a much greater slump in the prices of equity shares.

Whenever, therefore, investors see saturation approaching they must be particularly nervous, especially if the recent rate of growth has been rapid. Their caution must be abnormally great—

(a) If the boomlet has stimulated the setting up of much new plant,

(b) If the attrition period of the product is long—implying that the annual demand for replacement will be small.

Beware of bulges in demand due purely to a change in inventory policy.

Another point about which investors should be particularly careful is if there is a sudden wave of demand due purely to middlemen or private consumers increasing the size of their stocks.

If, for instance, middlemen normally sell 100 units a year and keep a stock of 40 units, the decision to enlarge stocks to 60 units will increase the effective demand by 20% for one year: the next year it may revert to normal, which will mean a slump of 17%.

Similarly, if private persons increase their private stocks of, say, shirts from four to five in one year, whereas only one shirt wears out each year, demand may increase 100% in the given year, and then suddenly revert to normal. Much new plant, however, may be thoughtlessly ordered by manufacturers, and there may be a violent subsequent slump. Little booms in this way often lead to much bigger slumps.

Always, therefore, beware of sudden boomlets in single industries, and consider carefully whether they may not be due purely to a temporary stock-changing demand, originating either among middlemen or among private consumers.

Beware of waves of instalment buying in industries whose products have long attrition periods.

Again, be particularly careful of industries whose goods are being sold in large volume on instalment. If the goods are durable, demand will certainly decline as soon as saturation has been reached and everyone has bought his gramophone, bedstead, refrigerator, etc.

Waves of instalment buying in any industry are particularly likely to be followed by long slumps—
- (a) if the attrition period of the product is long, and
- (b) if each family requires only *one* item, e.g., one gramophone, one wireless set, etc. (as indeed is the case in many of the goods sold on instalment),

so that even big reductions in future prices will fail to stimulate demand sufficiently to occupy existing plant.

* * *

On principle always stand clear of industries that appear to be in a dangerous position, either on account of bona fide demand, prospective supply, bargaining power or stock-changing policies.

Charts to keep as regards single industries.

As regards the raw material industries concerning which statistics are available, investors should, where possible, keep a chart of the following curves:

    Production,
    Consumption,
    Stocks,
    Prices,
    Prime costs (probable average for the industry); as in the following graph:

Investors should hesitate to buy while unsold stocks are rising, or if production is still absolutely larger than consumption, or if prices are falling.

APPENDIX A
PLATE XVII

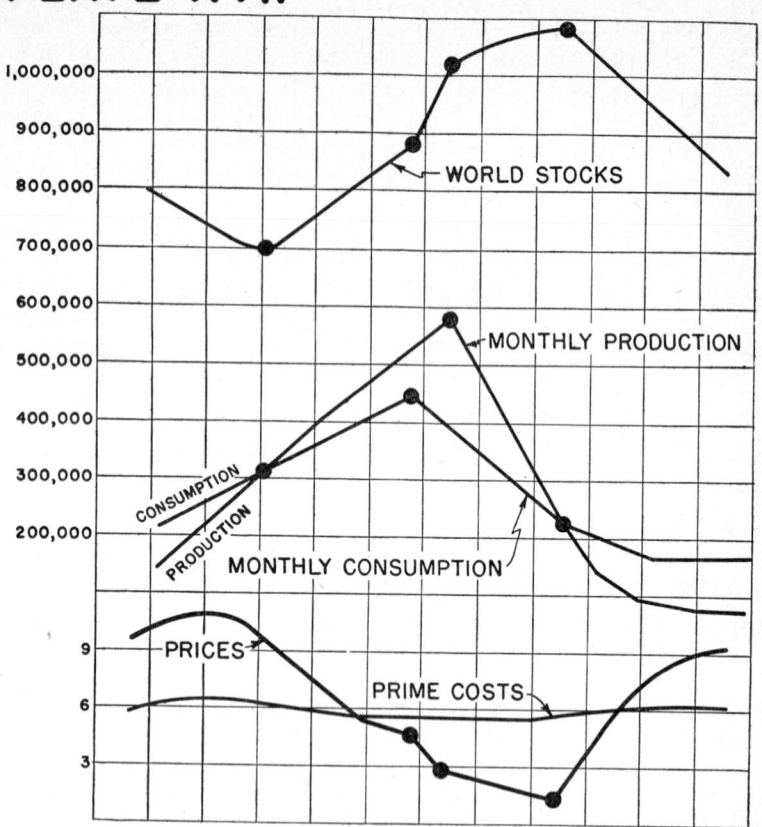

The vertical lines represent intervals of one year

The various favorable factors to watch for in slumping industries are:

(1) A flattening or downturn in the stock-curve.

(2) An upturn in the price-curve.

(3) A closer approximation of the consumption and production curves (or rather, a difference in the relative steepness, or in the direction, of the curves).*

(4) A fall in costs.

*Prices sometimes rise in anticipation of stocks falling; e.g., when the consumption curve is rising faster than the production curve,

INDUSTRIAL FORECASTING

"Deferred" replacement demand.

One important factor in the *early* stages of general industrial revival must here be noted, namely "deferred" replacement demand. This perhaps can best be illustrated by conditions similar to those existing in the American automobile industry in the early 1930's.

The aggregate demand for cars may be of five sorts:
1. "Expansion" demand.
2. "Normal" replacement demand (depending on life).
3. "Deferred" replacement demand (due to previous temporary lengthening of life, for economy's sake).
4. "Fore-shortened" replacement demand (due to the shortening of average life).
5. The export demand.

Deferred Replacement. If the car population of a country remains permanently stationary at say 21,000,000, and if the average life remains permanently fixed at say 7 years, normal replacement demand will be 3,000,000 cars.

But if during one year (of depression) people delay the scrapping of cars, so that the average life suddenly becomes 8 years instead of 7, there will, for that year (theoretically), be no replacement demand at all—although the accumulated or "deferred" replacement demand will, in the *following* year, be 3,000,000 cars.

If such a lengthening of life is only temporary, the results may be startling.

For instance, if, in the year after life lengthens from 7 to 8 years, life suddenly shortens again to "normal," i.e., 7 years,

even though production still exceeds consumption. (See the convergence of production on consumption in the second and third years on the above graph: suggesting an eventual crossing of the two lines, and a consequent fall in stocks.)

283

APPENDIX A

the total demand in that year will be 6,000,000 cars, i.e., 3,000,000 for *"normal"* replacement demand on a 7-year life, *plus* 3,000,000 for demand *"deferred"* from the previous year.

Thus car production, on total "replacement" demand account, may theoretically rise, in one year, from nil to 6,000,000, or at all events several hundred per cent.

Incidentally, it should be further noted that if life, in the second year, suddenly drops by *two* years instead of one, i.e., from 8 years to 6 years, the "normal" replacement demand of the third year will also be crowded into the second year, so that theoretical car production in that year will be 9,000,000 cars.

The following chart attempts to illustrate this theory (assuming always that the total car population remains stationary):

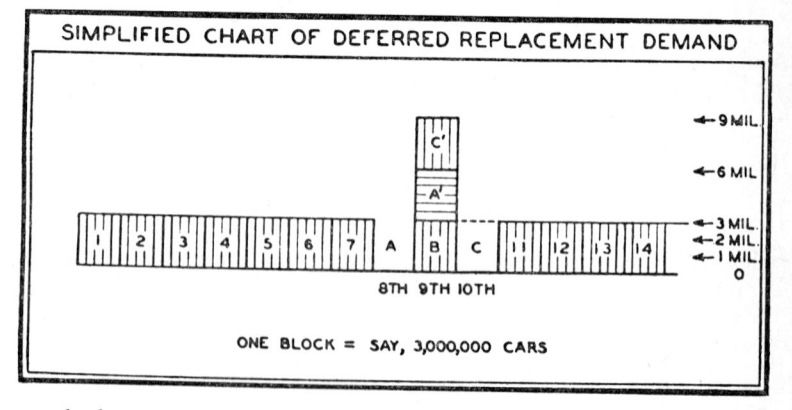

```
SIMPLIFIED CHART OF DEFERRED REPLACEMENT DEMAND

                         C'
                         A'
     2  3  4  5  6  7  A  B  C     11 12 13 14
                      8TH 9TH 10TH

            ONE BLOCK = SAY, 3,000,000 CARS
```
← 9 MIL
← 6 MIL
← 3 MIL
← 2 MIL
← 1 MIL
0

Block A represents the cars which, on a 7-year life, would "normally" have been produced in the *8th year* to replace the cars produced in the 1st year.

Block B represents the "normal" replacement demand, of the following or *9th year*—replacing cars that were built in the 2nd year, on a 7-year life.

Block C represents the "normal" replacement demand of the *10th year* for the cars built in the 3rd year, on a 7-year life.

But if, in the 8th year, the average life of cars is suddenly, *though only temporarily,* lengthened by 1 year, owing to consumers' inability to make normal replacements, there will pile up, in the 9th year, a "deferred" replacement demand (Block A′) over and above the "normal" replacement demand of the 9th year (i.e., Block B), assuming a return to a 7-year life, making 6,000,000 cars in all.

Further: if in the 9th year the average life is positively shortened from 8 years to 6 (instead of only to 7), Block C′ will also be superimposed on Blocks A′ and B, giving a total theoretical production for the 9th year of 9,000,000 cars.

N.B.—In the 10th year, however, if life re-lengthened to 7 years once more (from 6), there would be no demand whatever in that year, and production would decline from 9,000,000 to nil. (In the 11th year, however, under these circumstances, demand, on a 7-year life, might again become normal, i.e., 3,000,000 cars, namely those replacing those built in the 4th year.)

The above represents the Key Theory to forecasting the motor car industry, in a virtually "saturated" country.

In practice, of course, life does not "suddenly" increase or decrease by a year at a time, as suggested in the "Block" theory described above. In reality, it is a more gradual affair, increasing relatively slowly, perhaps month by month. Thus, in practice, a more accurate drawing would be somewhat as follows:

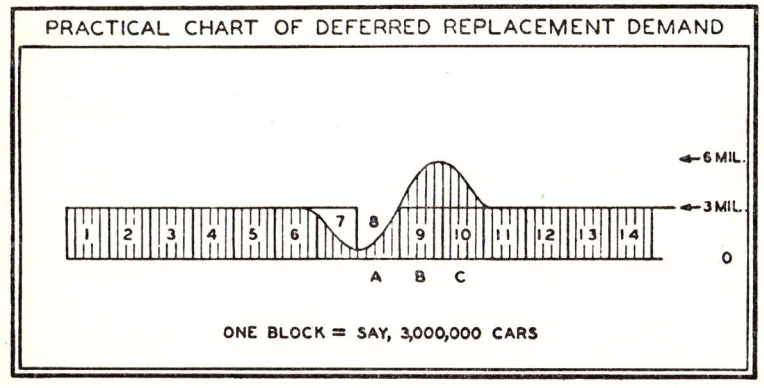

PRACTICAL CHART OF DEFERRED REPLACEMENT DEMAND

ONE BLOCK = SAY, 3,000,000 CARS

APPENDIX A

From the above graph it will be seen, that instead of Block A' *suddenly* jumping up on top of Block B, as it does in Chart I, a more likely occurrence is that—owing to life beginning to lengthen *gradually* in say the 7th year, and continuing to lengthen in the 8th year (and then eventually shortening again)—both *part* of Block 7 and *part* of Block 8, or A, will be wiped out, as per the "hollow" curve there drawn.

The unshaded area above this hollow curve (i.e., the top part of Blocks 7 and 8, or A) will represent the "deferred" replacement demand, which, *if* (and only if) life returns to the normal 7 years in the 9th and 10th years, will be superimposed, in the form of a "bulging" curve *of equal area,* above Blocks 9, or B, and 10, or C (thus creating a boom).

* * *

Actually the hollow and bulge have been drawn as if the complete development of, and subsequent correction of, deferred replacement demand were effected within two pairs of years.

In practice, of course, it is possible for these two curves to sweep over a longer period, so that the recovery in demand is not so sharp, or so closely concentrated as regards time.

The net result, however, may be a rise in demand from 25% of normal (during the slump) to say 175% of normal (during the deferred replacement demand boom), i.e., a rise of 600%.

When, however, the *deferred* part of replacement demand has been satisfied, and total demand reverts to normal, i.e., to "normal" or "pure" replacement demand only, production may decline from 175 to 100 (unless expansion-, export-, or "fore-shortened" demands take its place).

This downward oscillation is, in fact, a normal feature of a great many industries in about the third year of *general* cyclical *revival*. During the *general* slump they slump seriously—particularly if they are luxuries and non-consumption is easily possible; or if the life of the product can be easily extended, as in cars. During general revival they enjoy a *deferred* replacement demand boom—particularly if they are semi-necessities, like shirts; and if their life cannot be *indefinitely* lengthened. Then later, despite the probable continued improvement in *general* trade, these *deferred* replacement demand industries suffer a reaction peculiar to themselves, because of the satisfaction of the *deferred* portion of total "replacement" demand.

Such "normal" reactions will be particularly aggravated if the directors of such companies (not understanding the transient nature of the "deferred" portion of total "replacement" demand), over-enlarge their factories during the boomlet—as usually happens!

Moderate slumps, in fact, due (i) to the satisfaction of *deferred* demand, and (ii) to over-investment in new plant, are *normal* in the *deferred* replacement demand industries, in the middle stages of every *general* cyclical revival.

Conclusion: The deferred replacement demand industries are *particularly* promising in the *early* stages of general revival; and rather dangerous later on.

Various points to consider when making an analysis.

Finally when analyzing a company carefully consider the following factors:

I. The trend of demand.
   1. Is demand geometric or of only a normal character?
   2. Has saturation apparently been reached?
   3. Has the commodity a long attrition period?
   4. What is the likely volume of demand for "normal" replacement?
   5. What is the likely volume of demand for "deferred" replacement?
   6. What is the likely volume of demand for expansion?
   7. Is demand much influenced by price?

8. Does consumption depend on fashion?
9. Is a rival industry growing up?
10. Is durability increasing?

II. The trend of supply.
1. Can existing plant immediately expand its output, or is it already working full time?
2. Is much new plant now being built? How long will it take to come to fruition?
3. Is there a substitute product?
4. Can the product be reclaimed?
5. Is there danger from a second-hand market?

III. The active and prospective influence of *foreign* demand, *foreign* supply, and tariffs.

IV. Are there any fiscal or political dangers?

V. The extent to which the industry at home is monopolistic, or subject to fierce internal competition.

VI. Bargaining Power as between producer and consumer, e.g. The extent to which existing plant is unoccupied; and the trend of unsold stocks.

VII. The trend of costs.

A useful classification of industries.

Expert investors should classify industries every few months according to the stages which they have respectively reached in their own individual business cycles, e.g., *prosperous, top-heavy, collapsing, depressed,* or *reviving,* as follows:

I. Industries which are highly prosperous, but which are *still in a safe position.*

II. Industries which are highly prosperous, but which are now *approaching a dangerous position* (due to new plant coming to fruition, to saturation being approached, or to speculative middlemen changing their stock policy, etc.).

INDUSTRIAL FORECASTING

III. Industries which are *clearly falling,* and which should therefore be avoided for some years.

IV. Industries which have slumped for some years but which are now apparently *bumping on the bottom*—and are therefore likely to prove a good medium for long-run investment.

V. Industries which are clearly *beginning to improve* and which therefore are probably good for both short-run and long-run investment.

The investor should keep, and repeatedly re-adjust, a classified table of industries as follows:

CLASSIFICATION OF INDUSTRIES
According to phases of the cycle (apparently) reached by each

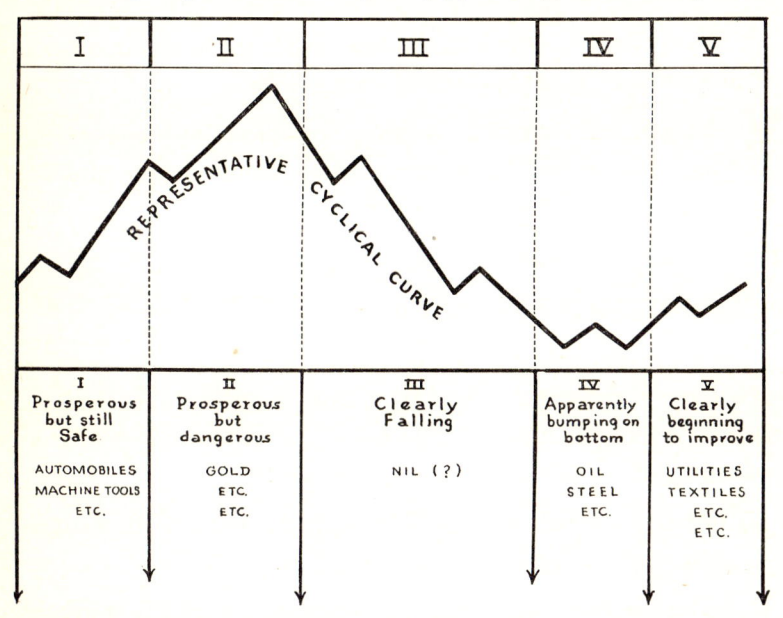

I	II	III	IV	V
Prosperous but still Safe	Prosperous but dangerous	Clearly Falling	Apparently bumping on bottom	Clearly beginning to improve
AUTOMOBILES MACHINE TOOLS ETC.	GOLD ETC. ETC.	NIL (?)	OIL STEEL ETC.	UTILITIES TEXTILES ETC. ETC.

REPRESENTATIVE CYCLICAL CURVE

Every few months the various industries should be re-classified according to what are, in the investor's opinion, their appropriate columns.

APPENDIX B

CAUSES OF THE BUSINESS CYCLE

This Appendix, from the fundamental point of view, is perhaps the most important portion of this book.

It is impossible, within a few pages, to give a complete description of the business cycle; yet to understand the business cycle, and its causes, is the essence of successful investment. The following are its principal features:

The vicious circle.

All economists are aware of the vicious circle which operates in periods of declining trade, namely:

Nervousness. Selling pressure in order to get liquid. Declining prices and declining profit margins. Hoarding of working capital by producers and middlemen through general fear. Hoarding of money by nervous consumers and a concomitant reduction in consumption. A general decline in security as well as commodity values. A resultant contraction of credit by the banks because the collateral for loans has shrunk in value. Forced sales on the part of the borrowers who are squeezed. A further decline in prices. Further contraction of credit by the banks. Still more forced sales and cumulative contraction.

Nervousness among middlemen about the future of prices. Attempts on their part to let inventories run low. Refusal by middlemen to give replacement orders to producers. A decline in manufacturing volume and in manufacturing incomes. An aggregate reduction in the purchasing power of workers. Fewer sales by the retail stores. Fewer replacement orders to producers, and a further decline in industrial incomes.

Consumption, production and prices thus cumulatively decline. Credit contraction, and hoarding, accentuate the momentum.

The virtuous circle.

On the other hand, a virtuous circle, as distinguished from a vicious circle, can operate during improving trade, namely:

A cessation of hoarding on the part of the general public. Increased purchases at retail. A gradual reduction of retail stocks. Increased replacement orders to producers. Increased industrial incomes. Increased purchases at the shops by industrial workers, probably *before* any new commodities are completed. Further reduction in retail stocks. Further replacement orders to producers. A general increase in industrial activity. Expansion by banks of commercial loans. A general "natural" reflation of credit. A gradual rise in the prices and costs of finished goods.

Attempts by retailers to enlarge their inventories before prices rise further. Additional orders to manufacturers. Additional borrowing from the banks to finance increased output. A further inflation of bank credit and prices.

A desire by consumers to buy before prices rise further. More buying on credit-from-the-shops and on the instalment plan. Further orders to producers, and an increase in incomes.

Eventually this increased activity in the consumer goods industries causes more orders to be given to the capital goods industries, and the general scale of production and consumption both grow.

* * *

Later on, however, these hitherto "virtuous" movements begin to assume a dangerous character, i.e.:

A gradual outbreak of speculation in commodities and securities and real estate, largely financed with borrowed bank money. An inflation of bank credit even faster than production. A rise in prices and profits, developing into boom. Strained banking conditions then appear. Nervousness spreads. Collapse eventuates.

* * *

What then are the causes of these violent fluctuations?

The business cycle is a monetary phenomenon.

The business cycle is mainly a monetary affair. The six stages are: Prosperity; boom; strained credit; collapse; depression; revival. And repeat. This cycle is primarily brought about by fluctuations in either the demand for, or supply of, money. These fluctuations in the demand for and supply of money themselves are reflected in variations in the monetary demand for goods and services.

Some people reject this monetary theory of the cycle. But inspect any row of shops. Does not their prosperity depend upon the willingness, and ability, of the public to spend money? And does not the prosperity of manufacturers depend on the orders which they receive from retailers?

The flow of money.

Since all modern trade is conducted with money, and since trade consists of the flow of money on to goods and services, perhaps the best way to study modern trade is to analyze this flow of money on to goods.

The flow is influenced partly by changes in the volume or supply of money; partly by changes in its velocity, i.e., in the so-called hoarding demand for it.

Definitions of money.

(i) *The Supply of Money.* By the supply of money we mean coins not used as backing for notes; *plus* notes except those used as backing for bank deposits; *plus* transferable bank deposits, i.e., current or demand deposits as distinct from fixed or time deposits.

N.B.—In the supply of money, we, of course, include bank credit as well as legal tender, just as when we talk of traffic we include motors, even though they are merely a "convenient substitute" for horses.

(ii) *The Demand for Money.* The demand for money proper is of two separate sorts:

(a) For use as a medium-of-exchange.

(b) For use as a store-of-value.

As regards the medium-of-exchange demand: This consists of the amount required in one's pocket or passbook as a medium-of-exchange for effecting those expected or unexpected items of expenditure which are likely to mature before the next anticipated replenishment of monetary income.

As regards the store-of-value demand: This consists of the amount required for hoarding purposes either so as to keep liquid or as a speculative investment against an anticipated general fall in prices.

[Let me here emphasize that the demand for money proper, must not be confused with loan-money, despite the convenient, though slip-shod, terminology of the (loan) money market.]

The supply of money as an influence on trade.

Variations in the supply of money can obviously affect trade and the price level as follows:

In a modern industrial community like America, 80% of all the money used consists of bank money; i.e., the scribbled credit entries in bank ledgers and pass books which are transferable by means of checks.

If the use of all this "bank credit currency" was made illegal overnight; or if it was suddenly all cancelled or deflated; the net result tomorrow morning would be that all of us who held credit bank balances, would no longer possess this money at all; nor could we spend it at the shops. Thus, if 80% of all money was deflated, either trade, or prices, would have to fall about 80%.

In both cases money profits would decline and industry would suffer a slump.

The demand for money as an influence on trade.

But prices and trade can be affected not only by variations in the supply of money, but also by variations in the demand for it—particularly the store-of-value demand.

For instance, if instead of the total supply of bank credit currency all being actually cancelled or deflated, the owners decided to hoard it (in their banks); i.e., not spend it for say ten years, the net result on prices and trade—resulting from this hoarding, or decline in velocity—would be the same as if there had been an actual deflation of 80%.

Thus either a decrease in the supply of, or an increase in the (hoarding) demand for money, can bring about lower prices, and bad trade, and unemployment.

Conversely, of course, an 80% or a 100% inflationary increase in the supply of bank money, pumped into people's pass-books over-night tends, with a lag, to have the effect of increasing trade and raising prices—because people, being "economic men," do not like keeping money idle without receiving any interest; so they therefore spend their surplus redundant holdings on either income-giving securities or enjoyment-giving commodities.

Thus, with a lag, an inflation of money first stimulates consumption, and then later when stocks of commodities have fallen, brings about a rise in prices.

Changes in velocity. Dishoarding.

In like manner the converse case must be noted, namely that the dishoarding of *previously* hoarded money (within the banks) will have a similar influence on trade and prices. Dishoarding, i.e., spending, after a previous period of hoarding, will have a reflationary effect, owing to demand of the store-of-value sort, having fallen, and caused an increase in Velocity.

All these factors are matters of fluctuations in either the supply *or* the demand for money, and it is these various types of monetary fluctuation which influence trade, general prices, business profits and unemployment.

* * *

There is, however, one feature about the demand for money of the utmost economic and industrial importance.

The net demand for money increases in bad trade (a cumulative disease).

The medium-of-exchange demand for money obviously increases and decreases with the general scale of industrial activity, rising in the rising half of the business cycle, and falling in the falling half.

But the store-of-value demand for money moves in precisely the opposite direction. That is to say, as trade declines people become nervous, and although they require less money for actual trading or medium-of-exchange purposes, they desire to be liquid—this nervous desire being stimulated by the prospects of falling commodity prices.

The result, in terms of money, is an augmentation of the store-of-value demand for money, which checks monetary velocity and reduces its general flow on to commodities. Thus, although the medium-of-exchange demand for money in general diminishes during declining trade, the store-of-value demand increases.

Moreover, since, as a general rule, variations in the storage demand for money are greater throughout the business cycle than the variations in the medium-of-exchange demand, you get the curious, though rarely appreciated, phenomenon of a *net* increase in the *total demand* for money occurring during each slump—thus making prices (and trade) fall *cumulatively*.

Conversely during revival, the combined demand for money decreases, owing to the store-of-value demand diminishing *even faster* than the medium-of-exchange demand increases. Prices (and trade) thus rise cumulatively.

Cumulative fluctuations in supply.

The foregoing "net demand" phenomena would be bad enough from an industrial point of view, even if supply itself remained perfectly stationary the whole while; but instead of supply itself remaining stationary, or being scientifically manipulated so as to offset net variations in aggregate demand, the reverse happens; and *as net demand increases, supply is positively decreased,* thus adding *further* cumulative momentum to every downward (and upward) swing of the business cycle.

To explain this point we must briefly describe one important feature of our curious modern banking and monetary system.

Inflation and deflation of bank credit currency.

As already stated, 80% of the money used by the public consists merely of scribbled credit entries in the pass-books of the public and the ledgers of the banks. People are content to take payment in this form, and scribbled credit entries constitute most of our modern money.

These credit entries, however, can (as was explained in Chapter VII) be decreased or increased at the option of the banks. For instance, if a bank calls in a loan and the borrower pays him off, the original credit entry is thereby cancelled and there is less so-called credit currency in existence.

On the other hand, if a banker makes a loan to a borrower (other than in the form of legal tender), the borrower has a credit entry marked up in his own pass-book which he can thereafter transfer to anyone else by means of a check. The total credit money of the country is thereby inflated. And the public have more money to spend and re-spend on commodities.

In fact, banks, by calling in loans (or selling their investments) can deflate the bank credit currency; whereas by increasing their loans (or by buying investments or bills) they can inflate the credit currency as used by the public.

Their policy in these matters depends partly on their own confidence, partly on fluctuations in the market value of the collateral pledged with them against each loan, and partly on the state of the legal tender cash *reserves* which they hold.

This phenomenon of the cash reserve ratio system of banking is a vital factor influencing the modern business cycle.

Let us therefore trace its influence (via the Supply of Money) on trade, keeping an eye throughout our discussion on such variations in the Demand for money as also normally occur as the cycle progresses, either *because of* variations in Supply, or for other reasons.

The bank credit cycle.

As legal tender moves into or out of the banks from public circulation, so are the reserves of the banks automatically strengthened or weakened.

During a trade boom, when companies become fully employed and retail prices get marked up, and when competition for labor is causing wages to be raised, more legal tender is taken out of the banks in cancellation of bank credits, for wage paying, pocket-money and till-money purposes. This constitutes an increase in the *medium-of-exchange* demand for a particular sort of money, i.e., legal tender.

The result of this increased medium-of-exchange demand for legal tender, is, other things equal, to weaken the reserve ratios of the banks, and if ratios are already strained, causes them to contract the *supply* of credit and raise money rates.

Collapse.

Now, tight credit, coupled with actual or anticipated credit deflation, has a frightening effect upon business men, and the more cautious element will decide to get liquid. That is to say, after selling either securities or goods they will hoard the money-proceeds in their banks, instead of respending them. This in fact constitutes an increase in the *store-of-value* demand for bank credit money, i.e., a decline in Velocity.

Investors, in fact, after selling securities will not reinvest in other securities; and manufacturers and middlemen, after selling goods, will hoard their working capital, and not replenish their stocks to normal. Middlemen will thereupon give fewer orders to makers (since their policy is to increase their stocks of money and decrease their stocks of goods); with the result that production itself will decline, and with it the scale of monetary incomes. This will frighten people still more, and the *hoarding* demand for money will grow cumulatively.

But worse things habitually happen than this.

Cumulative bank credit contraction.

As production declines, profits decline; and general industrial nervousness spreads. More and more people try to get liquid, and more and more goods and securities are thrown on the market. Prices in consequence rapidly collapse and the value of commodities and securities pledged with the banks as collateral shrinks.

Now a prudent banker, in the course of his duty towards his depositors, calls in loans as collateral values shrink. This leads, in consequence, to a wave of forced sales, and general prices fall still further. Still more bankers call in loans, and the decline in prices gains cumulative momentum.

This brings us into what economists call the "collapse" phase of the business cycle; which is accentuated by nervous consumers hoarding a large part of even the small monetary incomes they receive (owing either to their stock exchange losses making them feel poorer on paper, or owing to their being nervous lest they soon lose their jobs). Some consumers may even hoard money in the positive hope of falling prices; they may in fact obey what economists call the Law of the Falling Market, thus tending to depress trade even further.

Summary of the monetary causes of slump.

What then were the actual causes of the slump?

The initial cause of the trouble was an increased "medium-of-exchange" demand for a particular sort of money, namely legal tender. The secondary effect was a contraction, or prospective contraction, of the supply of a certain sort of money, namely bank credit. The tertiary effect was an increase in the second of the two sorts of "demand" for money, namely the store-of-value demand. And the fourth effect was a further contraction of the supply of bank money, brought about by the fall in collateral values which had resulted from the previous augmentations of demand for, and/or diminutions of supply of money. Demand and supply, in fact, reacted on each other in such a way as to make the depression *cumulative*.

Features of capitalism which foster a cycle.

"Institutional" factors either causing or giving momentum to the slump were (i) the cash reserve ratio system of banking; (ii) the collateral system of banking; and (iii) the fact that bank loan contractions, since bank credits are money, deplete the money as owned and used by the people.

The so-called Law of the Falling Market also operates: Consumers hold off the market either for fear of lower incomes, or in the hope of lower prices, or because their securities have slumped and they feel poorer on paper. Profit-seeking middlemen and producers also hold off the market, and hoard (i.e., retard the velocity of) their working capital

(a) because the fall in their profits makes them feel nervous, and

(b) because they are afraid to trade or produce on a falling market.

Thus the slump is caused partly by the behavior of consumers, partly by the behavior of producers and middlemen, and partly by the behavior of bankers.

Artificial prevention of slumps.

Looking back at the early stages of a cyclical depression—no matter whether initiated by a strained cash reserve ratio position in the banks leading to bank credit contraction; or merely by a fortuitous wave of fear leading to an increase in the store-of-value demand for money—it is possible, both in theory and practice, to counteract either an increasing demand for, or a diminishing supply of money, by deliberate artificial "manipulations of supply." Supply, in fact, can be used to offset, and influence, demand (and business psychology).

For instance, if the initial cause of the slump was an increase in the demand for legal tender on the part of the public from the banks, for use in public circulation, then, if there had been a Currency Controller or a Central Bank in existence who had it in his power to increase legal tender, pari passu with the industrial demand (provided prices were not rising), the various other subsequent monetary and industrial diseases might have been prevented at their outset.

Or even if this had not been done *in time,* and if a store-of-value demand for money had started reducing trade, then if the supply of bank credit had been quickly inflated to offset this hoarding demand, the collapse in prices might have been prevented at the outset; and the subsequent cumulative contraction of bank credit, due to falling collateral values, might have been scientifically prevented. (This might have been done in U. S. A. in 1930.)

Error of laissez-faire.

But instead of deliberate monetary management being exercised on these lines, the normal course is to let the normal disastrous reactions mature. Non-interference and orthodox laissez-faire thus prevent the slump being cured at its outset. The slump continues "naturally." And natural forces are relied on to effectuate a revival eventually.

It is, however, possible, both in theory and practice, for either Governments or Central Banks to intervene to check depressions in their early stages. It is also possible, as we shall later show, to stimulate revival before the slump has run its full or "natural" course.

Fear as an initial cause of depressions.

Eventually, as it happens, depression itself breeds revival: but before going into the details of how depression eventually stimulates revival *automatically* (just as periods of boom *automatically* breed slumps), let us retrace our steps for a moment, and examine an alternative way in which a boom can be converted step by step into a slump.

In the foregoing analysis of the monetary factors, both of demand and supply, which might initiate and accentuate a depression, we chose as our starting point a condition (which arises in *most* trade cycles) of the cash reserve ratios of the banks becoming strained.

APPENDIX B

Depressions, however, can be initiated not only by a scarcity of legal tender money in the banks, and by an actual or anticipated contraction of the total supply of bank credit money, but also by purely fortuitous increases in the store-of-value demand for money, resulting through either fear, satisfaction of wants, or threatened industrial dislocation.

For instance, if owing to political, economic, or military fear, people in general begin to get nervous, they may decide, even though bank reserve ratios are not yet in any way strained, to get more liquid than formerly.

They may therefore sell out their stocks of commodities and securities in order to satisfy their growing store-of-value or "liquidity" demand for money.

Indeed, the mere thought that markets are already too high or that industrial profits may soon fall, may set such a demand for liquid money in motion.

In other words, instead of the depression starting with a shortage of legal tender in the banks and a strained banking position, the depression may start with an increased store-of-value demand for money in general instead of with either an increased medium-of-exchange demand *for legal tender,* or a positive contraction of the supply of bank credit.

(It is also theoretically possible for a depression to start on account of money being hoarded as a result of most economic wants having been recently satisfied. But this cause is comparatively rare.)

All depressions assume a monetary character.

Regardless, however, of the initial causes of any depression, monetary or otherwise, all depressions, when once begun, tend to assume a purely monetary nature. That is to say: prices fall, credit is contracted, prices fall further, and nervousness spreads. The store-of-value demand for money increases, and prices in consequence fall still further. Monetary forces thus make the slump continue.

This general industrial contraction normally continues until there matures a state of general disorder and collapse.

Transition to revival.

Let us now see how collapse is followed by stagnation or depression; and then eventually by revival and prosperity.

Mathematically, of course, it is theoretically possible for the contraction of bank credit to continue progressively until bank credit as such has been wiped out and prices and/or trade have fallen perhaps 80%, i.e., to 20% of their former levels.

But long before this happens there will be a banking panic, say, when there has been a 20% deflation in the volume of bank money and a 40% deflation in trade and prices.

The bank panic will occur owing (a) to bonds and bank investments falling in value until they no longer exceed in value the deposit liabilities created against them; and owing (b) to numerous bank loans becoming frozen, owing to the borrowers being unable to raise the money they owe, and to the banks not being able to find buyers who will pay a price for sacrificed collateral equal in value to the originally made loans.

The public, on perceiving this state of affairs, will rush to the banks and encash their deposits.

Normally speaking, a ten per cent rush will cause the majority of banks to close.

Hereupon the government will *always* step in either with deposit-guarantees, or actual cash inflation; and these two measures will either restore confidence in the banks, or cause the expectation of inflation, thus checking the desire of the public to hoard money, and to some extent restoring business confidence (owing to rising prices) even though both money and the banks may still be distrusted.

Normal transition.

As a general rule, however, most cyclical collapses in trade end without the occurrence of a banking panic. This is due to the fall in retail prices, wages, and retail trade gradually causing more and more legal tender to be returned to the banks from public circulation.

Hereupon the banks, being profit-seeking institutions, will, since sound commercial borrowers are difficult to find during depressions, invest their surplus supplies of credit in first class Government bonds. This will tend not only to raise their prices, i.e., lower the long-term market rate of interest; *but also to pump more bank credit currency into the hands of the public.*

Whereafter the public, feeling richer on paper because bond prices have risen, and seeing that they hold more bank money as a whole (on account of the quantitative reflation brought about by the extra purchases of securities by the banks), will gradually begin to dishoard previously hoarded money; i.e., the bank money left idle in the banks.

The velocity of money on to goods in consequence grows; and very gradually retail stocks are lowered and at last trade revival is set in motion. For retailers, when at last inventories have been sufficiently reduced, start giving replacement orders to producers; producers pay out larger incomes to their employees; the employees spend the incomes at the shops; still more orders are given to producers; and a virtuous, as distinct from a vicious, circle of trade is at last set in motion.

Survey of the monetary causes of revival.

The initial cause of recovery was a reduction in the medium-of-exchange demand for the *legal tender* type of money; the secondary effect was a strengthening of banking reserves; the third effect was an increase in the supply of bank credit money, owing to the banks buying more securities; the fourth effect of this growing redundancy of money, coupled with a rise in the bond market, was a diminished store-of-value demand for money. Which eventually would be followed, as trade improved, by an increased industrial demand for loans from the banks, which on being granted, would cause the creation of still more bank credit money; and this inflation, by adding to monetary redundancy, would cause still more spending.

Higher prices and better trade are the consequences of these forces.

This process will normally go on until at last the continuous expansion of prices, wages and trade has once more strained the credit resources of the banks, and yet a new slump is set in motion.

Government intervention in revival.

Looking back at the technical details of revival it will be seen that what really cured the slump was first the improved reserve ratios of the banks, and second the *natural* reflation of total bank credit brought about by the banks increasing their investments.

The question thus arises, can a government do anything to hasten on these reflationary and depression-curing forces? The answer is obviously, Yes.

Firstly, a government can artificially enlarge the cash reserves of the banks either by note inflation or gold devaluation; secondly, it can enlarge the reserves of the member banks by getting the reserve banks to invest surplus credit in government bills or bonds; while thirdly, in order to force extra credit into active circulation it can borrow from the member or reserve banks for public works, relief, etc., so that what it borrows will pass into the bank books of the general public, thereby creating a monetary redundancy precisely similar to that which normally occurs *automatically* as a result of the profit-seeking banks buying extra investments voluntarily.

Such government action may fairly be termed "artificial" but it will certainly have the practical effect of hastening on recovery.

Improvement in trade will occur (i) because the government deliberately borrows from the banks, when industrial borrowers are absent, thus hastening on the process of reflation; and (ii) because the re-spending at retail, by government employees, and by the employees of government contractors, of the money they receive for their non-reproductive work, will reduce retail inventories and eventually set a virtuous circle of replacement orders in motion. Which, when trade has grown in size, will eventually cause business men to borrow still more from the banks, thus causing still more monetary inflation, this time of the *natural* sort.

In other words, artificial reflation produces, with a lag, the normal phase of natural credit reflation.

A government can without doubt thus prime the pump *artificially,* and set in motion the processes of *natural* revival.

A process of cumulative change.

Reviewing the business cycle, as brought about by the monetary factors already described, what we find is as follows:

The business cycle itself is what is known as a process of cumulative change; that is to say, one set of conditions so reacts upon the minds and behavior of money-spending and money-lending men as to induce them collectively to perform a series of acts, which give rise to another set of conditions.

These new conditions have a new influence, and produce yet another set of circumstances; and so the process goes cumulatively on until at last the original economic conditions, with only minor variations, are once more reproduced; and a similar cycle then repeats. Thus,

Prosperity breeds strain.
Strain breeds collapse.
Collapse breeds nervousness and general depression.
Depression itself breeds healthier conditions.
Healthier conditions give rise to confidence.
As confidence improves, revival begins.
Revival gains momentum, through credit expansion.
Eventually revival leads to prosperity.
Prosperity develops into over-confidence and boom.
New strains develop.

Ultimately collapse eventuates, and the whole cycle repeats, with only minor variations.

The influence of a changing value of money.

Money is an influence on prosperity, however, not only because its volume and/or velocity varies; but also because its exchange-value, or general purchasing power as measured by index numbers, varies.

Wide fluctuations in the value of money automatically produce unhealthy depressions and booms.

This is due to two particular features of the modern capitalistic system, namely:

I. That the aim of industry is to make *money* profits.

II. That the major part of industry and commerce is conducted with *borrowed* money.

The price-level in relation to the cost-level.

As regards I, namely *The Profits System:* Modern business is conducted for money profits; but money profits are the difference between costs and prices; and in most industries the general cost level is relatively fixed and inflexible. Items such as rent, mortgage interest, maintenance, and a good many salaries cannot easily be changed, even if prices and sales and profits are all falling.

On the other hand, whereas a good many costs and contractual obligations are fixed, the selling prices of the commodities produced are determined by competition, and if money is being deflated, prices will fall rapidly, and the price level may fall to below the cost level, so that profits are wiped out.

Now if profits are wiped out in this manner, business men will cease employing labor, with the result that initial monetary factors may reduce not only production but also employment.

As regards II, namely *Loan Finance:* A large part of the borrowed money with which industry is conducted is borrowed for a long period of years at a fixed rate of interest.

Take, for instance, the mortgage on a farm: If the arranged rate of interest is 5%, the farmer may calculate that with wheat at say a dollar a bushel he will have to sell 50 bushels a year to pay the money interest on every $1000 bond. But, if for monetary reasons, wheat falls to 50 cents a bushel he will have to pay interest equivalent to 100 bushels; and, in order to pay back his loan, worth 1000 bushels when borrowed, he will have to sell 2000 bushels. Indeed, his total "real" annual payments instead of being 50 bushels yearly for 20 years, i.e., 1000 bushels in all, will be 2000 bushels for interest and in addition 2000 extra bushels will be needed to pay off his loan, i.e., 4000 bushels in all, instead of only 2000 bushels. Thus the "real" interest and the redemption burden is doubled.

Unstable money may thus ruin the borrower and transfer his real wealth fortuitously to the lender, banker or landlord.

The importance of monetary policy.

It can thus be seen that in a capitalist system of long-term debts, stable money is one of the first essentials both on the score of profits, business prosperity and fairness.

And yet (without deliberate monetary management) the capitalist system, as we have shown, is subject to a self-generating business cycle, and also to a cycle of prices.

Fortunately, however, a knowledge of the business cycle, in so far as it is caused by money (and is preventable by monetary policy), is rapidly growing.

In future, therefore, the success of a forecaster may largely depend on his ability to judge the extent to which the Government or Central Bank will step in and successfully control the course of the cycle.

Monetary policy may prove the future determinant of the long-run cyclical movements in general business, interest rates, bonds, commodity prices, trade prosperity, and common stocks.

Indeed this is what I have worked for for some years.

APPENDIX C

THE MECHANICS OF GOOD AND BAD TRADE
(A further explanation of business fluctuation)

The circuit flow of money.

To obtain a clear picture of why trade becomes depressed in the Capitalist System, and of what factors can cause it to recover, it is desirable to visualize the circuit flow of money through industry via the four great groups of trading entities—namely Retailers, Wholesalers, Manufacturers and Consumers. These four groups, all of whose members are holders of money and buyers and sellers of goods or services, can be represented diagrammatically by four rectangles as in the next diagram.

The normal circuit flow of money is, of course, from South to East, to North, to West, and so round again. A few short circuits can, however, occur; e.g., some money drifts from retailers and wholesalers directly into the consumer rectangle, in the form of wages; while, conversely, some money in the consumer rectangle, instead of being directly spent in the shops, is saved and invested in buying more plant direct from manufacturers for other manufacturers, etc. The major part of the monetary flow, however, flows round the complete circuit.

In addition to the above four great groups of "trading" entities there are two subsidiary entities, namely, the Bankers and the Government, who are also capable of influencing the general circuit flow of money and trade prosperity. These have been represented in our diagram by two dotted squares.

To study the causes of good and bad trade, i.e., of a large or small circuit flow of money on to goods, and on to labor, the following is a convenient method, particularly for those aiming at instituting cures.

THE MECHANICS OF GOOD AND BAD TRADE

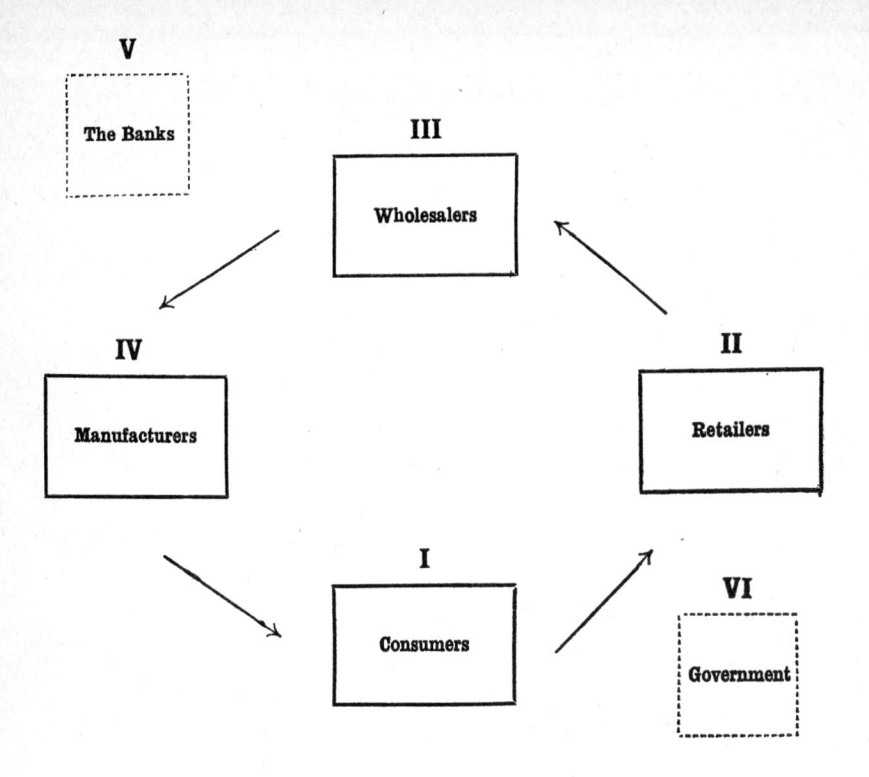

```
V                    III
The Banks         Wholesalers

IV                                    II
Manufacturers                      Retailers

            I
        Consumers              VI
                            Government
```

Take each of the six groups separately and consider what particular actions on its part will, by stimulating or checking the circuit flow of money, cause either good or bad trade. We shall thus have a bird's-eye view of the factors influencing trade as a whole; we shall also discover useful clues as to what should be done by each group, or by the government or the banks, so as to stimulate business activity.

The motivating forces in trade.

But before studying each of these groups in detail the following observations on the two motivating forces in trade, and in the circuit flow of money, are necessary:

APPENDIX C

I. Whether or not *Consumers* will part with any of the money they hold, depends on whether they think the goods in the shops are worth more to them than the money asked. If they do not think this, i.e., if they do not consider the bargains offered them good enough, consumers will hoard their money (i.e., continue to hold their wealth in the form of idle money rather than in consumable goods or real capital), and general incomes will come to a standstill. *Attractive bargains* must be offered to consumers or otherwise they will hoard.

II. Whether or not *Producers and Distributors* will part with their money in exchange for services and goods, thus propelling it onwards in its circuit flow, depends on whether or not they anticipate a profit from doing so. If they anticipate no profit they will cease buying goods and labor; and reproduction and general industrial incomes will soon come to a standstill. *Prospective profits* are therefore essential to the continued activity of retailers, wholesalers and producers.

As regards the three profit-seeking groups, i.e., retailers, wholesalers and manufacturers, it is important to notice that non-anticipation of profits on the part of *any* of the three groups may bring the circuit flow of money *as a whole* (and of goods) to a standstill; for it will mean that incomes cease at one point in the circuit flow and money will not flow onwards afterwards as usual.

* * *

But let us examine the six main groups of business entities— namely, retailers, wholesalers, manufacturers, consumers, bankers and the government—separately and in succession, with a view to summarizing what series of actions on the part of each will influence the circuit flow of money, either favorably or unfavorably.

Turn first to the Consumer group.

The influence of Group I, i.e., the consumers.

(i) *Hoarding.*—Consumers derive their incomes from wages, salaries, interest, rents, dividends and doles; and obviously consumers hold a large proportion of the total bank credit currency and legal tender in existence.

If they decide to hoard money, and do not spend it at retail, or invest it, the amount of money *moving* in the circuit flow is reduced. Hoarding is stimulated by either fear, the expectation of lower prices, or the recent satisfaction of existing wants.

Conversely if they try to reduce their average holdings, i.e., dishoard, the circuit flow of money is increased.

Dishoarding is stimulated by optimism concerning their own future incomes and the security of their jobs; by the expectation of higher prices, i.e., a declining value for money itself; or by gradual attrition of goods already in use.

(ii) *Bank Borrowing.*—Consumers can, however, influence the total amount of money in the Flow by borrowing from their bankers, either to buy goods at retail or in order to subscribe to new security issues (with the result that the money will be spent by the borrowers and thereby injected into the circuit stream of money either in the construction of new factories, bridges, houses, etc., or in the production or purchase of more goods or labor).

Consumers may also influence the circuit flow of money by borrowing to speculate on the Stock Exchange, the probability being that sooner or later most of the money thus borrowed will filter into the Industrial Flow either in the form of subscriptions to new issues by the investors who have recently sold securities to the speculators, or in the form of Stock Exchange profits spent on consumable goods (such profits being particularly likely to mature when newly-created bank money is speculatively spent on securities).

Incidentally, if consumers borrow from their bankers in order to pay taxes, the extra money is again likely to enter the Flow (unless the government uses the proceeds for paying off its own past bank loans).

(iii) *Instalment Buying.*—Another factor influencing the amount of money in the circuit flow is the buying of goods by the hire purchase system. Such purchases are usually financed by the retailers borrowing from their bankers the unpaid portion of the amount outstanding, and handing on this sum, coupled with the instalment already paid, to wholesalers. Thus the volume of hire purchase may itself be a powerful influence on the quantity of money in the circuit flow.

The influence of Group II, i. e., the retailers.

(i) *Stock Policy.*—If retailers decide to let their stocks run off, through political uncertainty, or because they expect a lower volume of sales, or because they anticipate a fall in prices, they will give fewer replacement orders to wholesalers, and wholesalers will give fewer orders to manufacturers. Manufacturers will therefore reduce their outputs, and since they will pay out less in wages, consumers will not be able to buy so much at retail as before.

Thus a change in the stock policy of retailers can reduce the circuit flow of money. Incidentally, it implies that the money which is not spent by the retailers on goods from wholesalers will be hoarded, or alternatively paid back in a deflationary manner to the banks.

Conversely, if retailers increase their stocks they will give more orders to wholesalers, and wholesalers will give more orders to manufacturers, so that the circuit flow of money will increase—the increase being financed either by dishoarding of previously hoarded money on the part of retailers, or by additional (inflationary) borrowing on their part from the banks.

(ii) *Wage Scales.*—Another factor capable of slightly affecting the circuit flow of money is the payments by retailers of lower wages and salaries; for less of their own money or of borrowed bank money will be paid out into the circuit flow, and the size of effective consumer demand will be thereby diminished.

(iii) *Reduced Bank Loans.*—It should also be noted that if the banks call in loans from retailers the latter will be forced to reduce their inventories, and also to give fewer orders to wholesalers; thus the squeezing of retailers by the banks will itself affect the circuit flow of money.

(iv) *The Hoarding of Profits.*—A minor point is that if retailers, after making profits, fail to pay out any dividends and hoard the money in their banks, the circuit flow of what would otherwise have been dividend-money will be reduced owing to the hoarding of their profits by retailers. (This, of course, also applies to wholesalers and manufacturers.)

The influence of Group III, i.e., the wholesalers.

The motives which cause wholesalers to reduce or increase the circuit flow of money are virtually the same as in the case of retailers, i.e.—

(i) A change in stock policy owing to fear or confidence, or owing to the expectation of lower or higher prices;

(ii) Increased or decreased borrowing from their bankers;

(iii) Lowering or raising wages;

(iv) Hoarding, or full distribution, of profits.

The influence of Group IV, i.e., the manufacturers.

(i) *Inventory Policy.*—In so far as manufacturers make for stock, without securing orders in advance, a change in inventory policy on their part will alter the volume of their manufacture and will consequently alter the amount they pay out in wages, salaries and other costs. Here, again, fear or confidence, or the expectation of lower or higher prices, will play a powerful part in governing their behavior.

(ii) *Wage Scales.*—A second factor influencing the total amount that manufacturers pay out into the circuit stream of money is an alteration in their scale of wages and salaries. A reduction in wage rates implies that the manufacturers hoard money, or borrow less from their bankers, and that the subsequent circuit flow to consumers is, in consequence, reduced.

(iii) *Hoarding profits* has a similar net effect.

(iv) *Bank-borrowing.*—Obviously in so far as manufacturers increase or decrease the amount they borrow from their bankers, either for manufacture itself or for repair of machinery, advertisement, or for paying taxes, the amount of money which they inject into the circuit stream will be influenced.

The influence of Group V, i.e., the bankers.

The influence of the banks on trade can be either (i) Passive or (ii) Active.

We have already described the *passive* part which banks may play in influencing the total stream of money by granting extra loans, on request, to retailers, wholesalers, manufacturers and consumers; and it follows that if at any time these four groups *voluntarily* repay outstanding loans from bankers, the quantity of money in the circuit flow will be thereby reduced, *unless* the bankers *actively* inject it into public circulation once again by deliberately increasing the quantity of their investments. Indeed it is mainly by changing the volume of their investments that the bankers *actively,* as distinct from *passively,* increase the total volume of money in the circuit flow.

Likewise the banks can *actively* reduce the total amount of money in the circuit flow by calling in loans—either because their cash reserves have fallen, because gold is being lost abroad, because the market value of collateral is shrinking, or because they are nervous about the future standing of their clients or about the future of prices.

It is sometimes said that the banks cannot *actively* influence industry and the price level, and that instead of their actions governing trade, they are merely governed by it. This is not entirely true. They can, and do, at times, play an active, as well as a passive, part in influencing the quantity of money, and industry.

The influence of Group VI, i.e., the government.

The government can also influence not only the quantity of money in the circuit flow, but also its Velocity.

(i) *The Quantity of Money.*—Assuming a country is not on the gold standard, and that the government controls the note issue, it can inflate the latter and inject extra money into general circulation either by increasing its total expenditure or meeting its budgetary deficits, not by taxation, but by the injection of inflationary notes into general circulation.

Similarly, by borrowing from the banks a government can influence the total quantity of money in the general circuit stream.

On the other hand, a government can, by increasing taxation or by borrowing money out of the *bona fide* savings of the public, withdraw currency notes, or pay off bank loans, thereby reducing the quantity of money in the stream.

(ii) *The Velocity of Money.*—As regards the speeding up of the Velocity of circulation of existing money, it is to be noted that, if investors in general are too nervous to purchase anything except government securities, a government can, by floating loans for public works, make the *bona fide* savings of the public (which would otherwise have been hoarded) flow more actively through general industry.

Summary.

Reviewing the circuit flow of money as a whole, the following points are worth noting:

(1) General trade, i.e., the movement or circuit-Velocity of money, can be stimulated (as well as checked) by action taken at *any* of the four main points of the compass on our diagram: i.e., by Retailers on the East; Wholesalers on the North; Manufacturers on the West; and Consumers on the South.

(2) Each of the four trading groups has it in its power to affect, not only the Velocity of the money in the circuit flow (by either hoarding or dishoarding), but also the total Quantity of money in the circuit flow, either by increasing or decreasing the amount it borrows from its bankers.

(3) It is also to be noted that the bankers themselves, without *passively* waiting either for voluntary repayments of old loans, or for new demands from business for extra loans, can *actively* influence the amount of money in the circuit flow by varying the volume of their own investments in securities and property, or by calling in loans.

(4) Furthermore, by inflating paper currency or by borrowing credit currency from the banks in order to balance its budget or to finance public works, etc., the government can also actively influence the total Quantity of money in the general circuit flow. Velocity can also be influenced by the expenditure of loans raised from the previously hoarding public.

(5) Although one or more of the six important groups (i.e., consumers, retailers, wholesalers, manufacturers, bankers and

the government) may be doing something which tends to diminish the flow as a whole, the other groups may simultaneously be doing something which tends to increase it.

(6) If, however, the six groups are all doing something which augments the general flow, trade will be good; while if all six groups are doing something harmful, trade will be bad.

(7) Finally, since trade in general can be made good or bad either by a change in the Velocity of the money already in the circuit flow, or by a change in its Quantity, the latter factor may be used to stimulate or offset the former. Monetary management, in fact, may be used as a weapon to stabilize prices, and to iron out such industrial fluctuation as is due to variations in the demand for money or in Confidence.

APPENDIX D

THE PROBLEM OF CONFIDENCE

It is not generally realized that there are at least four entirely different sorts of Economic confidence namely:

(i) Confidence in the government;

(ii) Confidence in the banks, i.e., the places where people (nominally) *keep* their money;

(iii) Confidence in money itself; and

(iv) Business confidence.

Let us consider these four forms of confidence separately:

(i) Confidence in the *government* entails a galaxy of ideas which vary with the political creeds of the persons affected. But, economically speaking, the matter very largely boils down to the balancing of the budget, the scale of taxation, and government interference in industry.

(ii) Confidence in the banks is, of course, essential to trade; otherwise the public will encash their deposits for legal tender and cause, first credit restriction and deflation (because of strained reserve-ratios), and then perhaps a run on the banks.

(iii) As regards confidence in *money:* it looks, at first sight, as if the more a government could increase the confidence of the public and of foreigners in the national money, the greater would be business confidence, and the better in consequence would be the state of trade. But this, as it happens, is frequently not so.

To increase confidence in money implies creating the general belief that money itself will appreciate in value rather than depreciate; which (i) from a domestic point of view implies the belief that prices will fall rather than rise, i.e., that a deflation will occur, and (ii) from the foreign point of view implies the belief that the currency of the country will appreciate over the foreign exchanges.

Neither of these beliefs is positively good for home trade. Indeed nothing is worse under the Capitalistic system, motivated as it is by Profits, than the expectation of declining prices. Moreover an appreciating exchange-rate—under paper, as distinct from gold—stimulates imports and checks exports, thus reducing profit margins and upsetting Business confidence.

The ideal, of course, is a suitable confidence in money, but not *increasing* confidence. The practical question is one of moderation and degree—for obviously *serious* lack of confidence in money should be carefully guarded against.

(iv) As regards *Business* Confidence: Business Confidence emanates from the belief among business men that they will be able to make profits; and such a belief is to some extent fostered by the anticipation of a rising, rather than a falling, price level. In other words, Business Confidence can on occasions be engendered by *slightly* destroying Monetary Confidence. It may sound exotic to make this remark; it is, however, true.

As regards the inter-relationship between business confidence and monetary confidence: I am far from saying that *all* prospective rises in prices are healthy. If, however, the general price level has recently been deflated below a relatively undeflated cost level, definite reflation on the part of the government is the only wise and sensible policy—even though, in terms of words, such a policy can rightly be stigmatized (*sic*) "as destroying Confidence in Money."

If, on the other hand, the price level has *already* been reflated into line with the cost level, I am *not* in favor of further inflation—i.e., reducing Confidence in Money *still further;* for if such a policy were pursued it would set up new dis-equilibrium in the opposite direction.

The fact remains, however, that at certain stages of the business cycle it *should* be the policy of the government to reflate prices—i.e., to destroy, rather than to increase, monetary confidence! (But such a policy, of course, should not continue *forever;* for just as a man can either eat healthily or over-eat, so can a government reflate healthily or over-reflate, i.e., inflate.)

Reflation should cease when the price level is again in line with the relatively rigid cost level.

A government should realize, however, that, in so far as its spokesmen declare that they are anxious to restore business confidence by raising prices, it is merely the same thing as saying that they are anxious, for the time being, to reduce to some extent (destroy, if you like!) Confidence in Money. To talk otherwise—though it sounds palatable—is to shun the truth.

The essence of the matter is that Business and Monetary confidence are to some extent in conflict. Business confidence is created by (mild) inflation and reflation. Confidence in money, on the other hand, is augmented by deflation—which destroys business confidence.

Note, incidentally, that if confidence increases rapidly, to the extent that the resultant increase in the Velocity of money causes an unhealthy inflationary rise in prices, the Currency Controller should deflate the quantity of money so as to counteract the unhealthy Velocity-inflation.

A control of quantity can (and, I think, should) be used to influence Velocity. The supply of money can be manipulated to influence the (store-of-value) demand for money, and therefore Velocity and Confidence.

Excursus.

Lest any reader might be tempted to describe me as an inflationist, please let me say that I am neither an inflationist nor a deflationist. I merely want to see the *Volume* of money and/or bank credit manipulated, so as to keep the *Purchasing Power* of money stable. In fact, just as the driver of an automobile should pull his steering wheel down to the right when the car is going too far to the left; and vice versa; so should those in charge of the currency and credit policy of a country turn the supply of money on and off, according as the tendency of money, when left to itself, is to fall or rise in purchasing power too fast.

Some people say that it is dangerous to entrust politicians (or their nominees) with the management of the nation's money. Drunken drivers, they say, are dangerous!

But surely nothing could be worse than a continuously moving car without any driver. Consider the 1929-33 slump in U. S. A. [And after all the drivers can quite well be sober.]

The alternatives are:
    (i) No control (as in 1932).
    (ii) Control by private (possibly vested) interests; or
    (iii) Political control.

Each country must choose between the three—although perhaps a satisfactory compromise between (ii) and (iii) is possible.

APPENDIX E
HOW TO CURE UNEMPLOYMENT
(An excursus)

1. *Democratic Governments are usually afraid of pursuing the policies necessary to Capitalism. The voting masses suffer.*

Much of the depression which occurs in modern industry could be prevented if democratic governments, who express themselves profoundly concerned with the problem of bad trade and unemployment, would realize that, although they are democratically elected and depend for their votes on a public which, for the most part, are not capitalists except in a very small way, their industrial systems are nevertheless still highly capitalistic.

Although they declare themselves anxious to improve trade and employment, most governments are so busy keeping an eye on the votes of the masses that they either cannot or will not see that what would really improve the condition of the masses most under Capitalism is a highly capitalistic policy calculated in the short run to lose votes.

Any government wishing to stimulate trade and employment in the capitalist system must appreciate that business men will not employ workmen unless they expect profits; and that, therefore, the first essential for curing widespread unemployment is to create the belief among business men, not only that high profits will be made, but also that the business men will be allowed to retain them.

To the unemployed workman it may, of course, appear that a policy of enriching the capitalist, prior to enriching the unemployed, is immoral and unsound; and many politicians, in their desire to please the electorate, hesitate to advocate any policy which is deliberately aimed at augmenting profits.

But the fact is that we still live under a capitalist system, and so long as this Profits System endures, governments must take the world as it is and *always* pursue a policy promising high profits to capitalist employers. Nor, in the long run, does this apparently unfair policy of favoring the capitalist matter either to consumers or wage-earners.

In the long run, capitalism, by its process of competitive investment, will always tend to reduce profits in any industry to a minimum; for if any one industry becomes abnormally prosperous and makes high profits, new capital, unless monopoly exists, will be attracted into it; and as soon as the gestation period of new plant is over, additional goods will come on the market. This augmentation of supply in a competitive market will soon reduce both profits and prices in that industry, so that the consumer will benefit in the wake of the capitalist.

Similarly as regards wages: other things being equal, employers are anxious to keep wages at a minimum in their *own* businesses. But if an industry, and industry in general, is making high profits, production will expand and more men will be wanted. Competition for men will grow, and trade unions will be able to obtain higher wages for their workers. Capitalists, however, *must* be making high profits *before* the wage-earners have a chance of higher wages. To amplify profits is, under capitalism, the latch-key to high wages and full employment.

2. *Profit margins must be protected.*

Therefore if wages and profits at any time are low, and unemployment is rife, the first duty of a government, under the capitalist system, is to create a profit reflation: An enlargement of profits is the *first* goal at which to aim.

Socialists may object, on political principle, to profits as such, and possibly to the social injustice of such a plan; but they must agree, on economic principle, that so long as capitalism endures, this is the most effective policy for governments to adopt, even though they may lose some votes on the part of those who think that all profits should be reduced to a minimum by government intervention.

APPENDIX F

THE INFLUENCE OF THE MARKET ON THE NATIONAL ECONOMY

In Chapter XI we showed that the prices of securities were governed, *via* demand and supply, *by* the Average Opinion of the Public.

To what extent is the public's purchasing power altered by falls and rises in securities?

What puzzles most people, however, is not so much that prices can move as a result of "opinion" (without "real" worth necessarily having altered) as that riches can apparently be augmented on the Stock Exchange by rises in securities, i.e., by changes in opinion.

Stock Exchange securities taken at market price are regarded as tangible wealth because Stock Exchange securities are supposedly saleable. A man, in fact, regards his securities (taken at market value) as being part of his personal reserves of wealth and as easily convertible into exercisable purchasing power.

Therefore if a man invests a certain sum of money on the Stock Exchange, and if a fall then occurs in his securities, he wonders where all his money has gone—and who, if anyone, has actually gained the money that he once clearly invested and now has apparently lost. On the other hand, if a rise occurs he regards himself as having "made" money and as having become definitely richer.

These various problems can best be unravelled by taking a simple hypothetical case.

Take a simplified economy where there are only two investors, A and B.

APPENDIX F

A has £1,000. B has 100 silk shares.

B sells his 100 silk shares to A for £1,000. Current price therefore equals £10.

Several weeks later B thinks he has made a mistake and wants to buy the shares back. A, however, will not sell under £12 10s. B, however, may now think them worth at least £12 10s.—probably £15. He therefore buys back 80 at £12 10s., paying the full £1,000. Price now equals £12 10s.

A, however, a short while afterwards also repents of having sold his 80 shares back to B at £12 10s. A, too, begins to think that future earnings are going to be much higher, and that the shares will eventually be worth, say, £25. A therefore buys back, say, 50 out of his recently sold 80 at £20 apiece (costing £1,000), thereby re-increasing his holding from 20 up to 70.

Thus A, instead of having 100 silk shares as originally, now has only 70, but since they are valued at £20 each he is worth on paper £1,400, instead of only £1,000 as originally, and his paper profit is therefore £400.

B, on the other hand, has again got back his originally acquired £1,000 in cash, but he has also 30 silk shares as well, worth £20 each, which means a paper profit of £600.

A thus "feels" richer by £400, B by £600.* (*Read the footnote.*)

* It will be seen that the foregoing process could continue indefinitely until the shares had risen to £40 or £80 apiece. Thus with only £1,000 of money, a capital appreciation of £2,000 or more could have been gradually effected. And if this thing had happened not only to the silk shares, but also *in succession,* with the *same* £1,000, to some hundreds of other securities, capital appreciation of perhaps hundreds of thousands of pounds could have been caused with the aid of only £1,000 of actual money. Thus a small amount of money, by flowing and re-flowing in the right way (i.e., if its velocity increases, as a result of confidence, more rapidly than that of shares), can, if opinions about values are changing, cause in succession an increase

Both are, in fact, richer *on paper* because share prices rose (opinion, of course, having caused the rise via Demand and Supply).

To go back, however, to our original case: the amount of money available throughout the original series of transactions was always the same, i.e., only £1,000; the amount of silk shares in existence was also always the same; and quite possibly the industrial earnings on the silk shares (i.e., the "real" values) did not alter in the least. Price, however, was altered by changing opinion, operating via Demand and Supply, i.e., by the relative flows or relative velocities of the two things called savings and silk shares. All parties made so-called money out of each other—purely because their average opinion happened curiously to change.

The impossibility of encashing paper profits faster than new savings accumulate.

If, however, both A and B (as referred to in our original argument) suddenly decided to encash their paper profits of in capital values on paper of many times its own actual amount. A money-capital of only £1,000 value can by beating upon shares in succession create paper capital values of millions of pounds in theory. [We are, of course, here neglecting the wastage caused by jobbers' turns, commissions, stamp duties, etc.] On the other hand, it might stop short at a much more modest figure. It all depends on how money flows as a result of what people *on an average* think.

Furthermore, it is immaterial whether only two persons are concerned in the circle of transactions, or whether the circle is enlarged to two or more million persons. If B buys silk shares from C instead of from A again, and if D buys from B, and so on, the same price-movements can eventuate in the market in the same shares with the same sum of money. Every share on the Stock Exchange can thus double in value, given the right flow of money and the right opinions. There need not be any more money about, and the Companies need *not* be earning any more.

APPENDIX F

£400 and £600 respectively (or, worse still, if profits had risen to £800 and £1,200 respectively and they still tried to encash them), the competition to sell the silk shares—to each other, in this case—and to get ready money out of each other, would lead to a serious deadlock.

£2,000 worth of shares (or more) would be for sale and only £1,000 of real money would be available (and incidentally in the above particular case B would hold it all).

B, however, would not be a buyer because he too was a seller; the market would thus be sellers only, and sellers would outnumber buyers. A deadlock would of course ensue, and nothing on earth (unless new savers came in) could enable them both to cash their paper profits for money. There would be no buyers; and the attempt to cash paper profits would obviously cause market prices rapidly to fall and the paper profits would entirely disappear.

Thus although a small amount of real money can cause enormous increases in paper-capital (if average opinion is sufficiently favorable), attempts to encash these paper values may suddenly cause them to vanish.

This is just the sort of thing that happens on the Stock Exchange. With the aid of a very small amount of newly saved money (or bank loans), jobbers' stocks can be denuded and prices can rise to any extent that people are optimistic enough to think the shares worth. (In fact even so small a sum as £2 million can, we believe, in London, cause a capital appreciation on paper of several hundred millions, merely as a result of denuding jobbers' stocks and being spent in *succession* on a large number of different securities.* *Read the footnote.*)

---

* It might be thought that denudation of jobbers' stocks and the marking up of prices, such as would result from the sudden expenditure of, say, £2 millions of public savings, might be cancelled as soon as the price-rise had induced the public to come in and sell, thus

INFLUENCE OF MARKET ON NATIONAL ECONOMY

If, however, people in general try to encash any part of these newly created paper profits, over and above, say, the £2 millions of cash originally made available, then unless extra new money of equal volume flows simultaneously into the Stock Exchange, selling orders will exceed buying orders and a collapse in the shares will be inevitable (and hundreds of millions of paper profits may suddenly be wiped out),* purely because people in general are trying to perform the impossible and take more money out of the Stock Exchange than is simultaneously available or put in.

Thus looking at the matter as a whole, although the public may enjoy their profits "on paper," they must not, taken as a whole as distinct from as individuals, ever try to enjoy these profits in practice. They must not try to encash nor expend them; for wholesale attempts to convert paper wealth into monetary wealth tends to cause the former to disappear.

The utmost the public can ever hope to get out in cash and enabling jobbers to replace their stocks (at the now higher prices). But it must be clearly realized that the money paid out by jobbers in replacing their stocks is received again by the investing public who can once more spend it and force up the prices of yet other shares. Thus the same small amount of money can, by again flowing into the Stock Exchange in the right manner, cause capital appreciation of many times its own absolute amount.

* This is what always happens in booms, say in rubbers, industrials, tins, etc. One or two million pounds cause a capital appreciation of, say, one hundred millions, and while the rise is taking place people hold hard to their shares. When, however, shares begin to look fully valued, a few people try to take profits, say to the tune of 5% only of the total paper capital appreciation of £100 million = £5 millions. Only £2 millions at most, however, is available, and even this may already have largely disappeared in commissions, subscriptions to new issues, and so on. The attempt, therefore, to get £5 millions out of the Stock Exchange may lead to a collapse—unless perchance new savings flow in either from the public or from abroad.

331

to spend (as a result of selling securities) is the actual cash that others are willing to put in. For the money which they have personally put in has more often than not been dissipated.

Money invested on the Stock Exchange is rarely withdrawable. It has usually flowed on from the Stock Exchange into industry.

If people invest money on the Stock Exchange it does not remain there permanently in an idle or liquid and withdrawable form, requiring only the sale of some security to make it immediately available.

Most of the money invested in *old* securities on the Stock Exchange flows on at second or third hand into industry in the form of subscriptions to new issues; and this happens regardless of whether the original purchases are made with permanent bona fide savings or with money borrowed only temporarily from the banks.

For instance, in 1929, over a thousand million dollars of new loans were made by New York banks against Stock Exchange securities either at call or short notice—and many writers, including bankers, complained that "industry was being starved of this money."

Money loaned to or spent on the Stock Exchange, however, disappears in the following five ways:

1. Commissions and expenses.
2. Withdrawals for private spending, after sales of securities.
3. Withdrawals for making repayments to the banks, ditto.
4. Withdrawals for foreign account, ditto.
5. Subscriptions to new issues on the part of recent sellers of securities.

It is undoubtedly true that some *small* part of the thousand million dollars loaned in 1929 to the New York Stock Exchange (over and above what was lent in 1928) was used up in the forms 1, 2, 3 and 4, but the major part certainly flowed, from investor to investor, eventually into industry in U. S. A., in the form of subscriptions to new issues.

A little, it is true, may have remained idle in the form of brokers' and investors' unexpended money balances, but most of it passed, after only short delays, into the hands of manufacturers and traders in commodities.

In other words bank money originally loaned short to brokers is eventually re-loaned long to, or sunk permanently in, industry by investors, either on the producer or the consumer side.

Industry thus receives, at one or two removes, almost the whole of any loans made by banks to the Stock Exchange. Industry, of course, is *not* starved of the money.

If, however, the banks suddenly call in these loans, then unless new bona fide savings are simultaneously forthcoming to an equal amount, selling orders will exceed buying orders and security prices must fall.

In fact, too rapid attempts at deflating Stock Exchange bank loans are mathematically bound to lead to Stock Exchange crises.

Similarly, it is impossible for the public to withdraw past savings previously invested *on the Stock Exchange* in the form of money faster than new money savings (or new bank loans or foreign funds) accumulate; because the bona fide savings will normally have been re-invested in industry quite quickly, and industrial companies as distinct from investors will have become possessed of the funds.

Money invested on the Stock Exchange does not in fact remain there permanently and thus build up a big idle pool or reservoir of liquid monetary purchasing power which can immediately be drawn upon; it flows rapidly away into industry so that if attempts at withdrawal exceed the tiny pool of money left in (plus the sums which accumulate as a result of *new* savings and new bank loans), there will automatically be a slump as a result of the attempt to perform the impossible.

Conclusions.

We thus see that although the investors composing the public regard all the funds they stand possessed of in Stock Exchange securities as easily realizable, their belief is in truth a misapprehension. Attempts to turn securities into cash faster than new savings flow in lead to the paper values of securities disappearing. Investors as a whole, therefore, as a result of trying in a body to do what they believe they can do individually, may lose as a body millions (on paper) although no one else gains, on paper, what they lose.*

Conversely, if a small surplus of money flows into the Stock Exchange while investors in general are optimistic, this small surplus may cause prices to rise to such an extent that everyone becomes much richer (on paper) without anyone becoming poorer.

* We must here protect ourselves by saying that we reject, for reasons which we lack space to enlarge on, the following popular though fallacious contentions:
1. That bears gain on paper or in cash *all* that bulls lose on paper.
2. That the people who sell high up gain all that buyers and holders eventually lose on paper.
3. That if securities fall in price, the exchange-value or purchasing power of money (and everything else) increases in proportion, and that, therefore, owners of money (and other things) gain all that shareholders lose.

For instance, in U. S. A. in 1928 share prices rose 50% above their previous highests of all time. Billions of dollars were thus made on paper, without anyone becoming a penny the poorer, either on paper or in cash (except possibly an occasional bear who had to pay out cash differences).

By the end of 1929, however, a third of this paper wealth had disappeared, and everyone felt much poorer. No one, at the end of this period, felt he had gained what others had lost.

This point is obvious in the case of any newly issued security which, as the result of a very few subsequent deals, suddenly doubles in price. Nobody loses what the holders have obviously gained on paper.

Conversely, if the same share eventually falls back to par, nobody gains on paper what the holders, on paper, obviously have just lost.

The foregoing remarks, however, have referred in the main to paper values. In terms of actual cash there is a somewhat different equation. If bears make money by selling short, it is true they have gained in cash what the bulls have lost in cash; but they do not gain all that the other shareholders, taken as a whole, lose on paper.

Then again there is the question of cash expenses. In England, Stock Exchange commissions, taxes and jobbers' turns absorb approximately fifteen million pounds of the public savings each year (i.e., roughly 6% of all savings invested in new issues); investors, therefore, *inevitably* lose this amount *in cash* each year and are *ipso facto* bound to become poorer to that extent *unless* paper values as a whole increase to an equal amount.

Rises and falls in securities do not, however, make the owners, or the country as a whole, absolutely richer or poorer, because paper values are *not* spendable and are not true wealth or purchasing power. They only make them "feel" richer or poorer. But let us go back to the problem of price movements.

Putting money "into" shares.

Some people say that for prices to rise by any considerable amount, it is necessary for a large amount of money to flow into the Stock Exchange. But as we have shown this is not necessarily so at all. What fundamentally causes prices to change is "average opinion," and this influences the willingness of owners-of-money to buy and of owners-of-shares to sell. If average opinion changes, these "willingnesses" change, and the offerings of both, i.e., the velocity of shares in relation to money within the market alters. Fewer shares get sold for the same money, or vice versa; hence there need not necessarily be any more money, or more shares, either dealt in, or in existence.

Buying exceeding selling.

Another popular fallacy should also be exploded. People talk loosely about Buying exceeding Selling; but for there to be a buyer there must also be a seller; and buying and selling are always equal.

The "quality" of the buying may, it is true, vary, shares passing from strong to weak hands, or vice versa; but the "volume" of buying in relation to the volume of selling does not vary except insofar as jobbers may slightly increase or decrease their middleman-holdings. Would-be sellers may exceed would-be buyers *at a given price,* but actual sellers or sales cannot exceed actual buyers or purchasers.

The wastage of savings.

It is also frequently, though fallaciously, stated, that a general rise in prices, if and when it has occurred, must have absorbed a large amount of the public's savings or of bank credit. But this need not be so at all.

If A has savings, and spends his savings on *old* issues of securities, as distinct from on new flotations, the seller receives the money which the buyer pays; and the amount of uninvested money on the sidelines remains identical, except for expenses.

In other words, money flows not into the Stock Exchange but through the Stock Exchange; and not *into* securities (except new issues), but *over* them. The buying of *old* securities does not absorb new savings, except in respect of brokerage and expenses.

New issues, of course, absorb part of the total amount of uninvested savings: the diversion in this case being on to the producer's side of industry.

Similarly, the selling of securities (either at a profit or a loss) to buy commodities, etc., also absorbs the public's savings: this time on the consumer's side of industry.

But the purchase of *old* securities does not absorb savings, nor *ipso facto* alter the amount of uninvested monetary capital, looking at the market as a whole.

The economics of brokers' loans.

For bankers to say that their loans to the Stock Exchange reduce the amount of short-term resources that they themselves might have lent for personally financing trade, by means of short-term loans, *is* true.

Indeed for bankers to say that brokers' loans absorb the credit resources of bankers is also true. But for them to say it diverts money from industry is untrue—because almost all of it flows on either into the producer or the consumer side of industry. It merely diverts money from the short loan market to other channels.

* * *

Nationally speaking, a dangerous feature about a large amount of short-term brokers' loans is that even though they may be well secured on paper, at the time of the loan, the money thus lent flows on into industry, either on the producer's or the consumer's side—assuming it is not held idle on the sidelines—and the result may be that if ever a wave of fear sweeps the country, the bankers may call in the short-term loans (even though the money has probably been re-invested long in industry). The only result can be a Stock Exchange crisis.

Indeed, in the period 1926-1929 the American banks lent seven thousand million dollars short to the Stock Exchange (most of which was re-invested in industry); and when the boom broke in 1929, four and one-half billion was called in, or voluntarily paid back, within three months, thus leading to panic and bank credit deflation and industrial disaster.

Collectively, the whole operation was foolish, although each banking loan was probably well secured at the time.

The influence of security price movements on trade.

To conclude, let us consider the influence of security price movements on trade. Since paper values, taken as a whole, are not spendable purchasing power, rises and falls in the prices of securities do not *directly* influence trade. Security prices do, however, make people "feel" richer or poorer, and thereby may influence "willingness to spend," "desire to save," and hoarding, i.e., the "velocity of re-spending of any money already received."

Rises in the prices of securities also increase the borrowing power of individuals—and if there is still some slack in the banking system, bank loans (and expenditure) may be increased as a direct result of the rise in securities. Trade may thus directly benefit. Conversely, a fall in security prices may lead to the calling in of bank loans made against share collateral, with the result that public savings that might have been devoted to new issues, and therefore to trade (for long-term purposes), may be devoted at one remove to the paying off of these bank loans, and a deflation of the nation's credit currency may result.*

Apart from this, however, and apart from the fact that when shares fall people feel poorer and tend to hoard their money and spend less rapidly, and vice versa, trade is not *directly* affected by general movements in security prices.

* Even if the bankers lend it out again, they will probably only lend it out "short," although in all probability it will be long loans rather than short-term advances that industry requires.

APPENDIX G

A METHOD OF ANALYZING SECURITIES

NOTE—*The contents of this Appendix, which are highly redundant, should not be read by anyone who has just completed this book. They are meant solely as a brief refresher for use in practice on future occasions.*

The ideal time to buy a share is:
1. When the industry is rising.
2. When the company is reviving. (Preferably during the second year as shown by a share-chart.)
3. When the shares are conjuncturally depressed, and yet are receiving renewed market attention, i.e., on the upturns.
4. When the shares are cheap on earnings.

Short- and long-run factors should all simultaneously be favorable; as also should internal and external factors.

* * *

When analyzing shares the following five main groups of factors should be considered:

GROUP A

FACTORS AFFECTING THE SINGLE COMPANY

I. The trend of the profits of the industry taken as a whole.
II. The trend of profits; and the finances and prospects of the particular company.
III. The characteristics, market price, and technical position of the actual share.

A METHOD OF ANALYZING SECURITIES

GROUP B
Factors Affecting Securities as a Whole

IV. Short-run conjunctural factors.

V. Long-run cyclical dangers.

In analyzing these five factors proceed on the following lines:

I

In analyzing the trend of any single industry consider:

1. Bargaining power as between producer and consumer, e.g. The extent to which existing plant is unoccupied; and the volume of unsold stocks.

2. The trend of demand, e.g.
    1. Is demand geometric or of only a normal character?
    2. What is the likely volume of demand for replacement?
    3. Is durability increasing?
    4. What is the likely volume of demand for expansion?
    5. Is demand much influenced by price?
    6. Does consumption depend on fashion?
    7. Is a rival industry growing up?
    8. Has saturation apparently been reached?
    9. Has the commodity a long attrition period?

3. The trend of supply.
    1. Can existing plant immediately expand its output, or is it already working full time?
    2. Is much new plant now being built? If so, when will it come to fruition?
    3. What is the trend of foreign supply? Is foreign dumping likely? Are tariffs likely to be lowered?

4. The trend of Costs.

5. Is the industry monopolistic or is it subject to fierce internal competition?

APPENDIX G

II

In analyzing the state of the single company consider:

1. Past profit trend.
2. Relative success compared with rival companies.
3. Extent to which the company is now fully employed.
4. Extent to which the company has recently enlarged, or is enlarging, its plant or commitments.
5. Current finances, debts, and so on.
6. Efficiency of management.
7. Reputation of directors.
8. Extent to which depreciation has been allowed for.
9. Extent to which earnings have been distributed.
10. Remarks made by chairman at the last meeting.
11. State of order-book and forward contracts.

III

When analyzing the condition of a share consider:

1. Freeness of the market.
2. Current yield.
3. Earnings on present market price.
4. Could the company easily have paid a higher dividend last year?
5. Equity leverage of ordinary share capital (reckoned at its current market price—not at par).
6. Existence of bull or bear account.
7. Position of present price on share-chart relative to apparent high and low parallels.
8. Apparent cyclical trend of the share.
9. Apparent trend for the last twelve months.
10. Normal range of conjunctural fluctuation.

A METHOD OF ANALYZING SECURITIES

11. Do directors or pools normally manipulate the shares?
12. Does the share belong to a share-group which is now over-popular and abnormally active?
13. Present position of index-curve representing the group of shares (if any) to which the single share belongs (e.g., Tins, Teas, etc.). Is this index-curve near its own high or low parallels?
14. When is the report or the dividend declaration due?
15. What is the apparent scope for rise in the shares?
16. What did the chairman say in his speech a year ago?

IV

When analyzing the short-run condition of the Stock Exchange as a whole, i.e., the conjuncture, consider:

1. Sentiment.
    (i) Economic:—Dangers looming ahead, and their likely dates.
    (ii) Political:—Ditto.

2. Volume of money available.
    (i) Trend of the banking position.
    (ii) Direction of the flow of international funds.
    (iii) Probable surplus or deficit between bona fide savings and new issues.
    (iv) Extent to which investments are likely to be realized with a view to obtaining cash. (Seasonal factors.)

3. Index curve representing ordinary shares as a whole.
    (i) Present position of the conjunctural curve in relation to its high and low parallels.
    (ii) Time for which, and extent to which, shares in general have recently been rising or falling.

APPENDIX G

V

In analyzing long-run cyclical dangers such as affect the Stock Exchange as a whole, consider:

1. General profit curve of the country.
2. General trend of conditions abroad.
3. Curve of domestic production and employment.
4. General trend of commodity prices.
5. Yield on ordinary shares in relation to bonds.
6. Height of bank rate in relation to bond-yield, and to the ordinary share yield.
7. Is the bank rate likely soon to be raised on account of conditions abroad?

* * *

The investor might here refer to Chapters XXVI and XLIII, where our general principles of investment were briefly summarized.

SUGGESTED RULES FOR BUYING AND SELLING

I Selection Rules	II Timing Rules	III Cartographical Rules	IV Mathematical Rules
Only buy the Market Leaders.	Never buy sharply falling shares; always wait for them to "saucer out."	Only buy near the lower parallels.	Only buy if present price is 15% below recent highest.
Prefer geometric industries.	Buy only in conjunctural depressions; but only on signs of revival.	Only buy on the upturns.	Hesitate to buy on top of an immediate rise of much over 10%.
Always beware of booming trades.	Beware of buying in cyclical depressions in single industries unless they have lasted four years.	Avoid all shares with falling means; never try to hit cyclical bottoms.	
Insist on earnings of 8%.			
Beware of companies if their profits have risen continuously for four years.	Beware of buying in conjunctural depressions unless they have lasted ten weeks.	But go with the tide when a *narrow* track is broken.	
Prefer the second year of revival.			
Avoid companies which lag behind rival companies.	Sell "prospect" shares when conjunctures waver.	Sell when old rising bottoms are crossed on the down side (and vice versa).	Sell on a loss of 20%.
			Sell if earnings fall 10%.
Sell on internal deterioration; or if dividends, or if the prices of products, are lowered.	Sell the bulk of your ordinary shares if national profits decline.	Avoid ordinary shares (except gold shares) as long as the national index of shares-in-general displays a falling mean.	Conserve two-thirds of paper gains exceeding 20%.
			Sell the bulk of your ordinary shares if the bank rate is raised to *over* 5%.

345

AN EXAMPLE OF APPLIED THEORY

The following circular, printed privately for the author and sent to his Stock Market clients in London at the bottom of the American slump in 1932, may indicate that sometimes the theories outlined in this book may be applied with profit in practice.

The index for English common stocks has, since this circular, (i.e., by February, 1936), risen 80%; the Dow index for American Industrials, 233%, i.e., from 44.7 to 150.

* * *

To the Clients of L. L. B. Angas only.

19 Throgmorton Avenue,
London, E.C. 2.

An Appreciation of the Investment Situation

4th June, 1932.

Many clients have recently written asking for a view on the present investment situation. The short-run position is difficult to assess; nerves throughout the world are frayed, and since modern bank credit currency is an inverted pyramid of purchasing power about nine times the size of the small basis of legal tender upon which it rests, there always exist the danger, in periods of bad nerves, of this delicate inverted pyramid collapsing. The quantity of super-imposed credit currency, on which we rely for our trade, depends on willingness to borrow, and willingness to lend; and these two willingnesses have been rapidly disappearing owing to nervousness; a rapid deflation of world prices has thus ensued, and could theoretically occur to one-tenth of the present level!

England, despite the advantages she reaped from the abandonment of gold in September, 1931, in the shape of an export bounty and import check, has been affected by these world deflationary influences; and the fall in gold prices in America of nearly 10 per cent. within the last six months, has dragged down sterling prices also, thus upsetting reviving confidence in England. There have also been shocks due to the Kreuger crisis, the Central European deadlock, and the collapse in the stock markets of America and Europe. The English position is certainly reasonably sound, but it has been seriously affected by these recent outside influences.

In January, 1932, I sent to my clients a pamphlet entitled "Stock Market Tactics," pressing them to buy during the market reaction which was then occurring after the previous off-gold boomlet—with a view to probable sales about Easter. By March 9th handsome profits were showing and the Paris and New York markets had also been booming. My clients, therefore, sold extensively, on the principle of getting in cash in the boomlets. They waited with cash idle for some weeks, but the market hardly reacted at all; so in many cases repurchases were made; but unfortunately too soon, for shortly afterwards the market began to react, and a downward zig-zag swing has continued throughout the last three months.

The timing of the repurchases was obviously inaccurate; my reason for suggesting them was that I was afraid to leave clients out of the Ordinary share market near the bottom of the cycle, when statistics were clearly indicating an improvement in internal British trade. (If I had relied on the graphic methods explained in Chapter V of "Stock Market Tactics," instead of on my own economic judgment, I would not have made the repurchases when I did. This provides yet one more example of the practical utility of the purely empirical Graphic Method of timing one's action in the market.)

An examination of graphs for indices of Ordinary shares in America, England, France, Holland and Germany for the last twelve months indicates that the short run "conjunctural swings" in these markets have become approximately simultaneous, the movements being governed by world sentiment (depending on commodity price movements and world politics) rather than by local technical market conditions such as in normal times are the determinants of the short run domestic swings.

Apart from European politics the chief determinant of world sentiment is commodity prices, and although President Hoover has instituted a policy of mild counter deflation in America, no immediate effect on prices has yet been manifested owing to the banks, which were put in possession of a larger credit basis, using the new funds to strengthen their own positions rather than to foster positive credit inflation. A lag of this nature, however, is normal in economics, but since it was not understood by the general public, the mischievous argument was put forward that since there were no *immediate* effects, the policy was bound to prove abortive. Confidence was therefore suddenly checked; the fall in prices continued.

In my own view, however, the American reflationary policy, which is occurring at the rate of £20 million a month, is bound, after a further short time lag, to have an effect on bonds, shares and commodities in that order. When commodities revive, world sentiment will improve, despite the political situation in Europe, and I look for a sharp revival in Wall Street where, within the last three months, the Dow Jones index for common stocks has fallen from 88 to 44.74, i.e., 48 per cent.; whereas the fall from the peak of September, 1929, has been from 382 to 44.74, i.e., 88 per cent. There has in fact been a virtual panic, super-imposed on a previous series of collapses, shares in general having fallen to nearly one-tenth of their 1929 high levels.

In September, 1929, the American investing public was borrowing on short term at 15 per cent. to buy shares yielding under 3 per cent.; now they are able to borrow at 3 per cent. and invest in shares of the very highest grade with earnings yields (on last quarter's basis—not on last year's) of 15 per cent. to 25 per cent. These are clearly panic conditions; conditions like these can never last.

In my view American shares are by far the cheapest in the world; the average dividend (as distinct from earnings) yield, according to Standard Statistics, was on 1st June 10.98 per cent. (with average earnings of over 15 per cent.); whereas the average yield on English industrials is only about 6 per cent.—and the long run economic prospects of America are much more favorable, I think, than those of this country. English shares would have to fall 50 per cent. to be on a comparable basis with America.

As an example of how cheap many of the shares are, I give the instance of Drug Incorporated which at $30 gives a yield of 13 per cent. and earnings of 18 per cent., as compared with the British subsidiary which it controls, Boots Chemists, which gives a yield of 5¼ per cent.

The rise that has taken place during the last few days is only a very small percentage of the enormous fall which has taken place during the last three years. This is an opportunity which comes in the life-time of but few generations to buy first class investments to give an enormous yield and having the possibility of capital appreciation usually only possible in the most undesirable type of speculative counters.

* * *

In England the Investors' Chronicle Index for ordinary shares in General Business has fallen from 158 in January, 1929, to 65.7 at the end of May, i.e. 58 per cent.; and the Financial News Index for 30 representative industrials has, since 9th March, 1932, fallen 20 per cent. (from 64.3 to 51.3)—one of the biggest percentage short-run falls in England in the course of the present depression.

Three great dangers confront the English investor in Ordinary shares:

1. Firstly, that political fear will cause a continuation of the present credit contraction in England; and that the Government will no nothing to counteract this tendency by a policy of controlled counter deflation, such as was positively recommended by the Macmillan Committee on Finance and Industry, and which is discussed in a pamphlet of mine being published this week. (Reflate or Perish.)
2. Secondly, that the pound will rise in terms of foreign currencies so that England is deprived of the export bounty and import check which she now enjoys as a result of the undervaluation of sterling; and thirdly,
3. The possible, indeed probable, departure of Central Europe from the gold standard, thus depriving us of a large proportion of our present competitive benefits.

As regards these dangers:

(1) A further collapse in credit is not impossible, although the Government seem to be swinging in favor of a policy

of deliberate counter-deflation and Reflation (which, if adopted, will cause a boom in Ordinary shares).

(2) It seems unlikely that the pound will be allowed to rise far owing to the recent institution by the Government of an Exchange Equalization Fund of £150 m.

(3) Departure of Central Europe from the gold standard seems far from impossible; and, although tariffs may save us from undercutting at home, tariffs will not help us in our export markets abroad.

These dangers have certainly been overhanging the English markets for some months, but despite being fully aware of their existence, I did not anticipate the recent sharp fall in share-prices in England; I made the error of anticipating more rigorous inflation in America, with favorable reactions in England; and I expected an earlier reflection on English industrial shares in Throgmorton Street of the cheapening of money in London and of the boom in gilt-edged, which I forecast in January in "Stock Market Tactics." I am, therefore, somewhat reluctant to express strong views about present market tendencies, even though in the last four tops and bottoms of the English short-run market luck was favorable as regards our timing. Since, however, an opinion is wanted an opinion will now be given.

Although I am fully aware of the possibility of London industrials acquiring still further downward momentum, owing to fear and progressive credit contraction, I am inclined to think that we are now about to touch the bottom of this recent swing in the English market. The present world slump will not be perpetual, and as soon as the governments of the world reflate with courage, the fall in commodities will come to an end. There is no doubt whatever that resolute inflation is bound, with a lag, to turn prices upward, and as soon as this movement gets under way—and it is openly advocated in almost all countries—the process of world revival will begin. English shares will thereupon benefit, for, besides being abnormally cheap on long prospects, they are reasonably cheap on current earnings, despite the minor recession in trade which has occurred within the last three months, despite our having abandoned the gold standard. In other words, I favor the English Ordinary share market and am disinclined to sell. (But see later.) I am strongly averse to switching into fixed interest stocks on the recent rapid rise lest one fall into the common error habitually made by investors at the top and bottom of each business cycle, namely, switching from fixed interest to Ordinary shares at the peak of the boom, and from Ordinary shares to fixed interest at the bottom of the slump. The investor's nerves, it is true, are frayed, but that is normally the right time to buy, not to sell.

* * *

Viewing the markets of the world dispassionately, it seems to me an indisputable fact that American shares are 50 per cent. cheaper on actualities and on prospects than those of any other country; and analysis suggests that it is prudent to switch immediately from the shares of England and other countries into those of America, especially as that country in addition to showing much higher current yields, has *already* adopted an active programme of reflation; and is not dependent appreciably on world trade, and is not particularly damaged industrially by the state of turmoil in Europe. The country's industries are highly protected; the currency is strong, though some banks are somewhat shaky; 110 million people trade internally without tariff walls; and the country is largely self contained. The budget it is true is heavily unbalanced, but unbalanced budgets, despite the popular view, are sometimes a cause of industrial revival, owing to the government borrowing from the banks and thus injecting credit currency into circulation and bringing about inflation.

To switch from English to American common stocks is, I feel convinced, wise and prudent—even though English shares themselves are quite cheap. The investor, however, should consider Relativity rather than Absolute levels.

By selling in England one is certainly selling cheap shares and abandoning the chance of partaking in the prospective improvement in England; but what one loses is more than regained by buying at panic prices in America, where yields are higher and where prospects of appreciation are, in my view, enormously greater.

Such action is not unpatriotic under a paper currency régime, because every pound spent on foreign currency is bought in the foreign exchange market by some foreigner and spent eventually on English goods or services. English exports are thus stimulated *pari passu* with every import of American securities. When on a gold currency, gold was lost and thus weakened our national position; under paper the economics of the matter are reversed.

As regards exchange risks: Personally I do not think America will abandon gold (see Chapter XII. of "Stock Market Tactics"); but since abandonment is theoretically possible, the purchaser of American common stocks should probably sell dollars forward and cover the exchange to the dollar value of his American shares. This will cost him about 3 per cent. per annum (less than 1 per cent. per quarter) and can be effected, and continued, by his stockbroker. Even so American shares will show him a higher average yield than that obtainable on English industrials.

Although immediate action of this nature seems obvious on the basis not only of real merit, but also of prospects, the private investor and trust company in the last several years has so often found that any action taken has turned out to be a mistake, that he has come, through experience, to the conclusion that since action has usually shown itself wrong, inaction is therefore wisdom. He, like a bird in the presence of a snake, has become not only paralyzed, but mesmerized, and his mental faculties of analysis have in some cases left him. Moreover, inasmuch as selling English stocks shows paper losses, the investor is further discouraged from positive action—even though American stock index has fallen 48 per cent. since March and the English index only 20 per cent.

I feel it incumbent upon me, however, to urge the desirability of an immediate switch of this nature.

Theoretically, since the short run stock-market swings throughout the whole world are now apparently governed by political sentiment and by world commodity prices, the scientific short run investor should refrain from buying shares in any of the countries concerned until the Ordinary share graphs of America, England, France and Germany have all saucered out and begun to turn upwards, thus indicating a check to the decline in world confidence and the probability of a renewed upward swing from the present low levels. To switch, however, from something fairly cheap to something much cheaper, although requiring courage and a mental effort of the highest order, should in my view be strongly pressed, especially as American shares are already steadying and are now showing signs of turning upwards. In addition, the delayed effects of Deliberate Reflation seem now to be beginning to manifest themselves openly. In my personal opinion the present moment presents an amazing opportunity. A switch to America would have been wrong throughout the last three years;* now, however, I consider it emphatically desirable (up to a Dow Jones index level of, say, 65; see the daily financial papers). It is an astounding position to find a stock market which has fallen 88 per cent. in three years and which gives earnings yields, based on last quarter's earnings, of 15 per cent. to 25 per cent., despite the low earnings of depression. This moment, in my view, is the opportunity of a lifetime; and yet nobody seems willing to act. They have learned that America is a dangerous market; and Nerves prevent resolute action being taken despite the conclusions of the Brain. Three hundred per cent. rises, however, within a few years, with increasing yield, seem to me not improbable, but most likely.

I would therefore urge all my clients to master inaction, and to switch wholesale from England to America at once, covering the exchange when they act.

If America comes off gold, this itself will stimulate a boom in American industrials.

L. L. B. ANGAS.

* * *

*The author perhaps may be forgiven for adding that at no time during the American slump, prior to 4th June, 1932, did he recommend to the investors whom he advises the purchase of American Securities.

A brilliant study of one of the most crucial economic questions of our day

THE PROBLEMS OF THE FOREIGN EXCHANGES

by L. L. B. ANGAS

No banker, economist, investor, exporter or importer can afford to neglect the subjects dealt with in this recently published work by Major Angas.

Unlike most standard treatises on foreign exchange, this book deals not only with first principles and the mechanism of foreign exchange but also with the controversial questions arising from the widespread collapse of the gold standard and the confusion into which the foreign exchanges have fallen. Eleven chapters are devoted to the theory and mechanism of the gold and paper exchanges, and seven to a comparison of gold with paper and to the case for and against the gold standard. These discussions are followed by an analysis of practical problems, including stabilization, variable gold standards, and the exchange and tariff deadlock. The study concludes with a survey of the present and probable future policies of the United States, Great Britain, and France, and the effects, especially in regard to inflation, that these policies will have on business conditions.

ALFRED A. KNOPF, *Publisher*, 730 FIFTH AVENUE, NEW YORK

MACMILLAN AND CO., ST. MARTIN'S ST., LONDON

270 Pages $3.75

Financial News: "Mr. Angas has written the most clear and searching criticism of the gold standard which I have ever read."

Finance & Industry: "Major Angas exhibits real brilliance in his attempts to solve the world's economic and financial problems."

American Economic Review: "The book is divided into four parts: Part 1, 'First principles'; Part 2, 'Mechanism of the gold and paper exchanges'; Part 3, 'Gold compared with paper' (the chapter on the six diseases of money is important); and Part 4, 'Practical problems.' In the concluding chapter the author reviews today's exchange problems of the leading nations. The analysis is keen and clear. A thought-provoking book."

Wall Street Journal: "The six diseases of modern money, says Major Angas, make it difficult to cure the nation's economic ills so long as it clings to the fixed gold standard. He makes, it must be admitted, a plausible case for a managed-paper currency system."

Investment News: "The book constitutes an excellent exposition, not only of the monetary problems connected with foreign trade, but of the general theory of money and its influence upon business as well. As such, it should be read by all serious students of trade cycles and depression phenomena."

New York Herald Tribune: "Major Angas's objective is Capitalist recovery. Major Angas is intelligent; the book is well written."

Journal of the British Institute of Bankers: "His summing up of the pre-requisites of a successful functioning of a free gold standard and of the practical difficulties of insuring that such essential conditions shall obtain, is masterly."